A City
Full of People

Men and Women of London 1650–1750

A City
Full of People

*Men and Women
of London
1650–1750*

PETER EARLE

Methuen

First published in Great Britain 1994
by Methuen London
an imprint of Reed Consumer Books Ltd
Michelin House, 81 Fulham Road, London sw3 6rb
and Auckland, Melbourne, Singapore and Toronto

Copyright © 1994 by Peter Earle
The author has asserted his moral rights

A CIP catalogue record for this book
is available at the British Library

isbn 0 413 68170 x

Typeset by Wilmaset, Birkenhead, Wirral
Printed in Great Britain
by Mackays of Chatham plc

'I proceeded on my Way to London, that great and famous City, which may truly be said, like the Sea and the Gallows, to refuse none.'

An Account of Lot Cavanagh, ON, 12 April 1743

Contents

List of Illustrations

Acknowledgements

The illustrations are reproduced by kind permission of the following:

Plates 1, 2, 3, 6, 12: the Guildhall Library, Corporation of London; plate 4: the Board of Trustees of the Victoria & Albert Museum; plates 5, 9, 11: the British Library; plate 8: the British Museum, Department of Prints and Drawings; plate 7: from the Pepys Library by courtesy of the Master and Fellows, Magdalene College, Cambridge.

Preface

This book started life as a study of the women of Queen Anne's London, but it was quickly discovered that both the subject and the time period were too narrow. One learns more about the lives of women if they are studied alongside those of men, since only then do the real contrasts in experience become clear. The book remains a major study of the lives of female Londoners, but it also has much to say about the lives of their male contemporaries in the metropolis.

The time period has been expanded to cover the century from 1650 to 1750 because strict confinement to the short period of the reign of Queen Anne (1702–14) would have meant that several important types of source material could not have been used. However, although material from the whole of this longer period has been included, most of the sources have been drawn from a much shorter period, from about 1695 to 1720, and the focus throughout is on the two generations of Londoners who lived in the city between these years. The approach has been static rather than dynamic, though the direction of change has been noted when this can be determined. Essentially, the book provides a snapshot picture of the lives of Londoners in the early years of the eighteenth century.

This period is a fascinating one in its own right, but it has been chosen because of the availability of some magnificent source materials which do not exist in the same quality and quantity for any other period. These are depositions given by witnesses before the London Church courts. Cases heard before these courts related mainly to marital relations, probate and defamation (slander), and material from the depositions has provided an important input to the book. However, it is the biographical information on the witnesses rather than the depositions themselves which has produced most of the data analysed here.

Witnesses were asked a varying number of questions in order to establish what sort of people they were. Such questions included age, marital status, place of birth, residence and change of residence over several years, wealth and so on. Much the most important question for the purposes of this book was a requirement for witnesses to say how they made their living or were maintained, sometimes simply at the time of the deposition, but often for several years preceding it. This question was asked most frequently between 1695 and 1720, which is why the book concentrates on that period.

The book is divided into two parts. Part One consists of five chapters which analyse and describe the basic framework of the lives of Londoners. Chapter 1 sets the scene by a discussion of the metropolis itself. Chapter 2 looks at the education received by Londoners and the geographical origins of that majority of the population who were born outside the city. Chapters 3 and 4 cover the very different subjects of men's work and women's work. Finally, Chapter 5 looks at the marriages and family lives of Londoners, their homes and the social significance of the neighbourhoods in which they lived.

Part Two uses the rich vernacular material in depositions and other contemporary sources to illustrate a number of themes in the lives of Londoners and also to convey to the reader some idea of their *mentalité*. This section consists entirely of quotations from documents, some very short, some longer, arranged under such headings as 'People', 'Lives' and 'Eating and Drinking'. The object is to use the voices of the Londoners themselves to put flesh on the framework of analysis developed in Part One.

The book clearly has some overlap with my previous book, *The Making of the English Middle Class*, published by Methuen in 1989. This was also about London and covered very much the same period of the late seventeenth and early eighteenth centuries. However, this new book uses very different sources and also focuses much more on the ordinary Londoner of the period, though middling people do get the occasional mention, while it pays far more attention to women than did the previous book. Where there is obvious overlap, as in the discussion of apprenticeship, I have attempted not to repeat myself unduly, while some subjects which were covered thoroughly before, such as the changing pattern of consumption, are not considered here. The two books are designed to complement each other, to look at London life from two very different viewpoints and thus to enhance our knowledge of this colourful period in the city's history.

In the text the word 'City', i.e. with a capital, means the ancient area within the walls, the same area that we call the City today. The word 'city', with a lower case 'c', refers to the whole built-up area, as does 'London', 'the metropolis', 'metropolitan' etc. Money is expressed in pounds (£), shillings (s.) and pence (d.); 20 shillings equals £1 and 12 pence equals 1s. The following contemporary expressions of coinage may be unfamiliar to some readers: a groat = 4d.; half a crown = 2s.6d.; a crown = 5s.; a mark = 13s.4d.; a guinea = 21s. Conversion of contemporary money to figures understandable today is virtually impossible, so great have been changes in relative values, but multiplying by a hundred will give a very crude approximation.

My thanks are due to the staffs of the London record offices and libraries where I have gathered my material, these being principally the Public Record Office in Chancery Lane, the Greater London Record Office, the Corporation of London Records Office, Lambeth Palace Library, the Guildhall Library, Westminster City Library and the British Library. I would also like to thank my friends David Hebb and Jane Waldfogel for constant encouragement and for reading sections of the book in draft, and my research student Tim Meldrum for many hours of discussion and for drawing my attention to some of the extracts which appear in Part Two. Students in my special subject and M.Sc. classes during my last years as a teacher at the London School of Economics have contributed more than they might imagine, as have members of research seminars in London, Hull and Cambridge, who provided useful criticism of two working papers on the male and female labour force.

One

Structures of
Life and Work

1   The Metropolis

'London is the Metropolis of Great-Britain, the Seat of her Monarchs, the greatest, richest, most populous and most flourishing City in Europe.'

'London . . . the chiefest Emporium, or Town of Trade in the World; the largest and most populous, the fairest and most opulent City at this day in all Europe, perhaps in the Whole World.'

'The most Spacious, Populous, Rich, Beautiful, Renowned and Noble City that we know of at this day in the World.'[1]

London was indeed the largest and most populous city in Europe, though not in the world, when the writers of these early eighteenth-century guidebooks penned their superlatives.[2] Paris, Amsterdam and Naples had been left behind as wealth and people piled up in the great city beside the Thames, that wealth made evident to all by the densely packed shipping on the river below London Bridge, the bulging vaults and warehouses of the merchants, the fine new shops and houses, and the pomp and splendour of the richer citizens and gentlemen whose coaches forced their way through the crowded streets. England was proud of London and wanted foreigners to appreciate it, so perhaps these writers may be forgiven for failing to mention the poverty and squalor behind the opulence and undoubted beauty of much of the townscape. The habitat of those ordinary Londoners who are the main focus of this book was hardly suitable subject-matter for the writer of a contemporary guide to London.

These guidebooks are useful if rather dull, composed as they mainly are of dry descriptions of institutions, buildings and monuments, scraps of historical lore, lists of office-holders and such information as the days on which wagons and coaches set out for various provincial destinations or the official rates which could be charged by watermen or hackney coachmen.[3] Some of the books incorporate illustrations and maps, but overall the reader gets very little idea of what sort of life was lived within the city they described and praised in such glowing terms. But anyone with access to a reasonable library can soon breathe some life into this prosaic framework of a city, for the London of this period has come down to us in a series of literary and artistic images, so detailed and apparently realistic that one feels one could almost walk in its streets.

At the beginning of the century covered here, it was the London so vividly brought to life in the diary of Samuel Pepys,[4] a bustling, busy and attractive city which suffered more than its fair share of disasters in the form of plague, fire and war with the Dutch, but one where an ambitious and energetic civil servant could enjoy life to the full, at the theatre, at home, in the streets and in the taverns which played such a prominent part in contemporary existence. Pepys was in many ways an admirable and hard-working man, but his ambiguous sex life may serve to remind us that his London was also the London of Restoration comedy, a place of wit and amoral intrigue, a home for idle and foppish young ladies and gentlemen with nothing but disdain for those so unfortunate as to have to work for their living, those 'cits' who so uneasily and pathetically tried to ape the 'wits'.

The contrast between West End idleness and vanity and City industry and social ambition is still present at the end of our period in the London of William Hogarth; he portrayed a corrupt and often sordid place peopled by the ugly and unpleasant, by fools and knaves, rakes and harlots, cynics and hypocrites.[5] This is a sad, grotesque city of hedonism and tarnished elegance, deception and decay, in which idleness, drink and vice lead inexorably to disgrace, madness and degrading death. There is of course another side to the world portrayed by Hogarth in which a sanctimonious apprentice can by constant diligence become a Lord Mayor or, more attractively, in which a rather stuffy family life can be enjoyed in a setting of decorum and dignity. But the images that linger longest are not those of the pretty Graham children or even of the jolly beer-swilling blacksmith of 'Beer Street'. They are those which portray London as a vicious, rotten city, the images of 'Gin Lane' and the rapid downward progresses of the harlot and the rake.

There is no shortage of literary vignettes of London between Pepys and Hogarth, a period when a new realism makes these pen portraits particularly vivid and memorable. But, since these writers aimed to amuse, instruct or maybe draw a moral, the city life they describe bears only a partial resemblance to the more prosaic lives experienced by the majority of the Londoners discussed in this book. Nonetheless, these vignettes create a collective image which is difficult for anyone writing about early eighteenth-century London to ignore.

One of the first of these writers was Ned Ward, whose rollicking prose and verse bring alive a lowly, noisy world of boozing dens, smoke-filled coffee-rooms, dives and taverns where a colourful and minutely observed crowd of jilts and cullies, blades and topers, strumpets and muckworms drink, gamble and smoke the night away.[6] Thomas Brown provides another lively guide to the 'miscellany of mortality' that peopled the London of 1700, a city of cheats, lechers, drunkards, fops and social climbers pushing their way through 'the confus'd noise' of streets cluttered with bullies and bailiffs, hawkers and porters, chairmen, carters and wheelbarrows full of nuts.[7]

This clamour and bustle also ring out in John Gay's poem *Trivia*, where clashing wheels, lashing whips, dashing hoofs, thundering wagons, hawkers' cries and the trampling feet of 'crouds heap'd on crouds' impress themselves by their repetition. If one can hear, see and feel the street in these evocations of the city, one can also smell it; and a foul smell it is, never more so than in Jonathan Swift's *Description of a City Shower* where 'sweepings from butcher's stall, dung, guts, and blood, drown'd puppies, stinking sprats, all drench'd in mud, dead cats, and turnip-tops come tumbling down the flood'. No wonder John Gay should beg his muse to 'bear me to the paths of fair Pell-Mell, safe are thy pavements, grateful is thy smell!'[8]

Where there was filth, there was inevitably vice, and the streets were peopled not just by hawkers and butchers, coalmen and carters, but by 'old letchers', 'skulking thieves', 'subtil artists' whose 'unfelt fingers make thy pocket light' and the inevitable harlots, 'who nightly stand, where Katharine Street descends into the Strand . . . with flatt'ring sounds she soothes the cred'lous ear, my noble captain! charmer! love! my dear!'[9] A few years later, in the 1720s, these pickpockets and harlots reappear in the London-based sections of the novels of Daniel Defoe, such as *Colonel Jack* and *Moll Flanders*. In his didactic works, Defoe displayed an immense knowledge of the trade and industry of London, and this is often reflected in his fiction. However, the images that stick in the mind are once again images of the street and of a noisy, vicious, amoral world similar to that portrayed by the writers mentioned above and by Hogarth, whose career was just starting as Defoe's was coming to an end.

These images are not totally unjustified, as the reader will discover, especially in the second part of this book where contemporary non-literary Londoners themselves describe some aspects of the world in which they lived. London was indeed a noisy, crowded city in which much of life was conducted in the streets or in the courts and alleys around the tenements of the poor. It was dirty, smelly and filled with smoke, from tobacco indoors and from coal both inside and out, an atmosphere sometimes so thick as to be a serious hazard to visibility and to health. It was a city of startling contrasts between immense wealth and utter poverty, between elegance and squalor, between the fine carriages and magnificent clothes of the ladies and gentlemen of the West End and the filth and degradation of those at the bottom of the heap. Inevitably, such inequalities bred prostitution and crime, both of which seem to have been on the increase if contemporary complaints bear any relation to reality. And, perhaps above all, London was a very drunken city where both business and pleasure took place in taverns and inns, alehouses and brandy-shops and in coffee-houses which by no means only served coffee. The first half of the eighteenth century has been called the Gin Age, and not without reason since national production of distilled spirits rose sixteenfold between 1689 and 1740 and a very high proportion of this was gin distilled and drunk within the metropolis.[10]

Nevertheless, the lives of Londoners were not entirely devoted to booze, sex and vice, and not everybody spent all their time in taverns or being jostled in the streets. Women were not all prostitutes, pickpockets or gin-sodden old hags, as one might be forgiven for supposing from the literary and artistic images of the period. Nor were all men lechers, thieves and drunkards. Most people of both sexes lived or tried to live hard-working, respectable lives in this apparently licentious city, even if some did conform to the lurid stereotypes sketched out above. Londoners drank and smoked heavily, took opiates to enjoy themselves or to relieve pain, mugged and were mugged, raped and were raped, rioted, stole and occasionally murdered each other. They enjoyed eating and going out for a good time, buying and wearing as fine clothes as possible and talking and shouting at each other in very vivid and often explicit language. All these aspects of their lives will be reflected in this book. But, for most of the time, Londoners had to work, and work hard, to maintain themselves, and much of the focus will be on that work and on other mundane subjects such as where they came from, their families and their homes. But, first, we need to look at the metropolis itself, that solid red-brick framework within which the men and women of London lived out their lives.

This London may have been the largest city in Europe, but it would seem very small to the Londoner of today. Countrymen might have felt overwhelmed by the forest of houses and the choking atmosphere, but for all that the Londoner was never far from lush pastures and gardens, made fertile by the rubbish from the city they surrounded. Dungheaps on the edge of town might be offensive to some, but no one need feel imprisoned in a city which in 1708 was said to be only five miles and twenty yards from east to west and a mere two and a quarter miles from north to south.[11] Urban batteries could be recharged with ease and a walk in the fields or gardens was one of the commonest and certainly the cheapest contemporary form of recreation.

In 1650, at the beginning of the century considered here, the metropolis had long outgrown the walls of the ancient City, but the extent of the suburbs was still remarkably limited, considering the number of people who lived in them. Westminster was still separated from London proper with 'but few houses scattered up and down between Temple-Bar and St James, which was then but a field or pasture-ground'.[12] The 'West End' was as yet little more than the fashionable suburb around Drury Lane, though the future could be seen in Inigo Jones's Covent Garden and in Lincoln's Inn Fields, the forerunners of the squares which would one day colonize the unbuilt fields of Westminster.

To the north-west, there was not yet much beyond St Giles Church and Holborn, while further east Gray's Inn and Clerkenwell Green marked the end of the town, the ribbon development up St John's Street towards the present Angel not getting very far before 'suddenly the buildings cease'. In the east there were few houses beyond a line from Shoreditch Church to the Tower of London, except on Ratcliffe Highway and along the riverside through the crowded sailor towns of Wapping and Shadwell to Limehouse, which eighty years later was still considered by most writers to be the end of the town.[13]

London was to thicken up and burst these bounds in the century that followed, but even in 1750 the city was still small enough for most of it to be seen from the top of the new St Paul's Cathedral if the coal smoke was not too dense.[14] Much building evades the historian's eye, especially intensive developments within the existing built-up area as new houses replaced old ones or as old gardens and yards gave way to teeming courts and alleys. Such work went on from year to year, but most building, and especially the extension of the city into the surrounding fields, was concentrated in two great periods of boom in the construction trades: the two decades or so after the Restoration of 1660 and the years following the end of the great war against France in 1713.

The first of these periods saw an astonishing degree of activity as expansion both east and west coincided with the rebuilding of some 9,000 houses in the City after the Great Fire of 1666. These years saw the beginning of the real West End, as aristocrats sought to profit from their ownership of fields around the town and speculators scrambled to assist them. Plots were staked out and houses rose in the squares of Westminster and St Giles, each forming 'a little town' as Evelyn called Bloomsbury Square, with its network of surrounding streets and market.[15] Soon, little town linked up with little town, alleys and courts appeared off the initial streets and whole areas became covered with brick and tile in St James, Piccadilly, Mayfair, Soho, St Giles and Bloomsbury. A lull during the French wars was then followed by the building of Hanover, Cavendish and Grosvenor Squares, the last standing in 1729 'at the furthest extent of the town, upon a rising ground with the fields on all sides; which, with the fine air it thereby enjoys, renders the situation delightful'. A few years later, streets had replaced these fields too and Hyde Park had become the western boundary of London, a fine open space on the edge of the town where 'gentlemen take the air on horseback in the morning, and it is common to see there on a summer evening two or three hundred coaches, and sometimes many more'.[16] Further south, round the great bend in the river, Westminster had spread out beyond the Abbey and St James Park into Tuthill Fields, and the Horse Ferry near the present Lambeth Bridge marked the end of the town.

Expansion to the north was rather less impressive. Oxford Street was now known as such and was no longer a border, having been breached by Cavendish Square and by developments at the southern end of Tottenham Court Road. The northern frontier then ran along Great Russell Street, Queen's Square and Great Ormond Street, with fine views north across the fields to the hills of Highgate and Hampstead. There had been some limited extension of the built-up area in Clerkenwell and Shoreditch, but this was nothing to what had been happening further east, where a whole new town had been built in Spitalfields pushing east into Bethnal Green and south into Whitechapel. Goodman's Fields, which had been the frontier in 1650, had been engulfed and the earlier ribbon developments along Ratcliffe Highway and the riverside were ribbons no longer. The East End had been born.

South of the river, too, there had been much expansion to startle the visitor brave enough to walk across London Bridge into Southwark, 'a suburb of London, but much worse and more mean'. From Deptford in the east to Rotherhithe, now 'effectually joyned', was a continuous line of docks and wharves and watermen's stairs, but the housing of those who worked there clustered close to the river with no more than a single street separating them from the fields beyond.[17] But in Bermondsey and Southwark there was a real town expanding inexorably towards Newington Butts in the south and Lambeth in the west, though the crush of building soon diminished as one moved a few hundred yards away from the river or from the great thoroughfare of Borough High Street. London Bridge remained the only route for wheeled transport across the Thames throughout our period – Westminster Bridge was not opened until November 1750 – and this central area of Southwark was as densely populated as anywhere in the city, another London over the water.

This then was the largest and most spacious city in Europe, a mere fraction of the twentieth-century metropolis, all of it contained within such modern landmarks as Hyde Park, the Angel, the Isle of Dogs and the Elephant and Castle, and by no means completely filling the area between these places even in 1750. It was a handsome city, as long as one did not stray too far from the main streets and squares into the alleys behind them, an adventure which might end in a well-paved courtyard fronting the fine house of a rich merchant, but was more likely to lead to a mean, unpaved, pestilent enclosure surrounded by the tenements of the poor. But the red-brick streets themselves looked fine with their well-stocked shops at street level and dwellings and garrets above, topped off by the famous Georgian skyline of tiles and parapets no more than forty feet above the streets; there were no great office blocks to spoil it, just the towering steeples of the new-built churches crowned by the masterpiece of St Paul's.[18]

Not many late seventeenth- and early eighteenth-century houses survive, but, if they did, they would not seem too unfamiliar to modern eyes since they were the direct ancestors of those properties called Georgian or early Victorian by estate agents today. Fear of fire dictated the increasing use of non-inflammable materials such as brick and tiles, while high urban rents encouraged speculators to cram as many houses as they could into limited street frontages, so that street after street consisted of narrow-fronted, well-proportioned brick houses of up to five storeys including basements or cellars, with two and occasionally three rooms on each floor. This uniformity was intensified by the increasing use of sash-windows from the 1690s and was in marked contrast to the anarchy of the streets that lay before the serried red-brick ranks of London housing.

This is not to say that all London houses looked or were the same. Even in the most uniform of streets, there was plenty of scope for a builder to express his individuality in the design of a doorway or a balcony, in the use of stone or stucco cornices or in the pattern of his brickwork. Quality, size and general ambience also varied enormously between high-street frontage and the alleys behind and between area and area, depending on the wealth and social status of the inhabitants, as can be seen in the brief description of streets given by John Strype in his 1720 *Survey of London*. Here is Downing Street, not yet a seat of government, but 'a pretty open place, especially at the upper end, where are four or five very large and well built houses, fit for persons of honour and quality, each house having a pleasant prospect into St James' Park'; or nearby Prince's Court, 'a very handsome open place, with a freestone pavement . . . For the security of the inhabitants, there is a gate with iron bars to shut up at nights.'[19]

Westminster was famous for its fine town houses, elegant homes for aristocrats and gentlemen and their ladies or for lesser men and women who aspired to such status. The old City, now rebuilt after the Fire, formed a second focus of wealth within the metropolis, its new housing conforming to the strict rules of standardization laid down in the Rebuilding Act of 1667.[20] This allowed for four classes of house, all to be built in brick and covered in tiles, the thickness of their walls and their ceiling heights being specified in the legislation. The finest of these houses were those on the 'high and principal streets', which were to be uniformly built in four storeys (not counting the garrets for the servants), and those 'of the greatest bigness', these houses of merchants generally standing back from the street with court-yards and gardens. And elsewhere in London, even in otherwise poor Southwark, there were similar fine houses, a square here, a street there 'of pretty good account . . . having trees before the doors, which renders it pleasant'; 'a clean handsome street pretty well built and inhabited'.[21]

Such elegant, clean and comparatively safe urban space was a world away from the hundreds of lesser streets dismissed by Strype with such epithets as 'very meanly built and inhabited', 'of small account', 'very ordinary,' 'very bad . . . fit for the reception of beggars'. Such was the typical ambience of the East End and other poor areas of the town whose narrow streets and courts were crammed with shoddy properties, usually of two storeys and often housing several families.[22] The well-to-do rarely ventured into such areas and few descriptions survive of the shabby housing of the poor; even Hogarth in his squalid street scenes tended to depict run-down neighbourhoods which had once seen better times and to ignore the low-rise housing of the really poor.

It can be seen that London was characterized by two foci of

wealth, representing the two cities which formed its double nucleus. In the west was an expanding Westminster, already called the West End, an area which had originally grown up around the Abbey, the Houses of Parliament and Whitehall to house and provide services for the court and the government. Such functions had naturally attracted the well-born and wealthy from their country homes and, by our period, the West End was not just an administrative centre but also the main focus of a leisured and pleasant urban life-style which had its roots in the cities of Renaissance Italy. As such, the area was a magnet not only for those who were already rich but also those who thought that access to the court and the wealthy might make them rich: young men in search of a patron or a place, clergymen, soldiers and scholars seeking advancement, ladies seeking a husband, as well as visitors who came as tourists to see and be seen. One such was John Macky who lodged in Pall Mall, 'the ordinary residence of all strangers, because of its vicinity to the King's palace, the Park, the Parliament-house, the theatres, and the chocolate and coffee-houses, where the best company frequent'.[23]

The pleasures of this best company revolved to a considerable extent round the movements of the court in and out of London, so that a regular season had developed, an ebb and flow of country money and country gentlemen and their ladies into the West End in the autumn and back again to their provincial homes in the spring or early summer. This seasonal flow was also reflected in the timetable of parliament and the law courts, both of which closed down for the long vacation, while even warfare had its campaigning season, so that the town was full of army officers and soldiers in the winter and largely free of them at other times of the year.

These tidal flows of the quality did not mean that the West End was totally deserted in the summer, but empty houses and departed dukes did cause great seasonal variations in the earnings and work-loads of the many thousands engaged in providing the services which made the London season such a pleasant and rewarding experience for those who could afford it. Many of these people lived in the great houses of the West End, right up at the top in the garrets, and these droves of male and female servants might find themselves at a loose end when their masters and mistresses returned to the country. Many of them were out of a place completely; others lived an idle but not very rewarding existence on board wages, a retainer which provided none of the tips and perks which had made the hard work of the winter and spring endurable. But servants, numerous as they were in the West End, must have easily been outnumbered by the great army of seamstresses, dressmakers and tailors, peruke-makers and sword-cutlers, caterers and confectioners, chairmen and coachmen, porters and prostitutes, who worked hard and long hours to service the wealthy during the season only to spend three months in idleness during the summer, unless they were able to find some alternative form of employment.[24]

The rhythms of the West End were to a certain extent reversed in the other great bastion of London wealth, the old City within the walls, whose economic life was driven mainly by trade and shipping, which tended to peak in the summer. This area had once been the whole of London but was now just a diminishing part, albeit a very important one, of the expanding metropolis. Vestiges of the City's past as a great industrial and residential area still remained. The occasional gentleman continued to maintain his town house in the City rather than the West End and several industries were still based there, the most important being the manufacture of high-class metalwares such as pewter, gold and silverware, and the finishing and dyeing of woollen cloth, London's most important export, which was spun and woven in the provinces.

However, the City was already anticipating its modern function within the metropolis and its business life was mainly focused on commerce, finance and other more arcane and intangible ways of making money. Cornhill and Cheapside were still important shopping streets, but it was the merchants who lived in the courtyard behind them whose wealth provided the main driving-force of the City economy. Most of these merchants, together with other rich City residents such as wholesalers and bankers, still tended to live on top of their counting-houses and were not yet commuters, though several maintained second houses in the villages and countryside outside London to which they sent their families in the summer. These rich inhabitants of the City were often as wealthy as anyone in the West End and they maintained in their turn large numbers of living-in servants, apprentices, clerks, warehousemen and book-keepers, as well as providing a major source of demand for many of the other people who ran businesses in the City: the owners of taverns, inns and coffee-houses, shopkeepers and market people and the suppliers of professional services such as scriveners and brokers.

The part of London which linked the City and the West End, the area along Fleet Street and the Strand and to the north and south of these major thoroughfares, included some very run-down neighbourhoods such as Bridewell and Whitefriars, but was mainly devoted to the provision of services which might be demanded by either of the two main centres of metropolitan wealth. Here, in the Temple, Gray's Inn, Lincoln's Inn and the other inns of court, were the enclaves of the lawyers, most of them rich or at least well-off themselves. The Strand and the streets that ran off it had also taken over from Cheapside and Cornhill as the most important shopping area, particularly for textiles and clothing. Much of this was made or finished ready for sale by the vast numbers of tailors and seamstresses, stocking-makers and peruke-makers, glovers and hatmakers, and a host of other manufacturers of clothing accessories who lived in the streets and alleys of Covent Garden and St Clement Danes. Hidden away too were pewterers and silversmiths, clock- and watchmakers, cabinet-makers, joiners, upholsterers and other furniture-makers who supplied the smart dealers on the main streets. And finally, as one is constantly reminded in the literature of the period, this area, particularly round the Strand, Charing Cross and Drury Lane, was the most important centre for public entertainment in the city, the location not just of the famous theatres but also of huge numbers of taverns and coffee-houses and more doubtful establishments such as brothels, bagnios and gaming-houses.

Most wealthy residents of London probably never strayed outside these three areas, which provided them with all that they required, whether this was a business contact, entertainment or the acquisition of clothes, furniture and other attractive items for their personal consumption. But this central belt of the metropolis, from the City through to the farthest reaches of Westminster alongside Hyde Park, probably housed less than half of London's population. The other half, poorer people in poorer housing, lived in a great horseshoe bordering the areas already considered, from St Giles, Holborn and Smithfield in the west, through the northern suburbs of Clerkenwell, Cripplegate and Shoreditch into the East End, and then back along the south bank of the river from Deptford and Rotherhithe through Southwark to Lambeth.

Some of the poor Londoners who lived in these neighbourhoods were engaged in work which took them to richer parts of the city, for example porters, coachmen, hawkers and carters, and the watermen who mainly lived on the south bank of the river but spent most of their working hours plying for trade on the richer northern bank. Many of those in the riverside parishes on both sides of the river were sailors, one of the largest of all occupational groups within London. Other people supplied services for the poor amongst whom they lived, for example chandlers and other poor shopkeepers, the owners of dram-shops and alehouses. But the majority of people in these peripheral areas of the city were engaged in a wide variety of manufacturing, for London was not just the administrative, commercial and social capital of England but also by far its largest industrial city, a role which is often overlooked.

The industries changed as one moved round the great sweep of poor suburbs to the north, east and south of fashionable London. St Giles, a notoriously poor area, had amongst other things the largest concentration of shoemakers. Smithfield was known, hardly surprisingly, for its butchers and the associated leatherworkers, while St Sepulcre and Clerkenwell had one of the main concentrations of metal-workers, with large numbers of blacksmiths and founders, braziers, pewterers, clock- and watchmakers, making this a more than usually smoky and noisy area of the city. St Giles Cripplegate was also important for metalworking, especially wire-drawing and associated crafts such as gold- and silver-spinning which produced the incredibly expensive threads of silk twisted with precious metal used to embellish high-class clothing and furniture. Cripplegate was also the beginning of the great weaving belt of north and east London. Weaving, mainly of silk, was the city's biggest industry and the homes of the weavers stretched through Shoreditch and Bishopsgate into Spitalfields and Stepney.

The East End had many industries, including stocking-knitting in the Bishopsgate area, gun-making east of the Tower,

sugar-refining and soap-making, brewing, distilling and cooper-
age, and a whole range of industries connected with ships and the
river: shipbuilding and such allied manufactures as sail- and
rope-making, and the baking of ship's biscuit, while many of the
wives and daughters of the sailors were engaged in silk-throwing,
preparing the raw silk imported from the Levant and Asia for the
weavers who lived to the north of them. Shipbuilding trades
continued across the river into Deptford, Rotherhithe and
Bermondsey, while Southwark and Lambeth, like the East End,
were the home of a wide range of different industries, the most
important of which were tanning and leather-dressing, hat-
making, dyeing, brewing and the manufacture of glass.

How many Londoners there were altogether is a subject on
which historians have failed as yet to come to complete agreement.[25] Nevertheless, the broad picture is fairly clear. The
population around 1650 was somewhere between 400,000 and
500,000. Nearly 100,000 were to die in the last terrible outbreak
of the plague in 1665, but these losses were quickly made up by
massive immigration and a spate of early marriages in the city, so
that by the mid-1690s the population had advanced on its pre-
plague level to rather more than half a million. By 1750, this
figure had increased still further, with most historians being
prepared to accept a population of 675,000, making London
without doubt the largest city in western Europe.

There were, then, three Londoners in 1750 for every two that
there had been in 1650, a growth over the century of about fifty
per cent. Few other European cities experienced any growth at
all during this century, a period when the population of Europe
as a whole advanced very slowly.[26] Even so, London's growth
was very modest compared with the century that preceded it,
during which the population at least quadrupled, and can have
put little pressure on the city's ability to absorb the increase in its
numbers. Indeed, by all accounts, the century between 1650 and
1750 was a good one for Londoners, and particularly for the
London poor. Beggars could still be seen in the city's streets, but
the mass vagrancy which was considered such a serious problem
before 1650 had largely disappeared and begging began to be
seen as just an annoying habit of the idle poor rather than as a
dangerous social phenomenon which might well overwhelm the
pleasant lives of the rich.[27]

Lessons learned in the hard times of the early seventeenth century also meant that the institutions designed to assist the poor, particularly the system of poor relief administered by the parishes, now worked much more effectively with the reduction of the pressure placed on them.[28] Relief was handled more efficiently, the sums paid out to claimants increased and the treatment of those deemed truly 'deserving' – the sick, the aged and orphans – was relatively humane, though the humanity of the wealthy was often tempered by a somewhat unctuous paternalism which seems offensive to modern sensibility but may not have been to the recipients. Fair treatment of the 'deserving' was however paralleled by harsher attitudes to the 'undeserving' poor, the able-bodied unemployed. Contemporary opinion believed that most of such people were voluntarily unemployed, idle in fact, and many efforts were made to shame or shock them into working, including the introduction of a regime into the workhouses which foreshadowed many of the attitudes of the notorious New Poor Law of 1834.[29] Nevertheless, no one was left to starve and the condition of the poor was an enormous improvement on what it had been a century previously, even in such harsh decades as the 1690s when the dislocations brought about by warfare and high food prices made life more than usually difficult for those at the bottom of the social ladder.

Such high food prices were in fact an anomaly in the century under consideration. Continuing improvements in agriculture, together with a relaxation of pressure on the land as England's population hardly grew at all, led to a gradual long-term fall in the price of grain and Londoners were able to buy their bread cheaper.[30] It also seems probable that rent, the other major cost in the budgets of the poor, was at least stable if not falling as well. The physical growth of the city during the century should have been more than adequate to cope with the modest increase in population. Many people lived in very poor conditions, but one does not get the impression that the poor were facing monstrous rents to live in desperately overcrowded tenements, as had been the case in the past and was to be in the future as the population began to grow much more rapidly again after 1750.[31]

Stable or falling rents and bread prices were made even more attractive by the fact that from the 1670s, if not earlier, there was a gradual rise in the wages paid within the metropolis.[32] London wages had always been much higher than elsewhere in England, perhaps double on average, which was one reason why young men and women flocked to the city. Now these high wages became even higher and, since the increase was not eaten away by inflation, the standard of living of Londoners gradually improved; money once spent on bread became available for the purchase of other things: drink certainly, as has been seen, but also more meat, better clothes and a better time generally. Such changes were not approved by many of the wealthy, who objected to the erosion of social distinctions as the poor dressed better and perhaps grew more boisterous and self-confident. The poor, it was felt, should remain poor, otherwise they would become arrogant and idle and spend less time working hard to make life comfortable for the rich.

One should not of course exaggerate this golden age for Londoners. The portion of income which went to the bottom half of society was inevitably small since the total was determined by the very low productivity of three centuries ago. Londoners were better off than the inhabitants of all other European cities, except possibly Amsterdam, and they were better off than other English people, but they were very poor by the standards of today. And, in any case, real wages are not the only criterion of a good life.

Health care was abysmal and the expectation of life was extremely low throughout the period, especially for the poor. Death was an ever-present visitor at all ages, but particularly so in infancy and childhood. Demographers have demonstrated that one in four, or even one in three, of the babies born in London did not live to see their first birthday, while over half of all those born would not survive into adulthood. This sad culling of the city's children is well known, but it is often not fully realized just how high the mortality rate also was for young adults.[33] London suffered its last visitation of the plague in 1665, but this relief from plague made little difference to the life chances of the city's population, who continued to die in large numbers in their twenties, thirties and forties, at just those ages when the Londoners of today might feel most safe. The rise in real wages may have made the lives of ordinary Londoners more pleasant, but high mortality rates ensured that those lives were often only too short.

2 Upbringing and Origins

'Difficile emergunt quorum virtutibus obstat
Res angusta domi.'
('It is hard to rise in the world for those whose virtues are
hindered by poverty at home.')
                    (Juvenal, quoted by Richard Gough)[1]

Some half a million people lived in London at any time during
the period covered by this book. About a third of this population
would have been children under the age of fifteen, if we can
accept the estimate of the contemporary demographer Gregory
King. Some of London's children had been born outside the city,
such as Rachel Beacham, born in Hull and 'brought up to
London very young, even while hanging on her mother's breast'.[2]
But most were born within the metropolis and so were subject
from birth to those appalling death rates which meant that less
than half would reach the age of fifteen. Mortality of children on
this scale resulted in the survivors forming only a minority, about
a quarter or a third, of the city's adult population.[3] All other
adult Londoners were immigrants.

This chapter on the origins of Londoners will reflect the demographic composition of the city by looking first at the upbringing
and education of children, both in London and the provinces,
and then going on to consider the geographical origins and
motivations of the immigrants who made up such a predominant
part of the adult population of the city. Both sections will draw
on biographical material relating to individual Londoners whose
experiences reflect the population of the city as a whole.

i The Education of Children

'Joseph Laycock . . . was born in Bishopsgate-street; his father,
who sold fruit at a tavern-door, gave him little or no education,

but employed him in running of errands, or any such little jobbs he had to do, 'till Joe thinking himself big enough, as well as old enough, to trade for himself, purchased a wheelbarrow and went about the streets selling oranges and playing with dice, by which method he sometimes was a considerable gainer.'

'I [John Kelsey] was born in the town of Greenwich of very reputable parents; my father lived in a genteel manner. I was tenderly brought up in the fear of God, and in the Christian religion. I was put to the best of schools that could be found, and when I was capable of reading tollerably, I was put to a Latin boarding-school where I continued three years 'till the death of my father: then I was taken home and continued at other schools 'till I arrived to a tollerable competency of learning, in writing, arithmetick and Latin, so far as to undertake any business within a common sphere of life. At the age of about 17, I was put apprentice to a surgeon.'[4]

Childhood poses problems for the historian since the chief witness, the child, is rarely heard at all and parents too are normally silent about their relationships with their children. One is left with a few hints from diarists and autobiographers, a few vignettes providing a glimpse of children at home, at school or at play, a large number of complaints about the bad behaviour of the children of the poor, and a whole library of moralistic and didactic literature telling readers what children and child-rearing should be like but not necessarily what they were like.

Most of this literature makes dull reading, but it does make clear how seriously society regarded the responsibilities of parents. It was understood that some children as individuals might be so depraved that no amount of effort could reform them; 'the best education and instruction are often of no effect to stubborn and corrupt minds.' But such essentially evil children were believed to be exceptional and the majority were seen as wax, 'ready to be moulded into any form, and receive any impression'.[5] This moulding was the duty of parents and should be carried out with a nice mixture of tenderness and discipline, both pampering and savage correction being frowned on, and should be directed to the preparation of children for both this world and the next.

Religious instruction should start very early, so that children would acquire almost with their mother's milk a fear of God and a sense of their duty to parents and superiors. Such admonition was to be continued throughout childhood and should be reinforced by regular attendance at church and, ideally, family prayers and constant reading from the scriptures at home. As children grew older, it was time to think of more secular matters and to decide what career they should be directed towards. This decision should not be affected by vanity or pride on the part of parents who wished to use their children as vehicles to raise the family 'out of its original obscurity'. Social ambition was laudable and understandable, but only if the child was suitable to fulfil such a role, and it was one of the most important duties of a parent to 'discover the child's genius and temper' so that a correct choice of future occupation might be made and the child 'well dispos'd of, well settled in the world'.[6]

School was expected to buttress the good work started by parents, most surviving curricula placing great emphasis on character, morals and piety. Early teaching was combined with continuous religious instruction so that reading, for instance, was taught almost entirely from texts derived from the Bible and the catechism.[7] This monotonous diet continued right through the child's schooldays, but was later combined with rather more secular instruction designed to prepare pupils for the place that they might expect to take in the world. Such a place would depend on gender as well as on the wealth and social position of their parents.

Most children who went to school at all were exposed only to what we would call very basic education. This was provided at a variety of establishments, variously called ABC, petty, dame, parish or free schools, which taught reading first and, when this had been mastered, writing and possibly basic arithmetic. Such schools were open to both boys and girls and were widely scattered throughout the country so that the possibility of such a basic education existed everywhere except in the most remote parts of the countryside, while in London no child would be more than a few streets from such a school. Quality varied enormously. Some petty schools were extremely good by the standards of the day and often served to prepare children for the local grammar schools. Some were no more than child-minding services provided by people with little education themselves. But the great majority seem to have been perfectly adequate to perform their fairly limited functions, so that most children who went to school for a few years would be able at least to read and probably also to write by the time that they left. Some of these schools were supported by endowment and were free, but most required fees of at least a few pence a week, sufficient to deter poor parents from sending their children to them, especially when these children might be earning a few pence themselves.

There was a considerable expansion in the availability of basic education in the early eighteenth century with the development of the charity schools. These were free schools for poor children and were particularly successful in London, where there were over 5,000 places for boys and girls by 1729. Such schools had their critics, who believed it was dangerous to give the poor any education at all, lest they get ideas above their station. Others felt that free education would give the poor an unfair advantage over slightly less poor children whose parents had paid for their schooling, but generally the charity schools were welcomed as a means of disciplining poor children who would otherwise have been left by their parents 'to play in the streets, and to linger and pilfer from door to door'.[8] Charity children received the absolute minimum of education, sometimes reading and nothing more, and were constantly reminded of their subordinate position in society so that they might later take their place in it as obedient and dutiful servants or menial workers.

Some writers felt that 'to divert children from useful labour until they are 14 or 15 years old is a wrong way to qualify them for it when they are grown up'.[9] As a result, some charity schools combined their basic instruction with industrial work and so were similar to the workhouses, the lowest form of educational establishment, which catered for poor orphans and abandoned children. Such unfortunates had previously been entrusted by parishes to nurses and foster-parents who were supposed to bring them up in their own families until they were old enough to be apprenticed. However, critics believed that such an upbringing was almost bound to lead to irreligion, vice and idleness and, from the early eighteenth century, more and more of such children were being directed to workhouses where it was hoped that they would acquire the discipline of a religious education as well as becoming inured to labour by being 'taught to work as soon as they are able'. By the early 1730s, there were nearly 2,000 children in London's forty-eight workhouses and working charity schools, most of them getting about two hours' instruction a day in reading and sometimes writing and arithmetic, while most of the rest of their time was devoted to such monotonous industrial tasks as spinning mop yarn or picking oakum from old ropes, with just an hour off at noon for 'dinner and play'.[10]

There were changes too in the provision of education for that minority of children, mainly boys, who went beyond the basics. Before 1650, this had been monopolized by the grammar schools whose classical curriculum consisted almost entirely of Latin, though Greek was also taught to a few of the more advanced pupils. For some boys, such an education was preparation for university and a professional career, but mainly this immersion in a long dead culture was seen as valuable in itself. Latin would not only keep the boys out of mischief and prevent them from becoming idle, but would also discipline their minds and prepare them to play a useful part in the commonwealth.

This obsession with Latin came under attack in the second half of the seventeenth century, for reasons well expressed by Francis Brokesby in 1701: 'That learning which is acquired at Grammar Schools is of little or no use to such as are set to ordinary Trades, and consequently that time might have been better spent in attaining some useful knowledge, nay much more profitably in learning to write a good hand, arithmetick, and other things of this nature.' Most boys were set to trades which had no use for Latin and they were increasingly catered for, especially in London, by the establishment of writing and mathematical schools where pupils were taught how to express themselves in their own language in an easily readable hand, as well as practical subjects such as foreign languages, mathematics, accounting, navigation and surveying. By the middle of the eighteenth century, a writer who echoed Brokesby's attack on the grammar schools – 'five or six years under the discipline of the rod, to acquire an imperfect knowledge of a few Latin words' – was able to note that 'this absurd custom is however less generally practised than formerly'.[11]

The trend towards a more practical education for children destined to be tradesmen was paralleled by a growth in boarding schools, many of which were just outside London or in the metropolis itself. These establishments were of all sorts, ranging through schools such as Eton and Westminster (which had already acquired their modern reputations as training grounds for the elite), other lesser grammar schools, private schools providing a classical education, schools teaching fencing, horsemanship, deportment and other military or genteel skills, as well as schools which specialized in the new subjects mentioned above. Boarding, as today, was believed to toughen the child, to create a healthy spirit of competition and to provide the opportunity for making useful social contacts.

There was a simultaneous growth in boarding schools for girls, though these offered a very different curriculum. Few had any intellectual pretensions and their functions were those of finishing schools where young ladies and girls of the middle and upper classes were taught music, dancing, singing and French, as well as the needlework, writing and good manners which were the staples of all education for girls. Such education remained second rate at all levels compared with what was available for boys. This was partly because a patriarchal society considered that girls were intellectually inferior; but it also reflected the vocational intentions of much early modern schooling. Girls received a schooling which was deemed a satisfactory preparation for the life they would live after school; in other words, they were taught the skills necessary for running a household or for 'women's work'.[12]

What was expected was reflected in the instructions given to her husband by an expectant mother in Cheshire. 'If [the child] bee a daughter . . . I desire her bringinge up may bee learninge the Bible as my sisters doo, good huswifery, writing and good work; other learning a woman needs not.' Many schools, especially those catering for the poor, would not even have thought it necessary for a girl to learn to write, but they all taught reading and 'work' (i.e. needlework) and often 'casting accounts', which meant simple arithmetic to enable some control to be maintained over shopping and household budgets. Most also taught housewifery, details of which were spelt out in *The Poor Girl's Primer*: 'Learn to spin wool and linen; learn to sew shifts and shirts and caps; learn to knit hose; learn to bake and brew and wash; learn to clean rooms and pots and pans.' All girls' schools also placed emphasis on 'good manners and behaviour, the grounds and principles of the Christian religion'.[13]

The teachers who gave evidence in the London Church courts reflect the range of education provided in the metropolis. At one end of the scale, there were people like James Maccubine who taught at a charity school in St Giles or Thomas Barter of Clerkenwell who had kept 'a school for the teaching to read and write for the last eleven years'. At the other was Thomas Bushell of the Strand who taught 'young gentlemen Latin and French'. There were also many writing masters, most of whom kept their own schools, as well as mathematics teachers, music, dancing and singing teachers, fencing masters like Daniel Kahan, a native of Carrickfergus, and William Atkins, a carpenter who taught his trade to the children in Bridewell. Teaching did not pay very well and several of these men had a second occupation, usually one requiring learning, such as public notary, scrivener, parish clerk or clergyman. The women teachers underline the indifferent education available for girls. The most academic-sounding was Joan Johnson, the wife of a Chelsea pensioner who 'hath kept a school for the teaching of children to write, read and cast accounts for many years'. Two teachers taught reading only, two needlework only, and two both; one taught French, one singing, while the widow Dorcas Jurin taught 'the girls in the workhouse in Bishopsgate Street to work and read'. Maybe she had also taught her son, who kept a writing and grammar school at the Hand and Pen in Little Moorfields.[14]

How many Londoners were able to benefit from the wide range of schooling available, whether they were those who came to London as immigrant adults or, more particularly, were people who grew up in the metropolis itself? And how well did the parents of London children fulfil their duty to bring them up in the fear of God and ready to take their place in the world? Such questions are difficult to answer since few records throw any light on the upbringing and education of children. People were quite often asked where they were born and what was the status or occupation of their father. There are also records which show when and where they were apprenticed. But nearly all sources are silent on the long period between birth and apprenticeship, so that most studies of education can go no further than to discuss the types of school available and the curricula and

teaching methods as revealed in manuals of instruction. Who
benefited or did not benefit from what was available remains
largely a matter of speculation.

There is however one source of information which can
enlighten us on the education of individual Londoners and
hence, by inference, of Londoners as a whole. This source, which
may at first seem an unlikely one, relates exclusively to people
who were hanged in the city. It was the duty of the Ordinary
(chaplain) of Newgate Prison to prepare the condemned felons
for their tragic end, by getting them to confess and if possible
repent their crimes before they faced their maker. From the late
seventeenth century, successive Ordinaries also interviewed the
convicts and prepared short biographies which were reproduced
in an *Account* which was put on sale to the public. These
published biographies were designed not as mere entertainment
but as morality tales carrying a clear warning of just how easy it
was to slip from small faults into greater ones (although it did not
require such a great fault to be hanged in eighteenth-century
London). Since the first fall from grace often occurred in
childhood, or shortly afterwards, most of these biographies have
a section which outlines the upbringing and education of the
felons. This section is usually very brief, but it is sufficiently
consistent in its content to enable some generalizations to be
made, especially during the period 1725–46 when James Guthrie
was the Ordinary.[15]

It may seem odd to use the biographies of criminals as a guide
to the education of Londoners as a whole, but in fact both
contemporaries and modern writers have emphasized the simi-
larities rather than the differences which existed between the
criminal and the law-abiding majority. 'They are simply
accounts of the commonplace, mundane culture of plebeian
England,' wrote E. P. Thompson of the *Accounts* of the Ordinary
of Newgate, 'notes on the lives of unremarkable people, distinguished from their fellows by little else except the fact that by bad
luck or worse judgement they got caught up in the toils of the
law.'[16] This seems essentially true.

Much of this book is based on biographical material from
another source, the depositions made before the London Church
courts. Where the two sources overlap, as in the description of
work and careers, it is clear that both include people right across

the social spectrum and that most of these people are as unremarkable as E. P. Thompson suggests. Those who were hanged follow career patterns which can very easily be duplicated from those who made depositions before the courts, that is until something starts to go seriously wrong, very often in the teens or early twenties, and the future criminal starts to deviate from the norm. The only real difference lies in the social balance of individuals in the two groups, the hanged tending to come more from the lower levels of society, though by no means exclusively. An education at Eton or Westminster was no guarantee against death at Tyburn.[17]

Since the *Accounts* were intended as a warning, one might expect that the parents of criminals would bear much of the blame for their children's depravity, if only to push home an obvious object lesson in the importance of parental responsibility. This was certainly true in some cases, such as that of William Burroughs of St Giles whose 'mean' (i.e. poor) parents 'gave him no education at school but brought him up to a pitiful idle life, and let him run about the streets as he pleased, as soon as he was able to do it'. Such an upbringing was almost bound to lead to trouble and the Ordinary can hardly have been surprised to learn that, after hanging around stables since the age of six, young William soon fell into the company of 'that dreadful society of gin-drinkers, whores, thieves, house-breakers, street-robbers, pick-pockets, and the whole train of the most notable black-guards in and about London'. The only real surprise in such a biography was that William managed to dodge the gallows until he was twenty-two. Many other lads who had got into that 'dreadful society' were hanged much younger.[18]

There must have been many children like William Burroughs in London, neglected by their parents or simply deserted, like Richard Eades whose father ran away overseas 'when he was but young'. His mother did her best for some time, but then she too 'went away and left him, and he never heard or knew what became of her since, so that poor Eades being now left to the wide World, or to the Parish, or in short to any body who would take him, was exposed a prey to the Black Guard Boys and Girls in the streets'.[19] The death of parents as well as their desertion was an obvious and sadly common danger for young children. Death of a mother not only removed a tender and important influence from a young child's life, but it might also lead to the wicked stepmother syndrome, as it did for Robert Perkins who 'lived very happily with his father, so long as his mother lived, and afterwards, till his father married again; but then being forbidden the house, his disasters began'. Death of a father was likely to lead to a serious fall in family income, which often meant removal from school and an early introduction to the world of work; it also exposed children to the unfettered fondness of mothers. Barbara Spencer, for instance, who was burned to death for counterfeiting in 1721, 'could not but impute her sad end to the too great indulgence her mother used towards her . . . being never curbed or restrained'.[20]

Death of both parents was potentially an even greater disaster, though society had created institutions to deal with this only too common problem. Thomas Wright, for instance, was 'put to nurse' at an early age, but he was fortunate in his foster-parents, who brought him up very well, his troubles not starting until after he left their home. Thomas Homan's bricklayer father died of a fall when he was two and his mother died a year later, but he was lucky enough to be taken in by a carpenter uncle who managed to get him admitted to Christ's Hospital 'where he remained near nine years'. Other orphans were not so fortunate. Richard Sheppard was left in 'a desolate condition' when his Yorkshire immigrant parents died. There were no friends or relations to help him and his only option was to scrape a living by cleaning shoes in the streets, 'till being harrassed by tormenting beadles, and often committed to Bridewell as a vagrant, he was resolved to take another course of living', a fatal course which ended on the gallows.[21]

These stories of neglect, desertion and parental poverty are what one might expect in the biographies of early eighteenth-century criminals, most of whom were in their teens and twenties when they were hanged at Tyburn, and it would not be hard to expand the examples of such deprived childhoods. But in fact a reading of the *Accounts* suggests that such stories were the exception rather than the rule and that most parents, even of criminals, tried hard and normally successfully to bring up their children according to the expectation of the age. Some parents were of course too poor to do much about the education of their children, a fact noted but not necessarily condemned by the

Ordinaries, who seem to have been reasonable men who did not think that poverty itself was a crime, even if it provided the background to much criminal activity. Many poor parents provided discipline if not education for their children, while others strove hard to provide schooling as well, such as the parents of Thomas Talbot who 'was taught to read and write, though born of parents of low degree'. John Dean, a country boy, reflects what must have been a common pattern of education for the poor: 'His parents' poverty preventing their paying constantly for his schooling, so that what little he learnt was by starts, sometimes going a day, sometimes a week, as they could muster money.' No doubt this education did not amount to much in total, but one feels that John's parents, like many others, were trying hard to do their best for the boy, since the pennies spent on schooling could well have been spent some other way.[22]

Nor were poor widows all doting or careless of their children's education. Thomas Andrews was the son of 'mean' parents from Gloucestershire, his father being a labourer who came to London to look for work and died soon after his arrival. His widowed mother got a place as barmaid in a tavern and 'was very kind and tender of the son, put him to school, and go him taught to read, write and cypher', an education which was not however sufficient to prevent him from being hanged at nineteen for highway robbery, having been 'totally ruin'd by keeping company with lewd women'. John Davis's parents moved from Portsmouth to London where his father also died, leaving 'him young. His mother was a careful industrious woman, and did what she could for the keeping of six young children. She put John to school'; but he too was to be hanged for highway robbery.[23]

Such sad stories prompt one to speculate on what went wrong after parents had tried so hard to educate their children and keep them on the right path. Speculation on the reasons for crime was as rife in the eighteenth century as it is today, but two reasons stand out in the *Accounts* of the Ordinaries. In their view many children were just bad, like John Davis, who, despite the care and trouble taken by his mother, was 'a cross, perverse boy, disobedient to his mother, would not keep the school'. There was nothing much that parents could do about children like this, who would almost inevitably go from bad to worse as they got older.

Such idle, disobedient children were likely to play truant and so get no benefit from their schooling. The parents of John Atkins of Holborn 'would have given him what education their circumstances could afford, but his inclination was not that way turned, and when sent to school, he chose rather to loiter by the way with any loose and idle company; so that he scarce ever saw the inside of a school.' Joseph Peacock was another London boy who 'for one day he vouchsafed to go to school, he played truant five days'. His parents, who were 'in a pretty good way of life', eventually got fed up with laying out their money 'to no purpose' and sent him to sea as a cabin-boy when he was eleven. Others who did go to school were just as bad, such as James Brown, who 'when at school he was full of play, and idle to the last degree . . . He says he believes he could read a little formerly, but disuse had effaced the idea of every letter of the Alphabet.' Of course, not all bad boys were bad scholars. George Basset was educated at the Welsh School in Clerkenwell where 'he was a pretty good proficient in any exercise he was to go through and left the school with reputation'. His problem was that 'he was a pick-pocket almost from his cradle and never expected any other fate, but to be hanged'.[24]

However, most young criminals were described by the Ordinaries as neither innately wicked nor brought up badly by their parents. They were simply too weak to resist the many temptations placed in their path. They received the education fitting to their station and left home to go to work or start an apprenticeship, and it was then, after leaving home, that they began to get into trouble. Early eighteenth-century London offered many enticements for young people just free of the constraints of school and parental discipline, and such attractions soon drew the weak into idleness, vice and depravity as they deserted the world of work or the 'slavery' of apprenticeship for the lure of bad company, gambling, drink, idleness, petty theft and 'lewd women'. Many older people turned to crime in desperation as they struggled against poverty and the misfortunes of the world, but most young offenders were drawn into becoming pickpockets and street robbers by a desire to join in the high living and excitement to which they had been introduced by 'bad company'. Or, at least, that was the Ordinaries of Newgate thought, and who can say they were wrong?

Since most of these hanged men and women received at least

some education and several of them were very well educated indeed, the *Accounts* enable us to make some generalizations about the education of Londoners as a whole, for it seems a reasonable assumption that those who did not die on the gallows were unlikely to be any worse educated than those who were hanged. The *Accounts*, particularly those written by John Guthrie, used a handful of adjectives to describe parents and these words can serve as a shorthand guide to wealth or status. Poor parents were described as such, or were labelled 'very mean', 'mean', or 'mean but honest'. 'Honest' parents referred to those who were artisans or small tradesmen, such people as tailors, butchers or cheesemongers. And, at the top of the scale, since the children of the middling and upper ranks of society were not exempt from the gallows, there were such adjectives as 'reputable', 'creditable', 'respected', 'genteel' or even 'of great honour'.

Several 'mean' parents', especially those who were the country parents of immigrants, were unable to give their sons any education at all. Some of these children remained 'quite illiterate', such as the shepherd boy John Ireland of Lincolnshire who later came up to London to become a servant. Others were taught by their parents 'to read and write a little', like Patrick Kelley of Connaught, though he had 'forgot all' by the time he came to London as a labourer. But it would be wrong to think that all sons of poor parents were deprived of at least some schooling, even if it was only as little as that acquired by 'Country Dick' Lee, who did not go 'above a month to school to an old woman, so that he could neither write or read'. Most of the poor boys whose schooling was recorded by the Ordinary as 'indifferent', 'very little', 'little or no education' or 'hardly any education' did rather better than this, with at least a couple of years at school and often more; 'not much education' in the case of John Johnson, the son of a London porter, was six or seven years in the Ward School in Friday Street. Such children had usually learned to read and could often write and 'cypher' as well, some of them having learned such skills in London charity schools.[25]

There was hope too for those whose education did not get this far, if they were as enterprising as William Dickenson, 'a poor silly country boy' who came to London in his mid-twenties. 'His parents dying when he was nine or ten years of age, he was put into a free-school . . . where he learned only to read and was then sent about his business', as a day-servant in husbandry. But later, 'he, together with some few others of his age and neighbourhood, employed a person after their day-labour was over in the long winter evenings, to instruct them in reading and writing; by which he got a pretty livelihood and they received considerable improvement; so that Dickenson was able both to read and write tollerably well'.[26]

Overall, 'mean' parents could provide their sons with only a 'mean' education, as the Ordinary sarcastically remarked of the Irishman John Cassody, and as one might expect.[27] Only a small proportion seem to have been totally illiterate, most being able at least to read a little. But it was also only a minority of such children who got a decent education by the standards of the day: about one in five of these sons of mean parents were educated 'fit for an employment' or had schooling 'sufficient for one who was to get his living in a mechanical way', this normally meaning the basic reading, writing and 'vulgar arithmetic' taught in a local free or charity school. Poor parents and a poor education also meant poor prospects. Few of these children were apprenticed to respectable trades and most took their place in the lower ranks of the London labour force, as errand boys, labourers, river workers, stable hands, sailors, servants, porters, market workers, chimney-sweeps or in such poor trades as weaving and shoe-making.

There were nearly as many hanged men whose parents were described as 'honest' as 'mean', and here we move into quite a different world. Almost without exception, these 'honest' artisans and small shopkeepers, both in London and the provinces, were able to give their children what the Ordinary described as a 'good' education. Such an education takes on a standard form in the *Accounts*, son after son being credited with the same sort of schooling (and often in the same words) as Cockey Wager, the son of a London butcher whose parents gave him 'good education, and kept him at school to reading, writing and arithmetick, in order to his being qualified to business; and not neglecting his real benefit, they instructed him in the principles of the Christian religion and in the knowledge of his duty both to God and man'. Even a huge family did not prevent such parents from doing their duty. Henry Cook's father was a leather-cutter who had 'a great number of children, at least 19 or 20, now but eight living, all which he has handsomely brought up'. Henry himself 'was put to school to a gentleman in Sandy Court, near Houndsditch, with whom I continued and was instructed till I could write tollerable well and learned arithmetick as far as the Rule of Three'.[28] These 'good' educations normally started around the age of six or seven and lasted many years, so long indeed that it was often a problem to know how to fill up the hours, since 'a boy has commonly a great deal of time to spare from his having learned to read and write to his being of an age to be put apprentice, and it is asked how he can be employed and kept out of mischief'.[29]

One obvious answer was to add to the basic free school education the sort of subjects taught at writing and mathematical schools. John Marsland, for instance, the son of a wholesale cheesemonger from Aldgate, learned navigation as well as the basic 'good' education and at the age of fourteen was sent to sea to serve in the Guinea slave trade. Richard Brabant, whose father was an honest grazier near Bath, spent two years in a Bristol boarding school where he learned book-keeping and acquired that skill in writing 'several hands very well' that was later to lead to his execution for forging bills of exchange. He became a solicitor's clerk after leaving school, but the great majority of these sons of honest parents were apprenticed to trades as their fathers had been before them, having had some seven or eight years of education.[30]

A few of the sons of 'honest' parents had done a little Latin at school, but such erudition was normally reserved for the sons of 'reputable', 'respected' or 'genteel' parents. Some of these latter boys got the same 'good' education as the sons of honest parents, but most got the very best schooling available, such as William Maynee who was brought up in Canterbury by his clergyman uncle and was 'kept at as good schools as any in the Kingdom and made good proficiency in Latin, Greek, casting accounts and writing, to fit him for any kind of business'. Several went to boarding school, such as John Kelsey of Greenwich, who went to 'a Latin boarding-school' for three years, or John Toon, the son of a Shoreditch dyer, who was sent to a boarding school in East Ham. 'No expence was saved in his education. After he had been some years at school and all necessary learning had been given him, both as a gentleman and one that was to engage in business, he was put apprentice to one Mr Burchet, an eminent iron-

monger in Foster Lane who had married his own sister.' The
most thorough education paid for by 'reputable' parents in this
small sample, or at least the one most thoroughly spelled out by
the Ordinary, was that given around 1700 to Thomas Bridge, a
surgeon's instrument-maker who later murdered his wife. He
was sent first to school in Bloomsbury to learn writing and
arithmetic, and then 'went to a Minister in Dyet's [Dyott] Street
to learn Latin and continued there till I read Erasmus'. Next he
was enrolled for two years at the famous writing school in Foster
Lane run by Charles Snell, where he learned 'writing and
merchants accounts . . . and went also to a French school at the
same time'.[31]

Money, 'reputation' and a very good education meant that
most of these boys were intended for respectable occupations,
though the depravity of some of them ensured that these
intentions were not always carried out. If they were apprenticed
to trades or crafts, they would be put with 'eminent' masters who
would give them the best training available and introduce them
to a reputable clientele. Many were intended for professional
careers, as attorneys, surgeons or chemists, while some were
being educated to be gentlemen or placemen, members of that
privileged minority who avoided the vulgar world of work
altogether. The wealth or poverty of parents and the education
that money or the lack of it could bestow on a child were
therefore of paramount importance in determining the material
fate of Londoners, though misfortune or the supposed evil genius
of the child could soon destroy the apparent advantages of birth.
The death or business failure of a father, bad luck, a taste for
gambling, drink, lewd women or some other form of depravity
could soon put the rich boy on the same level as the poor boy and
ensure that both would suffer the same fate on the gallows at
Tyburn.

Far fewer women than men were hanged, but there were
sufficient to enable a comparison to be made between their
education and that of the boys discussed above. The daughters
of 'mean' parents were even worse served than their sons, nearly
all of them being described as having 'no' or 'little or no'
education. What little meant is spelled out in the case of
Catherine Lineham, a Dublin girl whose parents 'taught her
indeed to read a little, but neglecting it, she soon forgot all', or

Catherine Connor, another Irish girl, who 'had no education but the needle'.[32] Few 'mean' daughters were taught to write and the best that most could hope for was to be proficient at reading and needlework.

The daughters of 'honest' parents, on the other hand, all went to school, where most of them had a 'good', 'pretty good' or 'decent and commendable' education. This was usually confined to learning to read and write, to sew and, most importantly, to be instructed 'in Christian principles'. Some of these girls were also taught to 'cast accounts', while Anne Hazzard, the daughter of a Poland Street tailor, was sent to boarding school in Sussex 'where she was taught French, dancing, musick etc.'. The daughters of 'creditable' parents were not likely to do much better than this. They might well get a lengthy education, but its content would be very different from what was given to their brothers. Sarah Wilmhurst, for instance, 'the daughter of creditable parents in Town . . . went to school when I was at a proper age to one Mrs Banks . . . where I learned to work at my needle and likewise to dance. I continued there about two years. After I came from that school, I went to Poor Jury-Lane by Aldgate where I learned all sorts of plainwork [i.e. more sewing] and continued there about three years. The last school I went to was to one Mr Busking, facing Creed-church in Leadenhall-street, writing-master and I continued with him some considerable time.' What she learned from Mr Busking is not stated, but it was probably writing and 'casting accounts'.[33]

It is rare to find direct evidence about the schooling of any but exceptional people and these short biographies of hanged men and women are therefore invaluable for any understanding of the education received by Londoners. They show that virtually all children, both boys and girls, whose parents were in the artisan class and above had been to school, often for several years, and that formal education was by no means unknown to the sons of poor parents, if not to their daughters. Some indication that these biographies reflect the general experience of the city's population can be obtained by analysing whether Londoners were able to sign their name or merely leave a mark when they were required to do one or the other to show acceptance of the accuracy of a deposition. This can be only a very rough guide to literacy and hence by inference to education, but it is the only guide that is available on any scale for the early modern period. Those who have studied the subject suggest that the ability to sign normally meant that the person could read fairly fluently, since reading was taught before writing at school. However, it did not necessarily mean that they could write at all fluently, a point which can be confirmed from many of the signatures looked at for this study, especially those of women, which are often very shaky and certainly appear to have been written by people who rarely used a pen.[34]

On the other hand, studies of Victorian literacy have suggested that as many as three-quarters of those unable to sign their names were capable of reading simple printed texts. This cannot be tested directly for our period, but there is certainly plenty of evidence that people leaving marks were quite capable of reading. Catherine Dybel, for instance, left a mark, but she also deposed that she knew 'ye nature and meaning of an oath and has got such knowledge by reading ye scriptures'; the Bible, as already mentioned, was the usual text from which people learned to read. Other witnesses, especially in probate cases, were specifically asked if they could read or write and their answers suggest that there were basically three levels of attainment – those who could read anything and could write, those who could 'read in print, but cannot write or read written hand' and those who could neither read nor write.[35]

Unfortunately, there are not enough of these cases for analysis, but the signature evidence on its own suggests that all Londoners, men and women, London-born and immigrants, were exceptionally literate by the standards of the age and were growing more so across the period studied. National studies indicate that about thirty to forty per cent of men and ten to fifteen per cent of women could sign their names at the beginning of our period, figures which had risen considerably by the 1750s to sixty per cent for men and forty per cent for women.[36] The rates for a sample of Londoners who gave evidence in the Church courts between 1660 and 1725 are set out in Table 2.1. These show the expected discrepancy between men and women, but the rates for both sexes are very high compared with the national averages. Such figures not only confirm that education in London must have been very good; they also suggest that it was on average the best educated provincial men and women, those

TABLE 2.1 Literacy Patterns of Londoners

| | % signing deposition | |
	Men	Women
London-born	93.1	56.1
Immigrants	85.7	47.8
All deponents	87.6	50.3
Deponents born before 1660	83.4	41.1
Deponents born 1660 & after	93.0	59.4

Source: Male and female 'origins' samples (see pp. 263–5)

who were the children of the 'honest' rather than the 'mean', who migrated to the city.

It would be impossible to compare this signature data directly with the impressionistic evidence gathered from the *Accounts* of the Ordinary of Newgate. The Church court sample was drawn from all strata of the London population, but witnesses tended to be 'respectable' rather than otherwise and so the analysis probably exaggerates the degree of literacy in the metropolis. The hanged sample was of course far from respectable and so will exaggerate illiteracy. Nevertheless, both samples suggest that the numbers totally illiterate were fairly small and that the written word was accessible to nearly all London men and a majority of London women. Indeed, both approaches indicate that Londoners, both men and women, were amongst the best educated and most literate people in the early modern world.[37]

The Church court depositions provide no evidence about the parents of deponents, but they do give information on occupations, which makes it possible to determine which people were more likely to be illiterate in London. In the male sample, some 400 people with eighty different occupations left a mark, suggesting that illiteracy was a fairly common experience at the bottom, drifting section of many trades. However, fourteen occupations contributed ten or more people to this sample of the illiterate. These occupations are listed in Table 2.2 and they are very much the same types of poor occupations engaged in by those hanged men whose 'mean' parents were unable to provide them with any education.

Illiteracy was much commoner amongst women, as has been

TABLE 2.2 Occupations of Illiterate Males

Servant	Waterman
Shoemaker	Tailor
Sailor	Soldier
Victualler	Coachman
Porter	Blacksmith
Weaver	Carpenter
Labourer	Butcher

seen, but illiterate women no less than illiterate men tended to cluster in certain poorly paid occupations, such as charring, laundry-work, hawking and the winding of silk, this last being an occupation largely monopolized by the wives and daughters of sailors in the East End.[38] It is clear that for both men and women it paid to be able to read and write in early modern London.

ii Migrants

'London, like the Ocean, that receives the muddy and dirty Brooks, as well as the clear and rapid Rivers, swallows up all the scum and filth of the Country.'[39]

'It is observed, that in most Families of England, if there be any Son or Daughter that excels the rest in Beauty, or Wit, or perhaps Courage, or Industry, or any other rare Quality, London is their North Star, and they are never at rest till they point directly thither.'[40]

London was not unusual in its numbers of immigrants. All great cities in early modern Europe shared the same demographic conditions which made massive immigration a necessity if they were to remain the same size, let alone grow. Overcrowding, poor water and a filthy environment, 'the smoaks, stinks and close air' of big cities, meant that many more people died in them each year than were born. This 'urban graveyard effect', as it has been called, was already understood by contemporaries. John Graunt, for instance, noted that 'London is supplied with people from out of the country, whereby not only to supply the overplus differences of burials . . . , but likewise to increase its inhabitants'. More recently, it has been estimated that a net figure of some 8,000 people would have had to make their way to London each year to enable the city's population to grow as it did between 1650 and 1750. The gross figure would of course have been even higher, since an unknown number of people left London each year to return to the countryside.[41]

What sort of people were these immigrants? Were they 'the scum and filth of the country', as the quotation from a very sour Daniel Defoe at the head of this section insists? Or were they the best of their countrymen and countrywomen, as the second quotation suggests? Where did they come from? Why did they come, if migration to London put them at such risk of an early grave? How well did they adapt to city life when they arrived? These are difficult questions to answer since most migrants remain largely anonymous and provide little information for the historian to analyse. This is particularly true of female migrants, who probably comprised a majority of the 8,000 or so people who made their way each year to the metropolis.

London had once had a large male surplus in its population, but, by the 1690s if not earlier, this situation had been reversed and early eighteenth-century London was a city in which women considerably outnumbered men. Contemporaries thought this imbalance was caused by the large numbers of men who went abroad and died there, by 'the wars, and the sea, and trade, and other incidents [which] have carried the men so much away that there is no proportion between the sexes'.[42] Such an explanation makes some sense, but is not really sufficient to account for a complete reversal in the sex ratio of the city, since male Londoners had been subject to such accidents abroad at least since Elizabethan times. It is much more likely that the change was brought about by a shift in the balance of male and female immigration into the city, a flow once dominated by men becoming one in which women formed the majority.

Many things might have caused this, but the most plausible reason is the change in demand for domestic servants. This took two forms: an increase in the number of those employing servants and a different gender breakdown of the domestic servant population. In the sixteenth and early seventeenth centuries, a much higher proportion of servants were male than they were to be later, a ratio reflecting an older type of household where servants were potentially armed men.[43] By the 1690s, however, about eighty per cent of all domestic servants in City households were female. Even in the West End, where large numbers of male retainers remained common, the balance was shifting towards the female sex.[44]

The experience of London was to be shared rather later by other European cities. In both Geneva and Paris, for example, there was a change from male to female servants in the eighteenth century, with a resulting effect on the cities' sex structure. Even that most aristocratic of early modern cities, Madrid, shifted from male retainers to female domestics in the second half of the eighteenth century, leading to a female surplus in the city's population for the first time in the early nineteenth century.[45] The change seems to be a particular form of 'the transition from feudalism to capitalism' in which the large male households of a more aristocratic or feudal past were transformed into the large female households of the more bourgeois eighteenth and nineteenth centuries, it being clear to male contemporaries that 'the proportion of women in an urban population constitutes a sure index of comfort'.[46]

A growth in demand for female domestic servants was just one aspect of that demand for comfort which has underpinned the development of the modern economy, but it made a fundamental change in the choices open to young women in the English countryside. Those who desired to leave their homes for the big city, for whatever reason, could now feel confident that an opportunity to earn their living awaited them. Tens of thousands took this opportunity and joined the flow of migrants to London.

'City-dwellers of long standing and newly arrived rustics were widely different in appearance and manners,' writes Daniel Roche of eighteenth-century Paris. 'The former were large and plump, pink and white, their complexion unspoilt by work in the fields, and their physical ideal was the round-bellied bulk of the self-made bourgeois . . . The newcomers were lean and tanned, burnt by the sun of the field and the highway, their bodies were deformed by hard labour, their clothes dirty and neglected.'[47] Such bucolic stereotypes are common in the work of historians writing about rural-urban migration on the continent. Indeed, such work insists that immigrants were not only different from the city-born when they arrived but that they remained different, this being reflected in such fundamental characteristics as marriage patterns, life expectancy, types of work undertaken, crime rates and the parts of the city where they lived.

Allan Sharlin, for instance, distinguished between 'citizens' and 'migrants' in an article attacking the concept of the 'urban graveyard effect'. He argued that such a blanket analysis masked an essential difference between the migrant and the native-born (or citizen). Natives, he thought, enjoyed a small natural increase. Migrants, on the other hand, were mainly servants who did not marry in the city and so did not contribute to fertility, while they were more likely than natives to die as they had not acquired the immunities possessed by survivors of an urban childhood. Migrants as a result had a very large natural decrease, with very few births and many deaths, even though most of them were clustered in the relatively low mortality age-groups of young adulthood. He concluded by arguing, paradoxically, that cities would have grown faster without immigration.[48]

A similar world is portrayed by David Ringrose in his discussion of the population of Madrid. He found that there were two quite different groups, this time called the 'core' of native-born, who monopolized commercial life and all the better paid or more skilled artisan jobs, and the 'envelope' of immigrants who were nearly all servants or did the dirty work of the city. Such people were quite often only temporary migrants who swelled the age-groups of the city population between the late teens and the thirties before returning to their villages with their meagre savings. Daniel Roche found a very similar situation in eighteenth-century Paris, while both these writers thought that there was little assimilation between the two groups and little sign of the 'melting-pot' which has been thought to be characteristic of nineteenth-century American cities with their plethora of immigrants. 'In short,' writes Roche, 'there were two cities confronting each other in a way that should not surprise anyone from the late twentieth century, when immigrants are playing a similar role.'[49]

Both these writers also emphasize that female immigrants were even less likely to become assimilated within the city than their male counterparts. Female immigrants were normally younger than male immigrants, worked mainly in domestic service and were much more likely than males to treat city residence as a temporary phase before returning to their villages to buy themselves a peasant husband with their city savings.

Female immigrants also tended to travel much shorter distances than male immigrants, most of them coming from the immediately adjacent areas which provided the cities with food as well as young women. Such findings are mirrored by Cissie Fairchilds in her study of servants in France, much of which is based on material from Toulouse and Bordeaux. She found that her female domestics tended to come from the poorest families in the poorest rural areas in the vicinity of these cities.[50]

A picture thus emerges from the continental literature of young female immigrants to the cities smelling of the farmyard and soon to return to it, if they did not die first; a flow of undernourished, unattractive and presumably uneducated country girls who added very little to the cities they dwelt in for a few years. Male migrants were slightly superior, but were also destined to a future as unassimilated second-class citizens in a world which despised them and allowed them to take only the very worst and most poorly paid jobs.

As Roche remarks, such a picture is not unfamiliar to those who live in late twentieth-century cities. Was it true of migrants in early modern London? The evidence is not easy to assemble, but the impression is that, although migrants to London had some disadvantages, they were not in the main the lesser beings portrayed in continental studies, as has already been hinted in the analysis of literacy in the first section of this chapter. It is true that most migrant women went into domestic service as their first job in London, just as they did abroad, but then so did most of the London-born women. It is also true that many migrant men could only find the lowest types of menial work, as porters, servants, labourers and coal-heavers, but this was equally the fate of many young men born in the poorer parts of London such as St Giles and the East End. Access to better jobs depended mainly on the wealth and status of one's parents and the education and upbringing that they provided. In this respect, Londoners were at some advantage since wealth was concentrated in the city and some of that wealth could be used to promote the future of the city's more privileged children. But neither privilege nor wealth was monopolized by London and there are plenty of examples of provincial parents paying out high premiums and finding good masters to ensure their sons a potentially profitable future in the city. Such country boys seem to have been treated by their city masters without prejudice, as indeed they were by the livery companies, which strove, somewhat unsuccessfully, to maintain their former control over the flow of apprentices to London trades.[51]

It is also unusual to find in London that emphasis on provincial origins which one finds for instance in Paris, where a person's *pays* was regularly used as a distinguishing feature, as well as to a certain extent defining expected character and occupation.[52] Londoners were certainly well aware of their origins and indeed proud to acknowledge them. News from their home counties or villages was eagerly sought from carriers and wagoners or in taverns and inns which specialized in serving those who came from a particular county or region. Clubs were formed from the middle of the seventeenth century for the same purpose, such as the Society of the Natives of Herefordshire. But such ties do not seem to have prevented assimilation both with native Londoners and with those from other counties. With the exception of the French and the Irish, it is difficult to find evidence that there were immigrant 'ghettos' within the city – streets or neighbourhoods in which most people came from Devon or Yorkshire, for example. Nor were immigrants normally singled out as such in common parlance, despite the fact that their origins must have constantly been apparent from their accents and their use of dialect. One gets the occasional Staffordshire Nan or Yorkshire George in criminal records but, for the most part, the London-born and the migrant alike were distinguished by occupation, marital and social status or appearance rather than by his or her origin, which is another indication that perhaps the melting pot melted rather better than it did in continental cities.

This is not to say that there was no prejudice. There was, of course, but it was mainly directed against those whose origins were not English at all, against the Scots, the Irish and the Welsh, the last being the common butt of jokes in chapbooks of the day. English migrants might be mocked as countrymen in a period which invented the phrase 'country bumpkin', but such condescension does not seem to have affected their assimilation within the city.[53]

Was migration to the city merely a temporary phase in the lives of those who came to London, as it is said to have been for the majority of continental migrants? It certainly was for some. There were, for example, many women who came to London each summer to work in the gardens and meadows surrounding the city and then returned to their country homes with much needed cash in the autumn. Many men too had only a fleeting relationship with the city, especially those in transport occupations – wagoners, pedlars, drovers and of course many of the huge population of seamen in the East End who might give a London address but very rarely live at it. Other male migrants used London earnings to maintain a family living in the country, such as Samuel Harris, tailor of Southwark, whose labours supported his wife and three children living in his house in Wiltshire, or Nathaniel Yeames, a river pilot who kept 'a house and family' in Suffolk.[54] Others followed the pattern of the continental stereotype by working for a few years in the city before returning home, perhaps to take up the family farm or to use their urban savings to secure a country husband. Another fairly common practice was for men to serve their apprenticeship in the metropolis and then set up as master in their native county with all the prestige of a London training in their craft. And of course there must have been many people who simply did not like London: Sarah Griffin left Worcestershire to become a servant in London but, 'the air not agreeing with her', decided to return to her 'own country'.[55]

Such examples and motivations could easily be expanded and there is little doubt that, for a considerable number of immigrants, their stay in London was not for life. Nevertheless, the impermanence suggested by studies of continental cities is not nearly so apparent in London. Most migrants to London intended to stay and most did stay, the majority of them eventually marrying fellow immigrants or native Londoners and establishing households similar to those established by the London-born. This cannot be proved directly, but an analysis of the age structure of the immigrants within the urban population suggests that it is probably true. In nearly all societies, the average age at which people migrate tends to be in the late teens or early twenties and this was so both of London and of continental cities in the early modern period. If most immigrants did not stay in the city population for very long, then this should be reflected in the relative contribution of immigrants to each age-group. They should dominate the young adult age-groups, but provide a smaller and smaller proportion of people in the older age-groups, by which time many would have returned to the countryside or, if Sharlin was correct, have died of city diseases.

This is in fact what happened in eighteenth-century Paris, where immigrants formed a declining proportion of the city's population in all age-groups over forty. The same was true of nineteenth-century Madrid.[56] But in London the situation was quite different. The percentage of immigrants in the city's population actually grows rather than falls in the higher age-groups, both for men and for women, as can be seen in Table 2.3. This suggests that most migrants stayed in London all their lives. It also suggests that they were less likely to die young than the London-born – the opposite of the Sharlin thesis. A country childhood may well have been a better guarantee of longevity than survival of the childhood gamble in the urban graveyard.[57]

Where did these migrants come from? Nearly all previous studies of migration have been based on the experience of men, and most of them on that of a particular sort of man – the apprentices whose places of birth were normally recorded either when they were first bound or when they became freemen of the City of London.[58] Such records show that, between the sixteenth and early eighteenth centuries, there was a considerable contraction in the migration field, with fewer apprentices coming from the north of England to London and a greater proportion coming from areas nearer to the metropolis. These studies tend to assume that what was true of apprentices was true of all migrants and much scholarly effort has gone into attempts to

TABLE 2.3 Proportion of Immigrants in the Population by Age

Age-group	Men % immigrants	Women % immigrants
15–24	61.3	55.3
25–34	67.2	69.3
35–44	75.4	74.5
45–54	81.5	78.6
55 & over	83.7	78.6

Source: Male and female 'origins' samples (see pp. 264–5)

explain the narrowing of the reservoir from which London's immigrants were drawn.[59] Very little work has been done on the migration of women to London but, as has been seen, continental studies suggest that most female migrants came from areas very close to the cities.[60]

These findings are counter-intuitive, since one would expect the migration field to expand rather than contract as a city got bigger and richer. It also seems probable that apprentices are not a very suitable proxy for male migrants in general. Their numbers were falling, both absolutely and relatively, across the seventeenth century and so increasingly they were becoming less representative of the male population as a whole. At the same time, the social status of their fathers was rising, a tendency which may have restricted the number of apprentices coming from poorer and more distant areas.[61]

The currently accepted hypothesis has been tested here by analysing the depositions of witnesses in the London Church courts, who were often required to give both their age and their place of birth. These deponents include both men and women and were drawn from the whole social spectrum of the city. Men and women have been treated separately and, to simplify the analysis, the birth places of migrants have been grouped in just four areas: 'near' counties (within 100 km of London), 'middle' counties (100–199 km from London), 'far' counties (200 km or more from London) and areas outside England and Wales. The percentage distribution of migrants from these four areas is shown in Table 2.4, together with the distribution of origins of freemen in 1690 analysed by David Glass, which can stand as a typical example of the results of a 'contracted' migration area. It is clear at a glance that the distribution of the Church court deponents is totally different from that of Glass's freemen, with much higher percentages coming from areas farther away from London and much smaller ones from areas closer to the metropolis. There are rather more women than men who came from the near counties and rather fewer who came from outside England and Wales, but it could hardly be said that the majority of women came from areas adjacent to the city. Most women, like most men, travelled a long way to come to live in London.

Indeed, on average, they were travelling farther and farther as can be seen in Table 2.5, where the migrant deponents have been

TABLE 2.4 Migration Patterns

Region of origin	Men 1665–1725 (n=1994) %	Women 1665–1725 (n=2121) %	Freemen 1690 (n=1548) %
Near counties[1]	30.7	34.6	42.4
Middle counties[2]	27.5	26.1	35.1
Far counties[3]	29.7	30.2	21.7
Outside England & Wales	12.1	9.1	0.8
	100.0	100.0	100.0
Total migrants	73.8	69.4	72.2
London	26.2	30.6	27.8
	100.0	100.0	100.0

Source: Men and women (1665–1725) from male and female 'origins' samples; freemen (1690) from Glass (1969), p. 387. Counties are defined as those whose midpoint is less than 100 km from London (near), 100–199 km (middle) and 200 km or more (far), as listed by M. J. Kitch (1986), p. 233.

1 Beds, Berks, Bucks, Cambs, Essex, Hants, Herts, Kent, Middlesex, Oxon, Surrey, Sussex.
2 Dorset, Gloucs, Hereford, Hunts, Leics, Lincs, Norfolk, Northants, Rutland, Suffolk, Warwicks, Wilts, Worcs.
3 Cheshire, Cornwall, Cumberland, Derbys, Devon, Durham, Lancs, Northumberland, Notts, Salop, Somerset, Staffs, Westmorland, Yorks and Wales.

grouped in three birth cohorts in order to see the direction of change across the period studied. The results are consistent for both male and female migrants and for all three birth cohorts. Far from contracting, the migration field was expanding, with the proportion coming from the two farthest areas increasing overall by seventeen per cent for the men and ten per cent for the women.

The most striking aspect of this change and the one which must have had the most impact on the people of London was the rapid growth in immigrants from outside England and Wales. These included increasingly large numbers of Irish, Scots and, of course, French Huguenots, who migrated in large numbers after the revocation of the Edict of Nantes in 1685. There were, however, immigrants from nearly every European country in this

TABLE 2.5 Migration by Birth Cohorts

a) *Male deponents*

| | Date of birth of deponents | | |
Region of origin	Before 1640 (n=492) %	1640–59 (n=629) %	1660 & after (n=873) %
Near counties	37.5	29.0	27.7
Middle counties	29.8	31.5	22.6
Far counties	25.1	30.2	32.2
Outside England & Wales	7.6	9.3	17.5
	100.0	100.0	100.0
Total migrants	77.0	78.9	68.3
London	23.0	21.1	31.7
	100.0	100.0	100.0

b) *Female deponents*

| | Date of birth of deponents | | |
Region of origin	Before 1640 (n=416) %	1640–59 (n=631) %	1660 & after (n=1069) %
Near counties	35.9	34.6	34.1
Middle counties	31.1	27.9	22.6
Far counties	26.6	31.2	31.1
Outside England & Wales	6.4	6.3	12.2
	100.0	100.0	100.0
Total migrants	75.0	75.1	64.3
London	25.0	24.9	35.7
	100.0	100.0	100.0

Source: Male and female 'origins' samples. Date of birth was calculated by subtracting the declared age of the deponent from the date of the deposition. Regions as in Table 2.4 above.

sample, as well as from the rapidly expanding English empire overseas, from Bombay and Calcutta, Boston and Barbados. It is in our period that London first became a truly cosmopolitan city, a new home for Germans and Dutchmen, Swiss and Danes,

Italians and Portuguese, as well as for the better known French Huguenots. It is also now that a Scots and Irish presence becomes increasingly obvious in London; the Irish in particular formed a distinctive community within the city.

It is relatively easy to analyse the geographical origins of the migrant population of London, since deponents were often required to give their place of birth. This information alone is of some interest and helps one to imagine what a Babel the metropolis must have been, with so many of its inhabitants conversing in mutually incomprehensible accents and dialects, not to mention those who spoke no English at all. But depositions normally do no more than state the fact of migration. To learn more, such as why so many should have chosen to migrate to London, it is necessary to rely on less systematic, anecdotal evidence.

Migration is often analysed in terms of 'push' and 'pull' factors, that is factors which might encourage or force people to leave the countryside, such as lack of land or destitution, and factors which might attract them to the city. Migrants within early modern England are also analysed in terms of another pair of labels used by Peter Clark, 'betterment' and 'subsistence' migrants, the former moving to towns with the aim of improving themselves, for example by apprenticeship or a good marriage, the latter moving simply to keep themselves alive from what charity, relief or casual employment the towns might offer.[62]

Subsistence migration had probably been most important in the century before the one considered in this book, a period of rapid general population growth and even faster growth of towns, particularly London, and of declining real wages. It was one of the worst periods of poverty and destitution in England's history and one when the institutions of relief were not nearly so well organized as they were to become later. Such conditions saw floods of desperate migrants on their way to London where they became a temporary or permanent presence in the suburban areas of the city.

The population of England ceased to grow after 1650, real wages slowly improved and conditions generally got better for the poor, so that vagrancy ceased to be seen as such a serious problem.[63] Nevertheless, London continued to be a focus for the poor and desperate, because of the legal and illegal opportunities that the city offered the newcomer and also because of its reputation for comparatively generous poor relief. Despite the existence of such destitute migrants, there seems little doubt that 'betterment' was a more likely motivation for the majority of migrants in our period and that the pull factors were generally more influential than the push factors.

London had many obvious attractions for provincial men and women of all classes. The rich were attracted to the city as the country's greatest leisure centre, where they could enjoy themselves amongst their peers, take part in sophisticated recreations, turn over the stocks of shops and maybe make a good investment or a good marriage. Those less rich might be drawn to London as the best place to undergo a skilled apprenticeship, the only place for many trades. They would also be attracted by the huge variety of work and the relatively high levels of pay. Men's wages in London were often double provincial wages and women's wages, though much lower, might well equal those of men doing similar work in the country. Women were also attracted by the prospect of a London husband, who was likely to be considerably better off than a country husband of the same status. Such obvious material motives for migration were doubtless predominant and it is easy to find examples of people like John Ireland who came to London 'with a view of rising above the common run of country servants; so that emulation, he seemed to insinuate, was the motive which induced him so to do'.[64]

Money and social improvement were obviously important, but they are not sufficient entirely to explain the constant flow of men and women towards the metropolis. It is clear that for many the constraints of a country life were extremely irksome, perhaps especially so for women, who were subject to very considerable restraint and surveillance in the small closed world of a rural parish. The commonest 'push' factor actually mentioned by female migrants was the death or business failure of their father leading to the collapse of the family as a viable economic unit. However, phrases like 'weary of restraint', 'weary of country business' were common enough and were echoed by male migrants like William Dickenson, who thought country work 'too much slavery', or Benjamin Beckenfield, who 'being tired of the labour of the field, he took it into his head to remove himself'. Such dislike of the slavery of country life leads naturally into the 'pull' element of the equation, as these migrants and thousands like them were drawn towards the freedom and excitement of one of the most vibrant cities in the early modern world, 'having an itching desire to see London', as Mary Young put it when she left Ulster for the metropolis at the age of fifteen.[65]

London was not just a place to make money and have fun. It was also an asylum, a haven for those in trouble, and many a migrant was drawn to the city for this reason. Several such cases can be found in the pages of William Gough, who wrote a fascinating history of his Shropshire village, Myddle, around the year 1700. Thomas Fardow fled to London after fathering a bastard on Black Nell, while Moll Guest, faced with a similar situation, was paid off by the father 'and soe shee went to London'. Thomas Elks 'tooke the roade directly for London' after murdering a child, but was caught on the way. Andrew Hall 'was so addicted to drinking that hee quickly gott in debt in Shrewsbury, soe that hee was forced to leave the Towne and went to London'.[66] Some did well and some did badly in their metropolitan haven, but all knew where to go in their hour of trouble. Londoners themselves tended to run away to sea or to the colonies in similar circumstances.

Migrants were of all ages and all types; widows came to town to spend their former husband's savings in a genteel environment, sailors came ashore in the East End after a lifetime at sea, middle-aged country shopkeepers sought their luck in Piccadilly or Covent Garden for a change. But most migrants were young, the majority making their first appearance on the metropolitan scene before they were twenty-five. Some of them came to London directly from their country homes, boys of fourteen or fifteen arriving to enter an apprenticeship arranged by their parents or guardians, girls going into a London service. Others were what demographers call step-migrants, people who had made one or more moves between home and their final destination. Most of these had already had experience of work before they came to town, perhaps a provincial apprenticeship or several years as a farm labourer. This pattern was particularly common for servants. Ellen Williams, for instance, was born at St Asaph in North Wales, 'from whence shee . . . being about the age of seaventeen or eighteen yeares removed and went to service at the house of Sir John Conway in Dyserth [two miles from her home]

. . . for about two yeares'. She then made the move to London, where she had been living for eight years when she gave her deposition, a period during which she had been a servant in seven different London households and also returned home to Wales for a six-week visit to her relations. Some cases of step-migration involved a veritable odyssey before the final arrival in London. Anne Berenet, for instance, was born and brought up in Paris, which she left to go to Maryland to serve 'the late Governor of Maryland's lady' for about six years before moving to Dublin, where she worked for Colonel de Fauver for two years, and then to England, where she worked first in Windsor before finally making the move to London at the age of thirty-one.[67]

Little evidence exists of how these migrants made their journeys to London. Many of those who lived fairly close to town probably walked, as indeed did some from far away, such as Andrew MacManus, a journeyman thread-dyer whose curiosity urged him to come to see England. 'Pursuant to this, I set out from Dublin and walked to Manchester, where I worked about half a year; from thence I walked to Staffordshire, and so to London.' Others rode up to town, as did a young man and his sister who on arrival sold their horses for eight guineas each and then advertised for places as a valet and a seamstress. But most people coming any distance probably rode either in a pack-horse train (the rider being charged as half a pack) or in the wagons of the carriers who provided regular services from most towns in England to London, a form of travel which was described as 'so tedious, by reason they must take waggon very early and come very late to their innes, as none but women and people of inferiour condition . . . use to travel in this sort'. Some journeys were tedious indeed, as Mary Milibell and Charity Elmes found when they left Cornwall for London in 1702, the journey by carrier from Falmouth taking them from 'a little time before Michaelmas' to 'the beginning of November'.[68]

The carriers normally had their London termini in inns and these could provide newcomers with valuable assistance when they first arrived in the big city, still very much country bumpkins, 'so foolish, so gaping and so engag'd in looking about them'. Innkeepers might recommend lodgings or introduce new arrivals to intermediaries who could help them to their first job if this had not already been fixed up from home. Such assistance needed, however, to be accepted with caution, since migrants, especially women, were at their most vulnerable immediately on arrival in the city, and stories abound of young immigrant girls procured for brothels by innkeepers and other helpful people. Many migrants were, however, in the fortunate but fairly common position of having relatives already in the city who could meet them at their inns, provide a bed, an information service and, most importantly, a character reference. Dorothy Catharell, for instance, arrived from Chester when she was seventeen and 'lived with her unckle' for a year before going into service, while the arrival of Arthur Rolph was eased by his brother Richard, who had preceded him and had got a good place as a cook in Lincoln's Inn Fields. John Carr, a Welshman who 'was kindly received' by his cousin in Holborn, took the opportunity for a little sightseeing. 'The first month was spent in going from place to place to see the town and country people I knew before they came to London, in which time near all what money I brought to London was spent.'[69]

Many other migrants, with no kin in town, would have known 'country people' who remembered their family and could give some assurance to potential employers or landladies that they could be trusted. With so many country migrants coming each year, there could have been few English villages without a representative in London. Most would have several representatives, as did the village of Myddle in Shropshire: in his description of his fellow villagers, Gough mentions nineteen families that had at least one son or daughter who had gone to live 160 miles away in the metropolis. In such circumstances, someone like John Adamson from Lynn in Norfolk must have been very unlucky. 'He some years ago came to Town, and having neither friends nor acquaintances here, he was put to great straits how to live.'[70]

Life was certainly difficult for the unconnected in a city where access to work often depended on reputation and personal contacts, but most people were able to procure some sort of employment. They might well find themselves in great straits at some time or other in their lives, but the majority were able to provide a positive answer when required to 'give a particular account of his or her particular trade or employment or meanes whereby he or she do live, subsist and maintaine him or herself'.[71] Such answers provide the main evidence for the discussion of work in the next two chapters.

3   Men's Work

'It is impossible that a Society can long subsist and suffer many of its Members to live in Idleness, and enjoy all the Ease and Pleasure they can invent, without having at the same time great multitudes of People that . . . will condescend to be quite the Reverse, and by use and patience inure their Bodies to Work for others and themselves besides.'[1]

Work in early modern cities tends to be discussed in terms of the tripartite structure of apprentices, journeymen and masters. Boys, and occasionally girls, were apprenticed at some time in their teens and served seven years unpaid in the household of their master, while they learned the mysteries of his trade. When their time was up, they became journeymen working for wages and often continued to live in their masters' houses until they got married. After some years, the wealthier or more enterprising journeymen became masters in their turn, took in their own apprentices and so perpetuated the system. One study of Elizabethan London suggests that some three-quarters of the male labour force fitted into this neat structure.[2]

This system still existed in the period covered in this book, but its dominant position had been seriously undermined. Changes in the economy and in the structure of work meant that fewer young people were apprenticed and also that fewer journeymen became masters. At the same time, several other work and career patterns had developed alongside the classic structure. These will be discussed in later sections, though it should be appreciated that there was much overlap and chopping and changing between the varieties of employment available in London, so that many people engaged in several types of work in their lifetimes. A high proportion of women were also engaged in gainful employment in the London economy, in addition to their household and reproductive labours. Women's work was, however, so different in its nature and organization that it will be discussed separately in the next chapter, while this chapter will be confined to the work done by men and boys.

Both chapters draw on a wide range of evidence, but the most important sources used were the records of the Church courts which often asked witnesses questions relating to their personal lives in order to obtain some idea of their status and reliability. One question quite often asked was 'how and by what meanes doe you gett your living or are you maintained?' and the answers to this or similar questions have provided most of the information for this discussion of work in the city. Some of the answers cover several years of the witness's experience and so provide an insight into changes in work over the life-cycle, a valuable addition to our knowledge since most discussions of work are unable to do more than analyse the structure of employment at a given point of time.

In all, the depositions of 1,794 male and 1,435 female witnesses who gave evidence between 1695 and 1725 have been used. The approach in the two chapters is rather different, men's work being discussed in very broad categories while the commonest jobs done by women are described in more detail. This is mainly because men engaged in such a huge variety of jobs that it would be impossible to describe even the most important in any detail, while women were employed in a very narrow range of occupations. It has also been possible to subject the work of women to more quantitative analysis than that of men, since the evidence suggests that the female witnesses more nearly approximate to a random sample.[3]

i Boys' Work

'[Josiah Cony] was brought up to no trade, nor had any
education bestow'd on him . . . He was employ'd sometimes in
drawing drink at an alehouse, and at other times in helping his
mother to carry and sell greens and flowers about the streets.'[4]

It is often assumed that the children of the past were forced out to work at very early ages by parents desperate for the few pence they could add to the family income. This certainly seems to have been common practice in the English countryside: one often reads of children as young as six or seven working in the fields, clearing the land of stones, scaring birds away or engaging in the simpler processes of such domestic industries as spinning, weaving and knitting. In London, too, some children started work very young, such as the orphans spinning mop yarn in the workhouses. Several of those destined to be hanged also started work early. John Clark, for instance, who was deserted by his parents, was put out to nurse by the parish when he was 'very young' and made to work for his keep by going 'from place to place along the waterside to pick up sticks, coals etc.'. William Burroughs was a post-boy at the age of seven and John Fellows was put 'to a weaver to be employ'd in what he was capable of' at about the same age.[5]

Such early experience of going out to work was however unusual. The biographical material in both the Church court depositions and the *Accounts* of the Ordinary of Newgate shows that the normal age to leave home in London, even for poor children, was in the early or mid-teens, with girls tending to go out to work at slightly later ages than boys. These findings can be confirmed from the Poor Law records of the large parish of St Martin in the Fields, whose settlement examinations for the years around 1720 provide unusually detailed information on the ages and whereabouts of the examinee's children. These are analysed in Table 3.1, which shows the proportion of girls and boys still at home or living with friends and relations at each age from ten to twenty. It can be seen that it was extremely unusual for either sex to leave home before the age of twelve, when boys began to leave in quite large numbers, though it was not till the age of fifteen that over half the boys had left home. Girls stayed at home even longer, the first major move coming at fourteen, though well over half were still at home at the age of sixteen and nearly a quarter at nineteen. Children still at home may of course have been working for their parents; indeed, a few of the girls in this sample were specifically stated to be working at home. It is, however, difficult to say just how common this was, since the sources usually have nothing to say about children (or indeed wives) who worked at home for no pay.

Boys, then, may or may not have been working to help their

Age	Girls at home %	Boys at home %
10	95	95
11	92	94
12	91	79
13	82	70
14	69	62
15	70	37
16	62	19
17	33	12
18	37	12
19	23	9
20	12	4

TABLE 3.1 Age at Leaving Home in London

Source: WCL F.5013–5020 (1718–27). 'At home' is defined as actually at home, at school or with friends or relations. Sample size = 298 girls and 291 boys.

parents from an early age, but most of them did not actually leave home to work until they were fourteen or older, the normal age to begin an apprenticeship, though there was a significant minority of poor and indifferently educated boys out at work long before that age. The range of jobs available for such juveniles in London was quite limited. Most skilled trades had no work for boys unless they were formally apprenticed, though sons might help their fathers in some trades, especially weaving. Unskilled work, such as labouring, portering and river work, usually required greater strength than these youngsters possessed, though there were exceptions, such as Thomas Whitehead who was set to making bricks at the age of nine, William Dean who started at ten as a labourer in the Southwark glass-house or Philip Poplett, aged eleven, who was 'at work at the Church on smoothing of stone'.[6] Nevertheless, there does not seem to have been any sector of the London economy which set out systematically to exploit the cheap, vulnerable and nimble qualities of boy labour, with the exception of the chimney-sweeps who can be found taking on boys of eight or nine as so-called apprentices.[7]

The two sectors of the London economy with fairly large numbers of early starters were domestic service and sea service, though here as elsewhere the usual starting age was fourteen or older. Most of those who left home early in the Poor Law sample discussed above were servants, usually working as pot-boys or drawers in alehouses or other victualling outlets, although some were foot-boys in private houses. These young servants often started work at ten or eleven and sometimes were merely marking time until they were 'of age' to be apprenticed. Henry Welsh worked three years in the household of Lady Bridget Osborne before being bound to an upholsterer at the age of fourteen and the enterprising John Newman saved up his meagre earnings as a drawer in an alehouse to pay his apprenticeship premium, 'knowing as he said that service was no inheritance, and thinking how he should be able to get his living when of age'.[8] Service at sea provided another opportunity for the adventurous youngster, or the runaway, both the Navy and the merchant service quite often taking on boys of ten or even younger, boys like John Awdry who went to sea at eight and 'served the Queen for the space of sixteen years' before getting into the trouble which led to his execution in 1714; he was the eldest of three sons of a St Giles publican who were all hanged at Tyburn within a single year.[9]

Most other young workers were to be found in the streets, watching horses, blacking shoes, crying milk or newspapers, hawking goods alongside their mothers and, commonest of all, running errands, like Kit Jordan whose 'chief employment while young was running of errands till he grew stronger, and then he sold fish or fruit and such like things about the streets'. Some of this work was perfectly respectable, such as that done by Jesse Walden who acquired 'a very good character' as errand boy to a hosier in Cornhill. Nonetheless, most shoeblacks and errand boys were treated with suspicion by middle-class contemporaries who tended to believe, like Defoe, that they belonged amongst the 'ten thousand wicked idle pilfering vagrants . . . called the black-guard', a nursery for young criminals.[10] In an ideal world, boys should be under the discipline of parents and schoolmasters until they were 'of age' and then they should be bound apprentice and placed under the discipline of a master.

ii Apprenticeship

'There are many good laws that require the lower sort of people to put their children apprentices, so that they may be provided for during the space of seven years . . . and be afterwards in a condition to maintain themselves by their own labour, in an honest way, which laws of late are not put in execution, but people are left at liberty to breed their children how they will.'[11]

James Guthrie was not the only commentator to note the decline in apprenticeship in the seventeenth and eighteenth centuries. A number of factors can account for this, apart from parental indifference and the hostility of children to the 'slavery' of the institution. Changes in the structure of work led to a growth of occupations in which apprenticeship was not the traditional form of entry or seemed irrelevant, such as domestic service, sea service and many labouring and carrying occupations. Most young people going to work in victualling outlets, such as alehouses or coffee-houses, went as pot-boys, drawers or servants rather than as formal apprentices, especially those with no ambition of eventually becoming a master. Shops too increasingly took on servants on a weekly or yearly basis rather than as seven-year apprentices, since, as critics pointed out, few shop assistants needed seven years to learn their trade and an apprenticeship was only valuable to those who intended to set up shop in their turn and trade within the City of London.

Manufacturing and artisan skills could also be learned without the formality and expense of an apprenticeship. Many boys were taught their trade by their fathers or other relatives, who saw no need to bind them apprentice if no one forced them to do so. Others were taught by strangers without being bound, such as Edward Irwin who learned the art of watchmaking while serving as a day servant to John Milbourne of St Sepulcre. Indeed, formal learning seems often to have been unnecessary, judging by the number of people who practised several trades. Jacob Moor, for instance, was in turn a tailor, a distiller and a brazier, and had certainly not been apprenticed to all three. William Johnson also practised 'divers callings', including being a butcher, a calico-printer, a corn-chandler and a surgeon in the Royal Navy. Thomas Clements was apprenticed to a glazier but later took up watch-spring making, 'which art he has learnt of his own accord, by seeing others working at that business'.[12] Such examples suggest that, even in traditional trades, seven years' training was often irrelevant. Meanwhile, those trades which had burst the bounds of the workshop type of organization, heavily capitalized industries with a large labour force such as brewing, glass- and soap-making, sugar and tobacco refining, tended to take on virtually no apprentices at all, relying for their work force on servants and labourers.

Slackness in enforcing the law, economic change and a realization that a long training was often unnecessary certainly led to a steep decline in the numbers of apprentices in London, both in absolute terms and relative to the population of the city. One estimate claims that, in 1600, between thirteen and seventeen per cent of the population of London were apprentices, an astonishingly high figure since few girls were apprenticed. By 1700, this proportion had fallen to somewhere between four and five per cent, suggesting a dramatic collapse of the institution.[13] In 1600, apprenticeship must have been an almost mandatory experience for young men joining the city's labour force; in 1700, if these figures are correct, only about a third or a quarter of such people could have done so as apprentices.

The mainly biographical sources used here do not provide information on the total numbers of young men starting work as apprentices, but they certainly suggest that the decline of the institution is exaggerated by such figures. Being 'bred to no trade' was seen by the Ordinary of Newgate as one reason why young people might end up on the gallows and he normally noted whether the hanged had been apprenticed or not. Many had not, but forty-eight per cent of the sample studied here had at least started an apprenticeship. Many failed to complete their term but there was nothing inherently criminal about this, since the drop-out rate amongst all apprentices was of the order of fifty per cent.[14] A rather higher rate of apprenticeship can be found amongst the sample of children from the Poor Law records of St Martin in the Fields, which show that nearly two-thirds of all boys between the ages of fourteen and eighteen were apprentices. Church court depositions with information on the employment of teenagers also indicate that well over half were apprentices.

Such evidence suggests that the figures normally quoted on the decline of apprenticeship are misleading. This may be because nearly all statistics are based on data produced by the

City government and the Livery companies, institutions which may well have had almost complete control over apprenticeship in London in 1600. The situation a hundred years later was very different, mainly as a result of the growth of the suburbs, over which the City and the companies had little effective control. It would be difficult, if not impossible, to count the number of boys bound apprentice to suburban masters who were not members of City companies, but it seems probable that such would have constituted a large minority of all London apprentices by 1700. These apprentices suffered the disability of not being able to trade or open a workshop within the City; indeed many would not even be able to work as journeymen within the City. But, since most industrial and artisan work was in fact carried out in the suburbs by 1700, this would hardly be a serious disadvantage, especially for that majority who had no hope of eventually becoming a master themselves. Such people were quite happy to serve a suburban master, who would normally demand a lower premium or even no premium at all. The skills acquired from such a man might not compare with those taught by 'eminent' masters in the City, but they were sufficient for the run of the mill work done by the majority of London's artisans.

These skills could also be taught in the provinces and many immigrants served their time in their native counties, coming to London as trained journeymen in their twenties. Such people had been encouraged to come to London after 1666 when the rebuilding after the Great Fire led to a huge increase in demand for building workers and a relaxation in rules requiring that those who worked in London had served their apprenticeship there. Once the gates had been opened, provincial workmen in almost any trade took the opportunity to seek employment in the metropolis. The Church court sample includes people who had been trained in well-known centres of their trade such as weavers from Norwich, needlemakers from Worcestershire, blacksmiths and file-cutters from Birmingham and Staffordshire, as well as those who had served their time in less obvious places. The majority of Londoners who served an apprenticeship, migrants as well as natives, served it in London, but a sizeable minority did their time in the provinces, presumably because it was cheaper or more convenient or because they had had no thought of migrating to London when they were fourteen.

A few of these country workmen were doomed to disappointment. Matthew Lee, for instance, served his time as a shoemaker near Boston in Lincolnshire, but was unable to find employment in London, 'being bred in the country [and] consequently unacquainted with the method of dispatching work either with that expedition or neatness that was necessary'. Others needed to enhance their skills in order to survive in the metroplitan environment, such as the country watchmaker and blacksmith who took a place as an unpaid servant with a London master in order to 'improve himself by watchmaking'.[15] But such experience was unusual. Provincial masters were normally perfectly competent; many indeed had been trained in London.

Apprenticeship may have been in decline from the levels of the late sixteenth century, but it was still the typical introduction to work for young male Londoners, whether they served their time in the City, the suburbs or the provinces.[16] Boys were normally bound for seven years and they typically started between the ages of fourteen and sixteen, most sons of 'honest' parents starting immediately after they left school. Apprenticeships can be found in virtually any trade or occupation, from the 'genteel servitude' which might lead to a prosperous life as a merchant, wholesaler, banker or big shopkeeper, through the run of artisan trades to such lowly or obscure occupations as chimney-sweep, rag-picker or mountebank, the last being the experience of Anthony Gearish of Newbury who was bound apprentice in London for seven years 'to learn the arts of dancing on the rope, tumbling, vaulting etc.'.[17]

Finding a master and putting their sons to a suitable trade was the last formal duty of parents and guardians as they sent their children out into the world. It was an important duty since the acquisition of a trade was seen as the best guarantee of a maintenance for life, as indeed it was in most cases, men with trades normally doing rather better in the uncertain world of London work than those without. Most parents carried out this duty conscientiously even though it cost them money, for nearly all masters demanded a premium to take on an apprentice.[18] Premiums could be several hundred pounds for a training carrying a passport to such middle-class occupations as merchant, woollen-draper or mercer, such expense coming on top of an expensive education. Artisan masters, too, could demand fairly high premiums if they were especially skilled in their trade, and sums of £30 or £40 were common for a training with such a man. Such premiums represented two or three years' pay for a poor man and ensured that there was no more equality of opportunity in the field of apprenticeship than there had been in that of education. Even the £5 or £10 commonly demanded by lesser artisan masters was too much for the really poor, such as the widowed mother of John Davis who 'being much straiten'd in her circumstances, was not in a capacity to bind him apprentice to a trade'.[19] Some poor children had their premiums paid by the parish or by charity, most charity schools, for instance, having funds for this purpose. However, such children were likely to serve their seven years (and often much longer for parish children) in the very poorest trades, thus effectively maintaining the social hierarchy of a city sometimes vaunted for the opportunities it provided for social mobility.

These years of service were normally unpaid, the apprentice working for his master in return for his keep and usually being supplied with such necessaries as replacements to his clothes and medicine. He was also of course supposed to be reimbursed for his labour by being taught the trade, though some masters were criticized for failing to attend to this basic requirement of the institution because they were idle or incompetent, or had no wish to train up future competition, or simply because they saw apprentices as a captive form of free labour who could be mercilessly exploited for seven years or until they ran away. Such attitudes were quite common, though overall the institution worked well enough as a method of transmitting skills from generation to generation while at the same time keeping a restraint on potentially riotous and idle adolescents.

Service in someone else's household was a common experience in early modern England and for those apprentices fortunate enough to have a kind and competent master or mistress, the experience could be both pleasant and rewarding. They were well taught and treated as well as any other member of the family, so well that many continued to work with their masters after their time was up; some indeed married the daughter of the master and took over his trade in the time-honoured manner. However, one gets the impression from the literature of the period that for most apprentices their period of service was at least galling, if not downright unpleasant, as is implied by the repeated use of words such as 'slavery' and 'restraint' to describe the institution. Few people today would enjoy living and working in someone else's house for seven years with no wages and the status of servant, and few people seem to have enjoyed it very much in our period, despite their greater familiarity with service. Londoners were restless people, constantly changing their jobs and their employers, as will be seen later in the discussion of domestic servants and journeymen, few of whom stayed with one employer for more than a year or two. Seven years' servitude was simply too long, especially since most trades could be learned in much less time. It comes then as no surprise to learn that, although many apprentices served their full seven years 'honestly and with approbation', many did not.

This was not just a matter of boredom, though this certainly played its part. Apprentices were forbidden by law and by their own indentures from doing virtually any of the things which adolescents wanted to do. 'He shall not commit fornication . . . He shall not play at cards, dice, tables [backgammon], or any other unlawfull games . . . He shall not haunt taverns or playhouses.' Complaints about apprentices suggest that such prohibitions were systematically ignored, though their very existence would be galling in a city so devoted to fornication, gambling and drinking as London. Many found it too much to bear, as can be seen in the biographies of the hanged who, like George Sutton, 'wearied of any further confinement, went to his idle company'.[20]

Many masters and mistresses were also far from kind or considerate to their apprentices, young lads who were often in a very vulnerable position. Complaints from apprentices obviously need to be treated with scepticism but they cannot be ignored completely, especially since they reflect no more than one might expect. There seems little doubt that many apprentices were exploited as cheap labour or made to do housework to save their masters the expense of hiring a domestic servant. Many were also poorly fed and ill-treated, beaten for petty misdemeanours or for no reason at all by sadistic or drunken masters. Some no doubt deserved chastisement, but even so one has no difficulty in appreciating why nearly all apprentices looked forward to the comparative freedom (and comparative insecurity) of life as a journeyman, and why so many were not prepared to wait seven years before they started that life.

iii Living by One's Trade

'He always distrusted his trade [barber and perriwig-maker] and quickly perceiv'd that it would not be in his power to procure a maintenance from it: that no body that had not felt the sorrow could guess at the dismal uneasiness and distraction of mind that tortures a man who has a wife and children he loves like himeself, and finds he shall have nothing wherewith to make them happy; but must be deaf to them when they urge him for victuals and cloaths and the common necessaries of life.'

(William Bond, executed in 1721 for returning illegally after being transported for stealing books)[21]

The social theory of the early modern period saw apprenticeship as the first step on a ladder which might lead to great riches, or at least a comfortable sufficiency, and also to a well-respected position within the community. Some apprentices, those with well-to-do fathers, might set up business in their own households as soon as they had completed their terms. Others served some years as journeymen, living either with their masters or in their own lodgings, before setting up for themselves, perhaps using their saved-up wages as their initial capital. And some – the poor, the incompetent or the unlucky – were never able to open their own shop or workshop and so remained journeymen all their lives.

Steve Rappaport, in his study of late sixteenth-century London, found that just over half of those journeymen whose careers he was able to trace eventually became masters.[22] This high proportion depends to a certain extent on the high drop-out rate of both apprentices and journeymen, who vanish without a trace from his records, but it is still impressive and suggests that the ambition to become a master was a realistic one for most young men starting work in Elizabethan London. This real possibility of improvement, suggests Rappaport, was a major factor in reducing social tension within the city, since journeyman and master were merely two steps on a ladder rather than opponents in constant strife with each other.

Masters were still plentiful in London during the century between 1650 and 1750, when the typical unit of production remained the individual master artisan working in his own workshop with his apprentices and journeymen. Such is clear both from inventories and from the biographical material in the Church court records, which include large numbers of small masters operating in this way. Nevertheless, the chances of becoming a master were considerably less than they had been in Elizabethan times, while many of those who did become masters no longer had the independence of earlier years.

One major reason for this was an increase in scale in many trades, leading to a need for capital far beyond the scope of a journeyman saving his wages.[23] Some industries, such as the larger breweries, soap-works and sugar-refineries, were organized almost like factories with extensive premises, impressive amounts of fixed capital and as many as a hundred men employed as labourers working for wages. Others used little fixed capital, but gained the benefits of improved supervision and division of labour by gathering together ten or twenty journeymen in a workshop under a foreman. Such organization can be seen in tailoring, hat-making, shoemaking and stocking-knitting. Small masters still existed in all these trades; indeed they probably still predominated. But their numbers were necessarily reduced by the presence of the big masters whose competition and ability to cut prices caused serious difficulties for the small men.

In many other industries where small workshops remained the normal form of organization, the masters lost the control over their product and the economic independence which they had once had. Sometimes, as in watch- and gun-making, this was because of subdivision of the production process, leading to each small master producing just one part of an artefact which was assembled by a wealthy and well-known master. Such subdivided skills were often easily learned, so that competition amongst small masters for the available work was intensified, especially since many of the parts could be made in the low-wage areas of the provinces and assembled in London. Being a small master in such circumstances was no great advantage, since subcontractors often waited a very long time to be paid for their work and they had no control over production decisions made by assemblers who would quickly reduce orders in response to a slackening of the market.

Similar problems for small masters can be seen in many other trades as a result of a growth in retail shopkeeping. There had once been a time when most small masters sold their products from the front of their workshops, a task often carried out by the master's wife. This practice became less common with the growth of large, well-stocked shops on the main thoroughfares which bought in stock as they needed it from scores of small masters in the alleys and lanes behind them, people like the glover William Devaral who 'wrought for the shops, himself keeping none'.[24] These small masters tended to concentrate on a very narrow product range or even on a single product, a decision which could reduce their unit costs but left them very vulnerable to changes in the market or in fashion.

Ironmongers, pewterers, jewellers, cabinet-makers and upholsterers, haberdashers and other sellers of ready-made clothing accessories were all examples of this trend. These shopkeepers required large amounts of working capital to finance their stocks and could easily be undermined by an accumulation of bad debt or by the very slow payment characteristic of their customers. Many shopkeepers became bankrupt or ended up in debtors' prisons as a result, but the small masters who supplied them were even more vulnerable. They too were paid slowly and could be left with no business at all as those on whom they depended cut back their orders for chairs or handkerchiefs or cast brass candle-sticks or whatever the small master produced.

These small men might style themselves master, but their function was similar to that of journeymen working on piece-rates, with the important difference that they were likely to have to wait much longer for their money: most journeymen received their wages every Saturday night. Even the fashionable bespoke trades supplying the West End market were often organized in this way. The aristocratic customer who received a new suit of clothes or a new piece of silverware for his table might well imagine that this had been made by the fashionable tailor or silversmith with whom he had placed the order. But, very often, some or all of the work had been done by anonymous small masters whose names can only be discerned from the account books of the more famous men who had subcontracted the work to them. The division of profit between the two masters was unlikely to be equal, though both would share the problems of supplying a market which included such people as Sir Edward Knatchbull whose refusal to pay a bill was justified by the remark that 'as I receive my rents once a year, so I pay my tradesmen's bills once a year which is not reckoned very bad pay as ye world goes'.[25]

Seven years' apprenticeship was not therefore a certain introduction to an easy life in this increasingly capitalistic and market-oriented city. Some people of course did well, setting up their own business immediately after their apprenticeship or after a few years as a journeyman, and then remaining in that same business and often in the same house for decades. The shoemaker Thomas Worthington, for example, had run his business from the same house in East Smithfield for thirty years when he gave his deposition in 1720.[26] Such an achievement required sufficient capital in the first place, a good wife (with a good dowry), competence, diligence, honesty and quite a bit of good luck, a combination of qualities which meant that such success stories, though not unusual, were by no means the norm.

Masters and journeymen are often seen to be two quite different sorts of people, mutually opposed in some eighteenth-century precursor of the nineteenth-century class struggle. There are certainly signs of this as economic change made it harder to set up as a master in many trades and forced more people into a realization that they were to be journeymen for life. Such changes led to the development of journeymen's organizations which ran 'box clubs' for the benefit of their members and sought to improve their conditions of work and pay by such means as strikes, which became increasingly common as the eighteenth century progressed.[27] Such disputes might be dramatic, but it would be wrong to exaggerate the class divisions that they seem to suggest. The economic gap between journeyman and small master was not large and it was constantly crossed in both directions. Many, probably most, masters had once been journeymen and many journeymen were former masters who had failed to make the grade, people like Philip Singleton, a journeyman brazier who had once kept his own shop in Harp Alley, or

John Bromley, who was 'very well known among the bakers of London, . . . having been bred to that trade and lived by it all his time from his youth, and was formerly a master'.[28]

A variety of circumstances might contribute to such disappointments. Running a workshop or other small business did not often demand much fixed capital, but it did require considerable working capital to pay journeymen or subcontractors, to buy raw materials and to last out the long wait for customers or shopkeepers to pay what was due. On top of this, most masters occupied and had to pay the rent of a whole house, together with the taxes which went with the dignified status of housekeeper. Many also celebrated this new status by the acquisition of a wife, or paid for it with her dowry, and so burdened their fledgling business with the costs of bringing up a young family. Such expenses were of a very different order from those of a bachelor journeyman living as a lodger and many young masters were seriously under-capitalized.

As such, they were vulnerable to any of the many accidents of life – sickness or injury to themselves, the death or sickness of a wife who played an important part in the business or acted as an unpaid housekeeper, medical expenses for sick children, default of debtors or the stops in trade which were a feature of the early modern economy. One or more of such problems could soon break a master or drive him out of business and so reduce him once again to doing journeywork and living as a lodger. Moral failings, such as drink, extravagance, idleness or simple incompetence, would of course force the master out of business even more quickly.

Even the soberest and most careful of masters might find it difficult to live by his trade, or might fear that it would become difficult at some time in the future, and a number of strategies were adopted to cope with such problems. If one trade failed to produce sufficient income, it was often possible to take up another, as did the weaver James Housdy of Stepney who 'fell into the employment of a baker' or John Smith, a former waterman who made a good living by supplying brandy and rum to the ships in the river, 'finding more benefit thereby than his proper trade'.[29] A very common practice was to run another business on the side in the hope that both would not do badly at the same time. This might be a second trade, but more commonly was a shop or a victualling outlet, for example the saddler who owned a chandler's shop, the baker who kept a coal cellar or the iron founder who ran the Woolsack alehouse.[30] Several of these second businesses were described in depositions as run by the artisan's wife and one suspects that this was true of the great majority of them. There was less opportunity for wives to assist in their husbands' trades in this world of economic specialization and subcontractors, as will be seen in the next chapter, but their earnings remained essential to the family economy. Running a shop or a victualling house was one obvious way in which their economic talents could be employed.

Diversification might be one way of surviving in the uncertain London economy, but many men preferred to give themselves security by withdrawing some of their capital from trade altogether. The profits from a good year or a windfall might well be invested in something producing a more certain return than their own trade, such as money-lending, houses or the increasingly attractive securities offered by the government.[31] Similar motives led many artisans and tradesmen to invest in the purchase of an office or place, so producing a sort of annuity in return for varying amounts of work. Parish clerk, sexton and beadle were offices commonly held by respectable masters and were often carried out in conjunction with their trades. But there were many others in a city where most salaried jobs were bought on the market, as can be seen from the deponents in the Church courts who include a bricklayer who was also Steward of Bernard's Inn, a weaver who was beadle of the Scriveners' Company, a pewterer who was Muster Master of the City of London and many others.[32] Such places required respectability and connections as well as money to acquire, but they provided an ideal solution to the problems of fluctuating profits and especially of the onset of old age.

Journeymen as well as masters very often found that they needed more than one job to survive with any comfort in London and they can be found adopting similar strategies. There were for example a variety of posts which might suit their more lowly status or pocket, such as watchman, constable, bailiff's assistant or chancel-keeper in a church. Two trades might pay better than one, as James Smith found when he got 'good bread' by combining the trades of needle-maker and silver-thread-spinner.

Others found they lived well if they combined a winter with a summer job, such as Simon Marshall who made candles in the winter and worked as a shipyard labourer in the summer.[33]

Hard times often forced the journeyman to abandon his trade altogether and try another, as did George Gibbons, a shoemaker who finding 'work growing scarce, he went to weaving', or James Buquois, a weaver who 'when the weaving business was slack and he was out of work, he wrought as a labourer to the bricklayers'. The sea offered another choice for those in search of a living or a bit of adventure; many a journeyman enlisted in the Royal Navy or served in the merchant service for a few years and then returned to his trade. And there was also of course the army, the choice of the Scotsman Alexander Duncan who told the court in 1711 that during the last seven years he had 'either belonged to the Queen's Foot Guards or followed the employment of a sadler and now belongs to the Queen's Guards'.[34]

The problem with such options was that they tended to be taken not just by skilled men in search of work but also by those many Londoners who had no trade at all. The lower end of the weaving and shoemaking trades, for instance, was notoriously easy to learn and so tended to be overcrowded and poorly rewarded, and the same was true of other occupations, as Henry Johnson discovered. He was bred a bricklayer, but 'because of the multiplicity of hands' he thought to better his state by going to sea, only to discover 'that the number of sailors made it difficult to get employment even at sea'.[35]

Even that majority of journeymen who stuck to their trade seem to have been addicted to variety, judging by the number of times they changed both their lodgings and their masters. The loyal, steady type of journeyman existed of course, people who worked and lived year after year with the same master. But they were easily outnumbered by the more peripatetic kind of workmen who notched up five or six different masters in as many years and rarely stayed more than two or three years with any one master. These moves might take them all round London and even out into the country and back again.

Such restlessness and such a variety of experience make it almost impossible to make any useful generalizations about the earnings of journeymen in London. Metropolitan wages were high relative to the rest of the country, guidebooks to London trades in the mid-eighteenth century suggesting a range of rates from about ten or twelve shillings a week for the less skilled and overcrowded trades to a pound or even thirty shillings a week for really skilled craftsmen.[36] This was certainly good pay by the standards of the day, but rates alone tell us little about annual earnings. A week's work was six days' labour, with typical hours of six in the morning to eight at night with an hour off at noon for dinner. But not many journeymen on daywork got six days' work in any week, let alone throughout the year. Many could get no work in their trade for months at a time, a period during which they might or might not find other employment. Many were on piece-rates so that their earnings varied, depending on the state of trade, their own productivity and their diligence, piece-workers being notorious for extending the Sunday holiday into Monday and often Tuesday as well. And even when journeymen were paid regular wages on an annual basis, calculation of their earnings is complicated by such problems as making allowance for the presence or absence of such perks as 'meate, drinke, washing and lodging', the provision of clothes and such custom-ary perquisites as 'cabbage' for tailors or 'chips' for carpenters and dockyard workers.[37] And even if a value could be put on all that, there would still be the problem of second occupations and the contribution to household income of wives and children.

All that can really be said is that, in good times, London's journeymen and small masters lived well and justified Defoe's boast that there was 'a class of your topping workmen in England, who, being only journeymen under manufacturers, are yet very substantial fellows'.[38] But neither for the individual nor his trade were times always good, as many a poor weaver or tailor could bear witness. 'As soon as the market stops they stop', it was said of the master silk-weavers of Spitalfields. 'If they cannot sell their work they immediately knock off the looms and the journeymen immediately starve, and want work.' 'They are as numerous as locusts,' wrote Campbell of 'the mere working taylors [who] are out of business about three or four months in the year; and generally as poor as rats.'[39] These were two of the poorest trades in London, but similar comments might have been made of many others. Living by one's trade was no more certain a way to economic sufficiency than the other patterns of work which will be described in the following sections.

iv Using the Seas

'He said he was about 20 years of age . . . and had been a loose liver, much addicted to swearing, excessive drinking, lasciviousness, and suchlike vices, too common among men of his profession, he being a seafaring man that had for these several years past been employ'd both in the Queen's Royal Navy and merchants' service at sea; and that he had little minded or regarded the wonderful works of God in the Deep.'
(John Gibson, executed for highway robbery in 1714)[40]

London's large community of sailors provided a striking contrast to the rest of the population of the metropolis. Their tanned faces, tattoos, distinctive clothing and rolling gait ensured that they looked very different from their stay at home contemporaries. They spoke differently too, in incomprehensible nautical jargon, not to mention their supposed addiction to swearing. Their numbers are difficult to compute, but one can hazard a guess that some twenty thousand Londoners 'belonged to the sea' in the sense that this was their main or only source of livelihood.[41] The vast majority of these men lived in the East End or south of the river. Some had only the most fleeting connections with the land, men like David Aubin who had been fifteen years at sea and 'was never on shore for the space of a month at the same time' or Joseph Gibson who was 'a seafaring man and being single and unmarried hath noe fixt habitation'.[42] But many mariners, especially those who were married, had permanent roots in London, often retaining the same homes in Shadwell or Rotherhithe for decades while they carried on their seafaring lives.

Most of London's sailors were born and brought up either in the city's maritime parishes or in maritime communities elsewhere, particularly on the east coast of England and Scotland and in the south-west. The origins of sailors were thus strikingly different from those of most Londoners, as can be seen in Tables 3.2 and 3.3 which analyse the birth places of sailors who had been resident in London at least one year. The prominence of counties such as Devon and Northumberland ensured that a much higher proportion came from 'far counties' than was typical of London's population as a whole. Many more came

from outside England and Wales as well – Irishmen, Channel
Islanders, Scots (who made up nearly ten per cent of the sailor
sample) and foreigners, who outnumbered even the Scots. Most
of these came from the maritime communities of the North Sea,
the Baltic and the British colonies in America, but sailors from
all over the world made their homes in East London, including
two in this sample who were suitably born 'at sea'.

Why did these immigrant sailors choose to live in London, a
city where rent and other expenses were probably going to be
very much higher than in their places of birth? In most cases it
was unlikely to have been for higher wages since seamen sold
their services in a national, indeed international, market and
one's home made no difference to the rate of pay, except for those
sailors who lived on the periphery of the main coastal and
international trading routes. Jeremiah Sullivan, for instance,
was a seaman from Cork who 'thought to get better wages by
coming to London and sailing thence'.[43] But this would not have
been true of the typical east coast sailor, who would have got the
London rate wherever he shipped from. The main economic
advantage of London was not the pay, but the vast range of ships
using the port since some two-thirds of all England's imports and
exports went through London and the metropolis also dominated the coastal trades. The problem for sailors, especially for
that majority working in the coastal trades and on the short-haul

TABLE 3.2 Origins of Sailors and All Male Londoners Compared

Region of origin	Sailors %	All men %
Near counties	14.0	30.7
Middle counties	17.1	27.5
Far counties	42.6	29.7
Outside England & Wales	26.3	12.1
	100.0	100.0
Total migrants	75.2	73.8
London	24.8	26.2
	100.0	100.0

TABLE 3.3 Leading Counties as Sources of Migrants	
Sailors	*All men*
1. Devon	1. Yorkshire
2. Northumberland	2. Bucks
3. Yorkshire	3. Oxfordshire
4. Kent	4. Northants
5. Dorset	5. Herts
6. Norfolk	6. Wilts
7. Cornwall	7. Warwicks
8. Somerset	8. Berkshire
9. Durham	9. Gloucestershire
10. Essex	10. Essex
11. Hampshire	11. Somerset
12. Suffolk	12. Surrey

Source: For both tables: 'all men' – same as Table 2.4 (p. 47); 'sailors' – all sailor witnesses in HCA 13/80–85 (1690–1715) who were resident in London and gave their place of birth (n=693). For 'near', 'middle' and 'far' counties, see Table 2.4.

routes to Europe, was to put together sufficient voyages to make a decent annual income, a problem more readily solved if one's home was in London rather than in Dartmouth or Sunderland.

An abundance of ships drew seamen to London, as did the unrivalled range of entertainments that the city afforded. Another major attraction of London as a base was the wide range of employment available for the wives of seamen. Single mariners could easily maintain themselves on their pay, but intermittent employment and slow payment of wages made it difficult to support a wife and children and most sailors' families relied heavily on the earnings of wives for their maintenance. For this reason, it seems probable that the majority of mariners who settled in London were married, a hypothesis supported by the age at which they first took up permanent residence in the city. Most sailors first went to sea in their mid-teens or earlier, but the median age of taking up residence in London was twenty-six, while over a third of all sailor migrants did not settle in the city until they were over thirty.[44]

Most sailors were 'bred to the sea', just as young men in inland communities were 'bred to husbandry', and this is sufficient to explain their choice of occupation. Their fathers, uncles, brothers and cousins were sailors or fishermen and there can rarely have been much doubt in their minds that, when they were 'of age', they would become sailors or fishermen in their turn. Not all sailors came from seafaring families however. Many, even from maritime counties, were born inland and chose the sea as one amongst many options for employment, one which was relatively well paid. Robert Willis, for instance, was 'brought up to husbandry' in Skelton, Yorkshire, near enough to the sea to know its potential. He told the High Court of Admiralty that he earned his living 'sometimes workeing about the coale workes, sometimes doing husbandry worke, sometimes going to sea with the fishermen' and sometimes on the coal boats going to London.[45]

Such an intermittent relationship with the sea was quite common, for Londoners as well as countrymen. Many men were in and out of sea service, especially those whose trades were relevant, such as shipwrights, sail-makers, surgeons, watermen or coopers, but men of any trade or none might find work at sea for a single voyage or a few years. Some were taken on in jobs requiring no maritime experience, as cooks or stewards for instance; others were able to carry on their land trade aboard ship, such as Sebastian Holdin who served three years as the captain's butcher on HMS *Pembroke* or William Innies who signed on as captain's tailor of the *Leghorn Frigate*;[46] but most of these landsmen served before the mast and learned the trade of the sailor as they went along.

Motives obviously varied. In this, as in all ages, some people went to sea for adventure or to see the world. A considerable number took refuge in a ship because the land did not seem to have anything to offer or was positively dangerous, the sea providing a convenient bolt-hole for many a runaway apprentice, unmarried father, deserting husband, debtor or fugitive from justice.[47] Most landsmen, however, went to sea because they were attracted by the money, a motive which meant that most of them became sailors during wartime.

England had too many regular sailors for them all to find employment during peacetime, but far too few to satisfy the demands of war, when a hugely expanded royal fleet competed with merchant ships and hundreds of privateers for the available sailors. The Royal Navy's answer to this manning problem was to use the hated press to force unwilling sailors into the fleet and to accept as volunteers landsmen who would never have been

taken on during peace – 'the scum of the world' to whom regular
food, a chance of prize money or plunder and a regular wage,
even if always in arrears, was an immense improvement on their
normal hand to mouth existence.[48]

Merchant ships also used force to make up their crews through
the medium of crimps who kidnapped or tricked unwilling men
to serve at sea. But their main recourse was to take every
precaution possible to save their men from the press and to
double the wages paid. Peacetime rates for able seamen were
normally between twenty-five and thirty shillings a month, good
pay in the provinces but not very good in London even when
allowance is made for free board and lodging. Wartime rates
fluctuated enormously, but were often over fifty shillings and
sometimes over sixty shillings a month, enough to tempt many a
poor baker or weaver to risk life, limb and the press, and sign on
for a voyage at sea.[49]

Service at sea offered a realistic chance of promotion and
improvements in pay to the steady, sober or well-connected man.
Some boys started as unpaid apprentices to officers who contracted to teach them navigation and other skills, most of these
apprentices having capital or connections which would ensure
fairly rapid promotion within the merchant service. The majority of 'younkers' began, however, as cabin-boys or ships' boys, as
servants to the officers, or were simply 'hired as a servant before
the mast', as was Thomas Kirby who sailed from London to
Archangel and back at the age of fifteen.[50] Boys' pay roughly
doubled on reaching manhood and would increase still further
when they were rated able seamen, able to 'hand, reef and steer'.
Such were the typical sailors, the foremastmen, most of whom
never advanced any further. But there was plenty of scope for the
competent to be promoted to quartermaster, boatswain, mate or
even master. Few sailors became masters unless they had good
connections ashore, but those who did were able to maintain a
very respectable 'middling' position in the community through
earnings which included not only their pay, but also commission
for acting abroad for merchants, profits from cargo they were
privileged to carry on their own behalf and often from part-
ownership of the ship as well. Such men were obviously only a
small and fortunate minority of the maritime community, but
many sailors of ability were likely to end up as mates, often

indeed reaching such a position in their early twenties. The pay of mates varied, but most earned two or three times as much as an able seaman in peacetime. Such rates put them in the same class as very skilled artisans.

The sea offered a huge variety of possible experience to the sailor. Some never went far from home, such as the master, man and boy who worked the coasting hoy *Content* between London and Maldon in Essex in the 1680s, averaging one round-trip a month. The Newcastle coal trade, the biggest single employer of sailors, was something of a lottery for seamen, who were paid by the voyage rather than by the month. A witness in 1692 claimed that a typical round-trip took six weeks, but that he had known colliers take as little as eighteen days or as long as nineteen weeks working their way through the dangerous east coast seas. Such short voyages would have seemed trivial to sailors on the deep-sea routes, such as those in the rapidly expanding American trades. The round-trip to America and back rarely took less than six months and often took eight or nine, much of the time being spent loading in American ports or creeks, a period during which seamen were often placed on half pay. Other sailors were away from home for years, sailing to China and India and back in the huge ships of the East India Company, which had crews nearly a hundred strong, or working in tramps like the *Cadiz Merchant*, whose books have survived for 1675–83. She made voyages to Newcastle, Amsterdam, Hamburg, Portugal, Norway, the Baltic, Jamaica and the Spanish Main during this period, as well as the two long trips to Cadiz and the Mediterranean which one might expect from her name. Winters were often spent in foreign ports and the crew might pass two years or more without ever seeing London.[51]

Some sailors had been everywhere; old tars like John Seagerts 'who used ye seas above 45 years and has been in almost all habitable parts of ye world'. However, the sources suggest that most sailors tended to specialize in particular trades or types of shipping, so long as they could get a berth. They worked in the Newfoundland fishery, in the slave trade from Africa to the West Indies, in the Newcastle coal trade or in the North American trades, like the black sailor Isaac George who had 'made eight or ten voyages between New England and London' before he was twenty-two.[52] Such constancy would be of obvious benefit to masters, who would thus gain a stock of knowledge about navigation and the trading conditions in particular ports. For the sailors it was probably more the result of inertia and the ease of getting a berth in a trade in which they were known by the masters. Sailors also liked to stick with a friendly ship if they possibly could. Discipline was not particularly harsh, but some masters and petty officers were brutal and sadistic men whom a sensible sailor would avoid if possible.[53]

Wherever the sailor sailed, it was a dangerous and uncomfortable but also exciting life. There are sailors in the sample who had been maimed in battle, shipwrecked, captured by privateers, marooned on remote islands, attacked by African slaves desperately seeking freedom, trepanned by Tuscan corsairs or pressed by the Royal Navy. Some had circumnavigated the globe, one had spent years in a slave prison in Tangiers, some, like William Hunt of Tower Street, had gone 'a buckaneering' in the West Indies.[54] Such dangerous lives, together with the accidents of shipboard existence and the fevers inevitable in close confinement, meant that many sailors died young even by the harsh standards of early modern London. Their mortality would be difficult to measure precisely, but some indication of the problem is given by the frequency with which their wives were widowed and remarried. The record in our sample was held by Anne Heathcott of Stepney, aged thirty-four, who had been married to five sailors, though such was the uncertainty of life at sea that the fourth husband returned to London several years after he had been reported dead by a former shipmate.[55]

Anne Heathcott earned her living by 'dealeing in the sale of seamans ticketts' and thus illustrates an important aspect of the East London maritime community: the support services provided by sailors' wives and widows and other landbound people. Seaman's tickets were promises by the Royal Navy to pay the wages of its sailors, promises often not redeemed for years, a scandal which enriched those with sufficient capital to provide sailors with ready cash by buying the tickets at discounts as great as eight or ten shillings in the pound. Merchant seamen often had similar problems in getting money from their employers and much of the business of the High Court of Admiralty as well as other courts consisted of their attempts, or those of their agents, to recover the wages which they felt they were due. Gerard Byrne, for instance, was an East End solicitor employed by the mariners of the ship *Colchester* 'to sue for their wages and [they] agreed to give the said Byrne two shillings in ye pound out of what should be received'.[56]

Mariners needed accommodation, food and entertainment as well as money while they were ashore. And when that money had gone, they needed to find a ship and prepare themselves for a new voyage. All these services were amply provided by the women of the East End who ran lodging-houses, bars and brothels, made and sold 'slops' for the sailors to wear, found them a berth and kitted them out for the months or years that would elapse before they returned. Sailors setting out on long voyages usually received an advance on their wages to enable them to pay the debts incurred ashore or to leave some money for the support of their families, but such advances were often not sufficient. Credit, however, was usually available, once again from the landladies and publicans of the East End, who secured their advances by a lien on the sailors' pay and even forced them to write wills in their favour.[57]

Some sailors continued to use the seas until they dropped, men like John Worley of Wapping who was still serving before the mast in the Newcastle coal trade at the age of seventy. But on the whole it was a young man's occupation.[58] This was partly because many sailors died young, but mainly because they tended to leave the sea in their thirties or forties, if not earlier. Landsmen returned to their families and their trades, as did Thomas Parr, a Westminster poulterer whose sales of chickens were no doubt enlivened by memories of his shipwreck in Bengal while serving as cook's mate in an East Indiaman.[59] Regular sailors reverted to other occupations, often those which had previously maintained them between ships, such as building work and general labouring, this being all that most strong men without a trade could aspire to. Those who were more fortunate set themselves up in business with their savings from the sea, often drawing on their wives' experience and skills to establish a slop-shop, an alehouse or a lodging house. Most fortunate of all were those former masters of ships whose earnings from the sea had been so great that they were able to establish themselves as merchants and shipowners, daily engaged in sending out a new generation of East Londoners to endure the dangers of the sea.

v By My Service

'The plough-boys, cow-herds, and lower hinds . . . desert their dirt and drudgery, and swarm up to London, in hopes of getting into service, where they can live luxuriously and wear fine clothes.'[60]

The comfort and elegance of early modern London depended on huge numbers of domestic servants, perhaps as many as fifty thousand by the end of our period.[61] Some four out of every five of these were women and girls, whose work will be discussed in the next chapter, but there was also a very visible minority of male servants whose powerful physiques and fine liveries made them as much of a feature in the streets of Westminster as the sailors in the East End. Most of the households which stretched to a male servant employed only one, as can be seen in Table 3.4. He would perhaps be a foot-boy like Tom Edwards who worked for Samuel Pepys, a porter or a general factotum of the sort employed by many a City merchant or professional man. But in terms of numbers, the employment offered by such households was dwarfed by the huge male staffs maintained by the aristocratic and gentry families of the West End, some of whom employed over twenty men and boys in their town residences.[62]

Very few of the male servants who worked in London were born there, the vast majority being country boys whose fresh faces, sturdy limbs and familiarity with horses made them desirable employees. Some went into service when they first left home, but many were former farm labourers who had tired of the toil of the field and decided to try what promised to be an easier life. A typical servant biography would include one or two places in the country as a servant in a gentleman's house and then a move to London in the late teens or early twenties. Many went straight into a London household on the basis of recommendations from their country employers, others found places through friends or kin in town or were hired from the inn where they put up on arrival in London. John Francis, for instance, left

TABLE 3.4 Numbers of Male Servants

Size of male staff	No. of households		No. of servants	
	N	%	N	%
1. WESTMINSTER				
One male servant	848	43.2	848	13.8
Two servants	382	19.4	764	12.4
Three servants	245	12.5	735	11.9
Four or more servants	490	17.9	3815	61.9
	1965	100.0	6162	100.0
2. REST OF LONDON				
One male servant	1870	60.0	1870	33.0
Two servants	652	20.9	1304	23.0
Three servants	352	11.3	1056	18.7
Four or more servants	245	7.8	1430	25.3
	3119	100.0	5660	100.0

Source: PRO T47/8. Returns of male servants' tax, 1780. The Middlesex figures adjusted to include London households only.

a gentleman's service in Warwickshire at the age of seventeen and came up to London where he lodged at the White Horse in the Haymarket and was there hired as a footman by the Hon. George Mordaunt.[63]

Four main types of work awaited these male domestics. The most important in terms of numbers was work relating to horses done by stable hands, grooms, postilions, jockeys and coachmen, all coming under the management of a Master of the Horse or Clerk of the Stables in the largest households. There were some 2,500 private coaches in London by the 1720s and each one provided work for at least one man and often for several.[64] Then there was the work of butlers and footmen: management of the cellar and service at table indoors, and display in the street, where a gentleman's status might be determined by the number and splendour of his footmen walking before his sedan chair, riding on the back of his coach or running ahead of it to clear the streets of lesser folk. The work of the kitchen was done in most houses by women, but a man cook was a sign of distinction and

could be found in many great houses, together with scullions and
scourers to assist him. Finally, there was employment of a more
personal and confidential nature, the work of valets and gentlemen's gentlemen, such as Archibald Hamilton, servant to his
kinsman James Hamilton, who 'dresseth him and waits on him
as his gentleman and does other business for him', or Bartholomew Hyatt, who was hired by the Hon. Benedict Calvert 'to bee
his servant, to dresse, shave, goe out with and attend on him as
hee had occasion for him'. Such employment shaded into the
work of a confidential secretary; George White, for example,
waited on Sir Thomas Meres, 'wrote his letters and received and
paid money for him'.[65]

The rewards for service were quite good, both in terms of the
psychological rewards of cutting a fine figure and the money.
Footmen typically got paid five or six pounds a year all found,
but would expect to enhance or even double their earnings by
'vails', tips from guests to the house, and by other perks such as
selling worn-out clothes or liveries. When one makes allowance
for the value of their free board and lodging, it is clear that male
servants made a good living, not much less than a skilled artisan,
and it is not difficult to understand why country boys should
desert the plough for the glamour of service in the metropolis.
There were also possibilities of promotion, from stable-boy to
groom to coachman, from foot-boy to footman to butler, from
page to valet, each step bringing advances in pay and status.
Male servants were notorious as lavish spenders, on their own
persons and in the taverns and alehouses where they displayed
themselves, but those who were careful could make very satisfactory savings after a few years in service.[66]

Some servants spent years, even decades, with the same
family, but fairly frequent changes of job were the typical
pattern. John MacDonald, a footman who served twenty-eight
masters in thirty years, was unusual in writing his memoirs
rather than in his apparent restlessness. Such a propensity to
move around was common among farm servants and also among
London journeymen, as has been seen, and probably signifies no
more than an eternal optimism that the next place would be a
better one. When a motive was mentioned, it was usually
financial. Servants moved for better pay or for promotion or they
left because the job did not pay as well as expected, like Joseph

Morrice who quitted the service of General Compton 'by reason of perquisites being taken from him which belonged to his place'. Such moves were not of course always voluntary. Many servants found themselves out of place at the end of the social season, the more fortunate being able to survive on board wages. Others were summarily dismissed, for quarrelling, for drunkenness, for insolence, for theft – like the footman Robert White who was dismissed by the Duke of Schomberg 'upon accusation of stealing some fruits out of his garden' – and for a host of other reasons. Richard Morris, for instance, was sacked by the general who employed him as *valet de chambre* 'for riding at too far a distance from his coach on Bagshot Heath', a place notorious for its highwaymen.[67]

Service, like the sea, was predominantly an occupation for young men. Elderly retainers could be found, men like the sixty-year-old John Dale who had been butler in the same family for twenty-four years or the amazing Adam Griffith whose career as a servant in the household of the Dowager Duchess of Sunderland only came to an end when she died when he was ninety.[68] But such cases were unusual and most men had left service before they were forty. This was partly because employers did not want middle-aged footmen or valets, but also because servants themselves tended to see the work as part of the life-cycle rather than a career for life. The opportunities for married servants were few, though they existed, especially for coachmen, and this would have been one motive for a change of career. The need for constant deference and servility may also have palled after a while, luxurious though the servant's existence was compared with that of most Londoners.

Former servants could be found in a wide range of jobs, but most did work which had some logical connection with the training and experience they had received. A habit of obedience and a good physique were suitable to a soldier as well as to a footman and many former servants enlisted in the army. Knowledge of horses was a valuable asset and many of London's hackney coachmen and stable-keepers had learned their trade in gentlemen's houses. A man who knew how to shave his master and keep his peruke in order could do the same for others and many servants became barbers. Commonest of all was the small shop or victualling outlet run by a married couple of former servants who pooled their savings to set themselves up in a business where servility and a willingness to please were likely to be positive assets. Some did well in such businesses, but few former servants were ever able to achieve again the standard of living which they had attained during their years of wearing livery.

vi Living by One's Pen

'One that can ingross well, and is fit for a lawyer's clerk, is also a good accomptant, and fit to be a clerk to a brewer, woodmonger, glass-house, or any thing like it, or to keep merchants' accompts, or to be gentleman or steward to a man of value; desires some such employment.'

(Advertisement in John Houghton's *Collection*)[69]

Many witnesses in the Church courts told the Registrar that they lived by their pens when he asked them how they maintained themselves. Such an expression suggests the sad world of Grub Street where impoverished authors laboured to produce the books, pamphlets, newspapers and other printed ephemera which flooded early modern London. A few of these men may indeed have belonged to this world of hopeful literati, but most were clerks, book-keepers and accountants, a new educated lower-middle class whose numbers rose in response to the demands of an increasingly literate society in which government, business and the law churned out more and more paper. The production of this plethora of words offered opportunities to a young man making his way in London which were very different in type and in esteem to those open to the servant, the sailor or the artisan. The pen carried status in itself and nearly all clerks styled themselves gentleman, however lowly their actual occupation and however mean its rewards.

The law provided the greatest employment for these pen-pushers. Much has been written on the upper reaches of this profession, on the attorneys and the barristers who were amongst the best paid men in London.[70] There were hundreds of these legal high-flyers, but the law provided a living for many

thousands more who had little to do with pleading or consul-
tancy and spent most of their time covering paper or parchment
with ink, often with considerable profit to themselves. A five-year
clerkship was the normal way into the profession of attorney or
solicitor, the legal equivalent of an apprenticeship, but many
men remained law clerks all their lives, men like Philip Taylor of
Gray's Inn who 'doth ingrosse most of Mr Martin Folkes'
business of ye said inn . . . by which he lives' or James Spooner, a
sixty-three-year-old gentleman of Chancery Lane 'who lives by
writing for country attorneys and other persons'. Legal clerical
work was done not only in the chambers of laywers, but also in
the parlours of justices of the peace and other law officers and in
the courts of law themselves. Here indeed it reached its greatest
profusion, with 'the multiplying of petitions, bills, answers,
pleadings, examinations, decrees and other forms and copies of
them, and extending them frequently to an unnecessary length':
several thousand sheets of fifteen lines each at eightpence a sheet
were considered quite normal in the Court of Chancery by 1730,
much of this being copied at a further eightpence a sheet.[71]

Much legal work was non-litigious: drawing up deeds and
wills, managing property or acting as intermediary between
borrowers and lenders. Some of this work was done by attorneys
and solicitors, but much was the responsibility of scriveners and
notaries public, two branches of the legal profession whose
members show up in large numbers in the sample used in this
book, taken as it is partly from probate litigation. These were the
men who drew up marriage contracts or brought the fair copy of
a will to a man's death-bed and many did well out of the
business, though the work was often too intermittent to provide a
comfortable income without a second occupation. Rowland
Pewsey, for instance, maintained himself 'by the business of a
scrivener, by collecting of rents and soliciting business in the
Court of Chancery and otherwise', while others combined the job
with running a writing school or other teaching work, like the
Huguenot Abraham Deblois who 'teaches youth to read and
write and practices as a scrivener among the French'.[72]

An expanding civil service provided another avenue of
employment for the scribe and one that was increasingly sought
after as the service became more professional. Security of tenure,
internal promotion, reasonable salaries and a rudimentary

pension scheme made even the lower levels of public administration an attractive option for young men of good birth but little capital. A lad like Miles Granger, who entered into a clerkship in the Treasury when he was fourteen, might never become more than one of the more senior under-clerks, but even such apparently lowly posts carried a salary of £100 a year and an entitlement to fees, more than the mate of a ship or a very skilled artisan was ever likely to earn. Treasury clerks were especially well paid, but most clerical posts in government service brought in at least £50 a year, enough to support a very respectable style of life.[73]

The range of such employment increased enormously during our period, and especially during the long wars against France between 1689 and 1713. Paying for a war of such a magnitude stretched the imagination of contemporaries to invent new taxes and each new tax brought in its wake employment for clerks and administrators, such as Richard Shirley, who became in 1697 one of the supervisors of marriages, births and burials for the so-called Marriage Duties Tax and then, upon its expiry, a surveyor of window lights for the Window Tax.[74] Every change in the customs and every new item subject to the excise swelled the already large numbers in these two branches of the revenue service, which was much the largest source of government employment outside the armed forces. The latter also had work for those who lived by the pen. Every new regiment or ship had its clerk or clerks, while the scope for those who served as paymasters or pay clerks was legendary, enough certainly to tempt Matthew Purcell to sell his place as Clerk to the Cofferer's Office and become a paymaster in the artillery.[75]

Private work for those with clerical or administrative skills was also growing, as the running of a business or a household became increasingly something done on paper rather than in one's head. A gentleman might employ a confidential secretary, as has been seen. Many people also employed rent collectors, men whose skills combined those of the bailiff and the clerk. Most large households would also have a steward or stewards, to oversee the management of the household and to run the estate. Henry Oldecop, for instance, followed 'the employment of steward to noblemen's families' and was in the service of the Duke of Beaufort when he made his deposition in 1709, his career having begun in the household of Lord Carlisle where he had been 'Clerke of the Kitchen'. Thomas Selby, who was steward to the Hon. Benedict Calvert, did rather different work, 'collecting and receiving of his money and rents and making payments of money for him'.[76]

Nearly all merchants employed a book-keeper and one or more clerks to keep accounts, copy bills and invoices, and write and copy letters, as did most wholesalers and the bigger shopkeepers and manufacturers. Goldsmith-bankers and joint-stock companies were a further important source of employment. George Barrett, for instance, was a former book-keeper to a banking partnership in Lombard Street who was serving as a clerk to the Royal African Company when he gave his deposition in 1713. Pay for the literate and numerate men who did such work ranged from some £20 to £100 or more a year, often with board and lodging, though many of these white-collar workers were true commuters, like Jeremy Bagshaw who was book-keeper to a wholesale silk hosier in the City but had his lodgings in Bloomsbury. Clerks working for the big brewers seem to have done particularly well, one of those in the sample being worth over £1,000. The deposition of Nicholas Webb, clerk to the brewer George Meggot, suggests how such a fortune might have been accumulated. He was paid one pound a week and received threepence in the pound for all the money he collected from his master's publican customers.[77]

The employment of a full-time clerk or book-keeper was a luxury which required a big business, but there was scope for the small businessman or woman to get such work done at less cost since many clerical workers operated as freelances. Thomas Leche of Covent Garden, for example, was 'a book-keeper to several master tailors in Burleigh Street', while Benjamin Hayne followed 'the buisnesse of writeing for any person who will employ him'. He described in his evidence how he went into a milliner's shop and asked the lady owner 'whether she had any thing for him to write or bills to copy (such being this deponent's employment for shopkeepers)'.[78]

Clerks tended to be loyal servants, whether they worked in government, business or the law, often staying with the same employer for ten or twenty years or more. But some shared that restlessness and itch for adventure or change characteristic of other workers in early modern London. Benjamin Hayne, the peripatetic clerk mentioned above, had previously worked for a notary public and had then enlisted as a clerk in the regiment of Lord Mohun. Thomas Gostlin served seven years as clerk to an attorney before deciding to go to sea as a clerk in the Royal Navy. The suitably named John Clarke arranged his career the other way round, leaving his home in Southwark to become clerk to the commander of HMS *Assistance* and then returning home again to work for his scrivener father. Francis Swaine was 'bred to penmanship' by his widowed mother who managed to get him a place as clerk in HMS *Colchester*. Two years later, he was working as clerk to the storekeeper in the newly acquired naval base at Port Mahon in Minorca, employment which no doubt helped him to the clerkship in the Navy Office in London which was providing his living when he gave his deposition in 1713.[79] Britain's expanding empire needed pens as well as swords, and clerks as well as sailors might want to see the world.

vii Victualling

'Nothing is more ridiculous . . . than for young drawers to imagine they are to live like the Company they see, and enjoy the same Delights with those they serve.'[80]

Drink, too much of it, looms large in any social history of London in the early eighteenth century, a time when 'one half of the town seems set up to furnish poison to the other half', as one man put it in 1733.[81] He exaggerated a little of course, but the sale of drink certainly provided one of the largest sources of employment within the metropolis. In the 1690s, Gregory King estimated that one in every twelve houses in London was taken up by the five main types of victualling establishment – inns, taverns, ale-houses, coffee-houses and brandy-shops. Forty years later, at the height of the Gin Age, one house in six sold drink, according to Maitland, who counted a total of nearly 16,000 outlets, over half of which were brandy-shops. Neither contemporaries nor historians have thought such numbers exaggerated. Indeed, if anything, they are probably too low, since strong drink was sold from cellars, garrets and even from wheelbarrows in the street, places unlikely to be called a brandy-shop, however loose the definition.[82]

The employment offered by these drink outlets varied enormously. Most brandy-shops provided only the crudest of facilities – a counter, some glasses and straw for those who had managed to get 'dead drunk for twopence' – and few provided work for more than the family of the proprietor. Alehouses, of which there were nearly 6,000 by Maitland's time, were rather more respectable. Now often called public houses, most served bread and cheese as well as beer, while many were fully fledged cook-shops offering a takeaway service as well as being the restaurants of the poor. A small house could manage with the labour of the owner's family, but alehouses of any size needed drawers to serve drink and pot-boys to carry beer to the workshops and dwelling houses in the vicinity, while a cook-shop would need kitchen staff and waiters as well. Coffee-houses were normally small establishments, but most employed a boy or two to distribute dishes of coffee, pipes and tobacco to the customers.

Taverns and inns were the largest employers. Taverns needed kitchen staff to produce the tavern 'ordinary', the fashionable restaurant meal of the day, and barmaids, drawers and waiters to service the bar and the large number of private rooms. A large house might employ a dozen people, but the average was much less. Inns, with their facilities for lodging and stabling as well as eating and drinking, might have an even larger staff. But only a few inns were really big and most employed about two or three men as ostlers, tapsters or chamberlains and perhaps rather more women.[83] London's eating and drinking establishments probably employed about 30,000 or 40,000 people altogether, including the proprietors, employment which was fairly evenly distributed between men and boys and women and girls.

Some youngsters started in the drink trades as apprentices, particularly in the larger inns and in the taverns, most of which were run by members of the Vintners' Company. Such lads normally had sufficient backing to anticipate becoming a landlord in their turn. Thomas Hall, for instance, was apprenticed at the age of thirteen to Mr Finch, landlord of the Cock and Hoop in Fetter Lane. He served his seven years and then did another three years in the same house as a journeyman before opening up for himself at the Ben Jonson's Head in Shoe Lane. John Willis,

who migrated from Cumberland when he was sixteen, worked
for thirteen years as apprentice and journeyman to the tavern-
keeper Hester Well, who died leaving £4,000 in wines and other
goods. Maybe she left some of this fortune to him, for eighteen
months later he was the landlord of the Crown Tavern on
Ludgate Hill and worth £1,000.[84]

Such careers are similar to those of any other artisan or
tradesman who made successful progress up the ladder of
London business. However, only a minority of servants in the
drink trades were apprentices, most being more analogous to
domestic servants. Many started work very young, as has been
seen. William Luddington, for instance, started at the famous
Young Man's Coffy House near Charing Cross when he was ten
and was still working as a servant there at the age of twenty-six,
though such devotion to a single employer was unusual. Such
servants were unlikely to aspire to the ownership of an inn or a
tavern, which required considerable capital, though they might
eventually becoming the keeper of an alehouse or coffee-house.

A pamphlet of 1729 described the process by which those 'bred
up' in coffee-houses became keepers themselves. 'The children of
destitute people, who at first are taken perhaps at eighteenpence,
two shillings, or half a crown a week, [are] promoted to the
dignity of waiters, and in process of time, scraping together a
little money by vails, and the bounty of their master's customers,
and joining themselves to a helpmate of the same quality',
manage to open their own establishment.[85] Such scraping
required great self-discipline and only a few of these servants
became masters, many being forced on to the casual labour
market as they grew older, since customers preferred young faces
to serve their food and drink.

Young men and women, bred to the drink trade, met much
competition from newcomers since the work required little
training and was open to anyone prepared to do it. Unskilled
migrants from the countryside, unable or unwilling to find a
place in gentlemen's houses, often drifted into service in victualling establishments. Peter Taylor, who migrated from Wales
when he was eighteen, became first a drawer at the Woolpack in
Birkin Lane and then a chamberlain at the Angel Inn. William
Dobson came down from Yorkshire when he was twenty-one and
served in seven different inns as tapster or ostler in the next seven

years. Such casual work also attracted soldiers and sailors or indeed anyone else looking for a temporary living, such as John Bumpus, who was 'too inclin'd to idleness' to serve out his time as apprentice to a peruke-maker and so 'serv'd for some time in a tavern, and after that did several other little things as opportunity offerr'd'. Most of these servants lived in and were hired on the same basis as domestic servants: a fixed annual wage normally paid quarterly, an expectation of perquisites such as tips, and free board and lodging. There are also signs of that love of subcontracting which has been noted above. John Stoakes, for instance, was a drawer in a 'tavern and rents the tap of [the landlady] and has not any wages of her'.[86]

The servants in London's 16,000 drink outlets were almost certainly outnumbered by the proprietors and their families. Some of these masters and mistresses had come up the ranks through the formal process of apprenticeship, as has been seen. But the majority of those who ran the smaller establishments had moved into the business as adults; these were the artisans, sailors or servants already met in earlier sections, who either ran an alehouse or dram-shop on the side or had given up their previous occupation and made the drink trade their main livelihood. Many of these small businesses were run by wives, with or without assistance from their husbands, and most relied for their labour force on the immediate family and perhaps a single servant, usually female, who combined domestic work with helping out in the bar or kitchen.

Those running any drink outlet, except dram-shops, had to satisfy increasingly stringent licensing requirements, and if they wished to take over a house in the City might need to become a freeman, if not one already. William Higgins, for instance, a former coachman, bought his freedom in the Haberdashers' Company before taking over the Black Raven Inn in Coleman Street.[87] But such formality was not necessary in the suburbs, nor indeed did one need to be a freeman to run such lesser establishments as alehouses or coffee-shops within the City, while there was no licensing of dram-shops at all until 1729 and no effective licensing till 1751. Since the capital requirements were minimal, anyone could open a dram-shop and anybody did, the Middlesex magistrates complaining in 1736 that the trade in spirits was conducted by 'chandlers, many weavers, several tobacconists, shoemakers, carpenters, barbers, tailors, dyers, labourers and others'.[88] Former or current members of all these trades, and many others, appear in the sample not just as owners of dram-shops or brandy-shops but also of the more respectable public houses and victualling houses. Frederick Dennis was a surgeon who also kept 'a brandy shop in Bishopsgate and there sells brandy and strong waters'. John Blake was a scrivener whose wife kept a victualling house in Dover Court, Lombard Street. He lived 'by his profession and the business and trade of his house'. Joseph Pratt kept the Bear Inn at the Horse Ferry and was 'likewise in His Majesty's Household Troop of Guards'.[89] Drink sustained Londoners in more ways than one.

viii By My Labour

'Jonathan Denby of the parish of Stepney, labourer, . . . said that he follows sometimes the employment of a porter and sometimes that of a labourer, but was bred up to the businesse of husbandry.'[90]

Not many urban workers styled themselves 'labourer', though the numbers were increasing, and it would be easy to assume that the residual element of unskilled and casual labour in the urban economy was quite small. The situation was certainly not yet like that in late Victorian London where many thousands of labourers, especially in the East End, competed for scraps of work in the dirtiest and most exhausting types of manual labour. Most of these unskilled men would be lucky to average a day or two's work a week, the occasional week of fairly full employment being sandwiched between weeks and sometimes months with no work at all.[91] Early eighteenth-century London was not like that, but there was already a very considerable demand for unskilled manual labour. Some of this was supplied by people for whom such work was their only occupation, but much was done part-time by those who could find no work in their regular line of employment. Sailors between ships, soldiers, servants out of place, gardeners out of season and temporary migrants from the countryside provided much of the muscle that the London economy required.

The docks were to be the main focus of the late Victorian casual labour market and the unloading of ships and lighters was already an important source of such work in our period, though there were as yet no docks. All overseas trade came ashore at the nineteen 'legal quays' lining the north bank of the river from London Bridge to the Tower. These quays did not have water deep enough for a ship of any size to come alongside, so most goods were transhipped into lighters in the middle of the river, thus ensuring that the bulk of London's imports had to be unladen twice and then carried across the wharves to warehouses or waiting carts.

The labour force handling this work was provided by gangs of regular porters whose earnings were such that individuals had to pay entrance fees to join a gang.[92] The foremen of these gangs negotiated rates with merchants, shipowners and the whar-fingers who ran the quays and they employed in their turn much casual labour to meet the peaks of work. Similar casual work could be obtained up and down the river unloading coasters, barges and lighters engaged in coastal and riverine transport. The biggest demand of all came from the coal boats, which were unladen in the middle of the river opposite Billingsgate. This was extremely hard and unpleasant work done by gangs of coal-heavers armed with shovels who threw the coal from platform to platform within the hold until it could be thrown into a vat to be measured for taxation purposes by officials called coal-meters. The coal was then tipped over the side into lighters and taken to the wharf at Billingsgate where it all had to be shovelled out again. Such hard work was in theory very well paid, but the casual worker was at the mercy of the foremen or other middlemen who took him on, many of whom were publicans who ensured that their thirsty workers took much of their pay in drink.[93]

Carriage on the land provided another opportunity for a strong man with no trade to make a living. Porterage was supposed to be the monopoly of the 'uptown ticket porters', burly men who carried loads of up to three hundredweight and touted for work from individual stands, of which there were nearly a hundred by the middle of the eighteenth century. Such a monopoly was difficult to maintain and there were unofficial or casual men engaged in similar work, many specializing in a particular field, as chairmen or wine-porters perhaps, or in the markets; Serjeant Griffith, for example, despite a 'very good' education at Christ's Hospital, delighted 'in doing business for the butchers, carrying carcasses and such servile offices'.[94]

Porterage was very well remunerated according to Collyer, who claimed in 1761 that 'all the porters in general, however slavish and servile their employment, get more money than many of the most ingenious artificers; and will not be employed by the day without being paid a crown [five shillings] for their labour'. This may have been true of the official ticket-porters, especially those with a particularly good pitch, like Joseph Bull who worked at the Custom House Key and told the Registrar of the Court of Arches that he was worth £50 and was the owner of a pub called the Ticket Porter in Moorfields. Some casual porters also did well. Samuel Ellard, a returned transportee who was hanged in 1744, worked 'as a porter to the market people . . . and has earned sometimes (as he says) thirty shillings a week', a huge sum for a manual worker but one which reflects the daily rate claimed by Collyer. Several of the porters in the sample were former artisans who may have made a positive choice to do such arduous but profitable work, but most in fact seem to have been men down on their luck who did the work for lack of anything else and it is doubtful if many earned such rates. Richard Gascoyne, a ticket-porter who needed to supplement his earnings by mending shoes, or Gilbert Havers, 'at this time very poor', were probably more typical of the generality of London porters.[95]

Porterage, on the river and within the town, employed at least 5,000 men more or less full-time in the early eighteenth century, and many thousands more on a casual basis.[96] The other main demand for manual labour came from the building trades, which employed an increasing number of unskilled general labourers as the period continued. This was the sort of work most commonly done by those described as living by 'day labour' or 'working at labouring work'. Few labourers started their working lives as such, unless on a farm, most being former artisans or engaged in other occupations, like Duncan Laman, a Scottish soldier who became a labourer after his discharge from the army at the age of fifty-four. He may well have had previous experience of the work, for soldiers often worked as labourers while still in the service.

Henry Tasker, for instance, was 'a soldier . . . lives by his pay and some labouring work that he does some times when he can gett worke'. Sailors too were drawn into labouring, either between ships or when they left the sea, like John Higgins who after 'tumbling on the ocean' became a 'bricklayer's labourer by day, and by night could not help following the deeds of darkness'.[97]

When there was no work in the building trades, there were other tasks to which the labourer might turn, such as the mending and making of roads, grave-digging and the scavenging of the streets. There was also summer work to be had in the market gardens and meadows surrounding the city, though much of this was done by women or by seasonal migrants from the countryside and later from Ireland. The demand for most of this labour was intermittent and casual, but there were also many industries in and around London which kept a more permanent body of unskilled labourers employed, such as brickmaking (which was mainly a summer occupation), brewing, shipbuilding in the royal yards, glass and soap manufacture, most of the work in the soap works being described as 'drudge work and labour that was done by labourers'.[98] There was also fairly permanent work for the strong or unscrupulous as bailiff's assistants, taking people into custody or seizing the goods of debtors, while many who laboured by day served as watchmen by night, this citizen's duty having been largely given over to paid substitutes by the eighteenth century. Finally, if all else failed, there was a wide variety of poorly paid unskilled work in the streets, much of it normally done by women or boys, such as minding horses, running errands, hawking, cleaning shoes or collecting such debris of the city as ashes, rags, broken glass and human and animal excrement, which in this green age were seen as valuable raw materials rather than rubbish.

The unskilled labourers of London might have been illiterate and despised by their betters, but they were not necessarily destitute. Some of the work was very well paid, as has been seen, though it might require the dovetailing of a variety of jobs to produce a decent income overall. Patrick Kelley, for instance, was an Irish labourer who came to London with his family in the 1730s. 'He provided for them by working about the river, going on errands as a porter, or any way he could honestly earn a penny under the masons, bricklayers, carpenters etc. and by such means he got good bread for them.' John Peacock of Ratcliffe, a former servant, got 'his living by travelling with gentlemen, by looking to horses, and working on ships in the docks and river, and porterage, and such kinds of labour'.[99]

Such chopping and changing might ensure 'good bread', but there were inevitable problems for casual labourers so that many of them alternated between comparative plenty and absolute want which could only be relieved by charity, crime or by the credit and savings built up in the days of plenty. Winter was nearly always a bad time, with little or no work in building, market gardening or the brickyards and fewer ships coming into the river. A really bad winter could be disastrous, as one was for Richard Quail and Philip Lipscomb, both 'brought into great straits by the hard weather' of the winter of 1740 and both hanged for burglary in March 1741.[100] Any stop in any trade was likely to cause difficulties, as unemployed metal-workers or weavers swelled the numbers looking for work. Worst of all was the transition from war to peace when discharged soldiers and sailors flooded the unskilled labour market, many of them turning to crime when they discovered they were unable to get a living by honest work.[101] Such communal problems were compounded by the frailty of the individual, whose possibilities of work were severely circumscribed by his strength and health. Ruptures, rheumatism and falls, from houses or into holds, were commonplace disasters for men engaged in such hard outdoor work, while all who survived were subject to diminishing strength as they grew older. Few old men could continue to carry loads of three hundredweight and few of them earned as much as a crown a day.

ix Retirement and Old Age

'I had . . . nothing to do but to saunter about like an idle person, of whom it may be said, he is perfectly useless in God's creation; and it is not one farthing matter to the rest of his kind whether he be dead or alive.'

(Robinson Crusoe's reflection on his life as a gentleman of leisure)[102]

A chapter on work cannot ignore a fundamental paradox of early modern England. In a society sometimes seen as ushering in that magic ingredient of capitalism, the work ethic, few people worked if they could afford to be idle. The poor were constantly lambasted for what liberal economists call their leisure preference, a preference described more bluntly by contemporaries as idleness. Middling people might work more willingly, but the ultimate object of their labours was to accumulate sufficient money to retire and live on a rentier income, to live in fact like the gentlemen of leisure who were the role models in this somewhat hypocritical society.

There were many such gentlemen in the sample, men like William Louis Le Grand, esquire, who 'lives upon his estate next to ye passage in Spring Gardens leading to St James Park . . . and at his seat at Sunning in the county of Berkshire', or Lodwick Fenwick, 'by profession a gentleman', or Vincent Peers of Leather Lane, 'not bred to any profession or business being born to an estate'.[103] Those not fortunate enough to be bred to idleness were quick to adopt it if they got a chance. On 7 June 1709, William Jones of Holborn was serving before the mast in HMS *Cornwall*. Next day he changed his style from mariner to gentleman, being discharged from the Navy 'and is not in any employ but is going to live upon an estate lately come to him by the death of his father'. Nicholas Jennings of St Clement Danes was a clerk at Mr Tarrant's brewhouse in the Tyburn Road until Christmas 1715. But then, at the age of thirty, his life changed for the better and he could report that he was 'maintained . . . by an allowance from his father who is a gentleman and lives on his estate'.[104]

Such changes of fortune were common enough, but most Londoners had to work and save in order to achieve that desirable condition of living on their estate. Many achieved this very young, especially merchants, most of whom started rich and with luck got richer. Thomas Harris, an early 'nabob', made sufficient money in India to retire when he was thirty-four. Francis Chaplin was the same age when he wound up his business as a Turkey merchant. But one did not have to be a merchant to take an early retirement. William Gransdon was only twenty-six when he told the Registrar that he had served his time as an apothecary, 'but at present lives upon his estate', a change of status symbolized by the deletion of the word 'apothecary' in the introduction to his deposition and the substitution of 'gentleman'. Henry Smith kept the Mitre Tavern in St James Duke Place until the ripe old age of thirty; he then sold up and retired on an income derived from money-lending. These examples were all exceptionally young, but it was far from unusual for tradesmen or professional people to wind up their businesses in their forties, many taking several years to do this as more and more of their assets were transferred from their business into housing, land, stocks and shares and personal loans. Not much sign of the puritan work ethic there, though perhaps the case of William Buckland is one to set on the other side of the ledger. He was bred an attorney and practised till he was forty-eight, when he retired to live on his very large private income, though 'sometimes accepted attorney's practice to keep out of idleness'.[105]

Prolonged idleness for artisans or labourers was, however, normally involuntary, the result of unemployment, sickness or 'being out of order', and few ever earned enough to afford the luxury of selling up and living on their estate. Indeed those who did retire to live on their savings commonly used another expression, living 'on that hee hath gott', which does not suggest much luxury. Many of course left their trade, as has been seen, to move into victualling perhaps or to live off a 'place', as did the shoemaker Samuel Coleman when he became a parish clerk at the age of thirty. However, one way or another, nearly all those below the middling ranks were condemned to work until they could no longer, 'by reason of age and weaknesse', as William Ison, a sixty-eight-year-old former carpenter, put it.[106]

Neither artisans nor anybody else were very likely to reach the age of sixty-eight in this high mortality city, but few of those who did were able to be idle, however weak they might happen to be. Apart from William Ison, there were thirty-nine men aged sixty-eight or more in the sample, of whom ten were living on their estate, on an annuity or 'on what he formerly acquired by his business'. Another man was maintained 'by the benevolence of his freinds', two were currently in debtors' prisons, one was a disabled soldier supported by a Chelsea pension, one was maintained by a pension from the Armourers' Company and also

'by his own industry in carrying a water tankard' and just one
was kept by the parish, Adam Griffith, the oldest man in the
sample at ninety-one. The other twenty-three old men were all
maintained by their work when they gave their depositions.[107]

Such old men did a variety of jobs, including running shops
and pubs, driving coaches, making mathematical instruments,
shoes or gin, carrying letters and running errands or, in one case,
tending a flock of she-asses in Hyde Park. Some were presumably living in some affluence, such as the two physicians. Others
were in abject poverty, such as Joshua Brooks, a former button-
maker who now got his living by 'tagging of laces', John Adson
who had worked as a shoemaker for fifty-seven years and was
'not worth five shillings' or William Jaques of Southwark who set
needles for glovers and 'was not worth a groat [fourpence]'.[108] It
is likely that the Church courts were prejudiced against witnesses
in receipt of alms, so that Poor Law pensioners would be under-
represented in this sample, but there is little doubt that the
experience of most poor old men was to work until they dropped.
The poor might express a leisure preference by taking a day off
from work every now and then; the rich could express it by taking
a few decades off or by never working at all.

x Accumulation

'What are you worth in your owne estate your debts paid?'[109]

This chapter has demonstrated the great variety of work done by
men in London and the different types of career structure which
they might experience. Little has been said about the rewards of
labour, partly because there is little evidence on this subject and
partly because those wage rates which can be recovered are often
misleading. The wages of sailors, for instance, were often
reported in depositions, but these give only a very partial
indication of sailors' earnings. For an accurate assessment, one
would need to know how much was deducted from the sailor's
pay for goods sold to him by the purser or other ships' officers
during the voyage, these deductions sometimes being so great
that the sailor owed the shipowners money at the end of the
voyage rather than the reverse. One would also need to know

how much of the year the sailor had been employed and how long
he had had to wait for his money, delays in this respect often
leading to losses in interest payments or discounts to people
prepared to buy a sailor's right to his pay. The net results of such
considerations would obviously be very much less than twelve
times the sailor's monthly pay rate.

Similar problems govern the estimation of the earnings of most
other workers. Servants were another group whose annual wage
rates were quite often recorded in depositions, but actual
earnings were likely to be different, enhanced by tips and other
perquisites, reduced by deductions of various sorts, not to
mention the fact that servants shared with most other workers
the problem of getting any of their pay at all. A craftsman might
have an impressively high weekly wage rate, but this might again
be subject to deductions for wastage of raw materials or hire of
tools or working space. His wage might also have to cover
payments by himself to subcontractors, assistants or labourers,
while once again there is the problem of knowing just what
perquisites he received and how many days or weeks he worked
in a year.

The earnings of self-employed men or piece-workers are even
harder to estimate, since in such cases there is not even a nominal
wage rate with which to start the calculations. These workers,
together with such small businessmen as shopkeepers and
victuallers, were likely to have widely fluctuating earnings and
hoped to balance weeks or years of absolute loss by good periods
when earnings were sufficiently positive to allow savings to be
accumulated to cover the next period of bad trade. Few of these
people kept good accounts, and in any case few accounts of any
sort have survived, so that there is really no way that the
historian can make any useful generalizations about their annual
income.

It may be impossible to learn much about the net earnings of
Londoners, but evidence does exist for analysis of their net
wealth since one of the questions quite commonly asked by the
courts was 'What are you worth in your owne estate, your debts
paid?' There are obvious problems in accepting self-estimates of
wealth at their face value. How many people would know exactly
how much they were worth? Were deponents consistent in
making allowance for bad debtors or in estimating the amount of

their own debts? Were they consistent in valuing their household goods and other possessions? Such consistency would be too much to expect, but for all that these self-estimates of wealth do have advantages over the post-mortem valuations for probate purposes which are normally the only guide to the wealth of people in the past.

First of all, the fortunes of the dead are likely to be biased upwards by their comparatively high age and possibly downwards by fortunes being reduced during a long final illness. Secondly, most probate inventories value only the assets of the deceased, a fact which can be seriously misleading in considering the fortunes of Londoners, most of whom can be assumed to have had considerable liabilities. Last and most importantly, probate valuations leave out most of the poorer members of the population since the wealth of those worth less than £5 was normally not inventoried. The statements in the Church courts were made by the living, were estimates of personal fortunes after debts had been deducted and they covered everyone, the range in the sample running from the fortune of £100,000 claimed by George Joachim von Podewill, a Pomeranian army officer who came over with King William as a Captain of Dragoons, to Thomas Barrington, a sailor worth tenpence, and large numbers of poor people not even worth that.[110]

Many of those asked to state their worth by the courts declined to do so, either saying that they did not know what they were worth or claiming that there was no legal requirement to answer such a question. Such shyness is unfortunate and may possibly bias the results, although just how and in what direction is difficult to say. Nevertheless, 662 men in the sample, over a third of the total number, did answer the question, thus providing a figure or in some cases a range of figures to express their net wealth. These figures reflect the sum of a number of different ways of making money. They reflect the accumulation of savings made from wages, fees, perquisites, profits and other earnings, such accumulation being evident in the fact that average wealth tended to rise with the age of the deponent, at least up to some age in the fifties, after which there were signs of dis-saving.[111] The estimates also reflect the injections of capital which the more fortunate of Londoners received, as portions or advances from parents or guardians, dowries from wives and other legacies or windfalls, several of the deponents referring to such expectations in their statements. James Atkinson, for instance, was an apprentice to a poulterer in St James's Market and told the court that he was 'worth but little . . . but has an expectancy from his father'. The lawyer Thomas London had 'expectancy of some estate was left him in the Indies', while the shoemaker Nicholas Knapp was currently 'sueing in the Court of Chancery for a right in an estate of £40 per annum'. Such windfalls or expectations were an important aspect of the process of accumulation, as of course were the losses and disappointments recorded by many less happy deponents, such as the former tobacconist James Walcot of Charterhouse Yard who was 'not worth anything, having had misfortune'.[112]

Age and inheritance, competence and idleness, good and bad luck, size of family, will all obviously affect the reported wealth of any particular deponent, as of course will optimism or incompetence in accounting. Nevertheless, these depositions do enable something like a hierarchy of metropolitan wealth to be established, a hierarchy which allows the fortunes of such professional groups as doctors and lawyers to be compared with those in the commercial and manufacturing world. This is done in Table 3.5, where the percentage of men whose declared fortune fell into five different wealth bands is calculated for a number of occupations or occupational groups. For comparison, 186 widows and spinsters who declared their wealth have been included at the foot of the table.

The table provides few surprises and accords well with work done previously on post-mortem inventories.[113] It is hardly astonishing to discover that the richest group in London were those who 'lived on their estate', those men of independent means whose way of life was everyone's ambition. It is no surprise either that it paid better to be a doctor or a lawyer than a shoemaker or a porter, though it is worth noting the long tail of poverty even in otherwise profitable occupations, these low fortunes representing those in humble ranks such as journeymen or clerks as well as young beginners and the old, the sick and the unsuccessful. Similarly, it is worth remembering that not all people in 'poor' trades were poor. Weavers, tailors and shoemakers, for instance, were normally poor men at the bottom of the hierarchy of manufacturing workers, people like the tailor Peter Jansen of

TABLE 3.5 Percentage of Occupational Groups in Wealth Bands

Occupations (men only)	*Declared wealth (£s)*					
	1000 & over	*101– 999*	*50– 100*	*10– 49*	*Under 10*	*No. of cases*
Lives on his estate	52.0	40.0	8.0	0.0	0.0	25
Medicine	41.9	32.3	9.7	3.2	12.9	31
Dealers	22.0	40.7	22.0	5.1	10.2	59
Officials & officers	19.6	26.1	28.3	15.2	10.8	46
Lawyers	16.7	39.6	18.7	10.4	14.6	48
Victuallers	10.2	26.5	34.7	8.2	20.4	49
Food shops	7.1	28.6	16.7	21.4	26.2	42
Manufacturing/building	8.4	18.7	15.4	22.0	35.5	214
Male servants	0.0	13.3	16.7	36.7	33.3	30
Tailors & shoemakers	0.0	13.7	7.8	21.6	56.9	51
Sailors & watermen	0.0	0.0	22.6	32.3	45.1	31
Porters/soldiers/labourers	0.0	0.0	10.3	10.3	79.4	29
All men	12.7	23.0	18.3	15.7	30.3	662
Widows	6.9	11.9	12.9	21.8	46.5	101
Spinsters	1.2	3.5	7.1	31.8	56.4	85

Source: Male and female employment samples. 'Little', 'very little', 'not much' and 'nothing' have been defined as under £10. Investment incomes per annum have been multiplied by 15. Where a range of declared wealth is stated, the higher figure has been analysed.

Covent Garden who was 'worth nothing but what he dayly works for'. There were also, however, some wealthy masters in these trades, such as the shoemaker Richard Sill, worth £500, or James Brent, a weaver of Peter Street off Bishopsgate who was worth over £1,000.[114]

To provide some illustration of this variety of fortunes, the occupations of those deponents who claimed to be worth exactly £1,000, £100, £10 and nothing are set out in Table 3.6. Here we can see that a scrivener, a physician or an exchange broker down on their luck might be worth nothing, while a cook or a clerk might be worth £1,000. The occupation and fortune of a man might be largely predetermined by his education and the wealth of his parents, but there was still plenty of room for upsets and surprises in the world of London work, rather more so perhaps in the world of men's work than in that of women's work, which was more predictable and is considered in the next chapter.

TABLE 3.6 Occupations of Deponents with Selected Fortunes

1. *Deponents worth exactly £1,000*
Apothecary (6), attorney (3), bombardier at Tower of London, brewer (2),
brewer's clerk, bricklayer, butcher, carpenter & pressmaker, City Marshal,
cheesemonger, clergyman, grocer (2), gunmaker, independent means, JP's
clerk, linen-draper, master cook to the King, merchant, pawnbroker,
peruke-maker (2), pewterer, printer, public notary, royal servant, saddler,
scrivener, stationer, steward, surgeon (3), tavern-keeper (2), upholsterer,
weaver, wine-cooper, wine merchant.

2. *Deponents worth exactly £100*
Apothecary, attorney (2), baker (2), barber & peruke-maker (2), book-
keeper, brewer, carpenter, chandler, clerk, coachman (2), cook, debt
collector, fellmonger, founder, gentleman's gentleman, glazier, horse dealer,
ivory turner, jacksmith, joiner, lighterman, livery stable keeper, Marshal's
Court officer, needlemaker, pawnbroker, Penny Post carrier, print-seller,
publican (4), reed-maker, sailor, servant (2), ship's captain, ship's mate,
shoemaker, silkthrower, snuffbox-maker, soldier, solicitor (2), stocking
trimmer, surgeon, tailor (2), teacher, tobacconist, upholsterer, victualler
(3), weaver (2).

3. *Deponents worth exactly £10*
Barber & peruke-maker, butcher, chancel-keeper, footman, glazier, ivory
turner, joiner, leather-dresser, parish clerk, porter, sailor (2), scrivener,
servant (3), ship's carpenter, shoemaker, silk-weaver, silver-spinner,
soldier, tailor, tidewaiter, tobacco-cutter, turner, waterman, wine-cooper,
writing-master.

4. *Deponents worth nothing*
Apprentice (5), baker (3), beadle, blacksmith (2), butler, chairman, Chelsea
pensioner (2), clerk, coachman (3), coach painter, costermonger, exchange
dealer, felt-maker, fisherman, fruiterer, gardener, glover, grave-digger,
joiner, labourer (3), needle-setter, painter, patten-maker, perfumer, peruke-
maker, physician, porter (7), prisoner for debt (4), prison servant, publican,
running errands (2), sailor (7), salesman, scrivener, servant (3), shoemaker
(6), silver-spinner, soldier (2), solicitor, tailor (3), tavern servant, theatre
box-keeper, tobacconist, water-carrier, weaver (3).

Source: Men's employment sample. Numbers in parentheses are the numbers in that
occupation, if over one.

4 Women's Work

'The conditions under which the obscure mass of women live and fulfil their duties as human beings have a vital influence upon the destinies of the human race, and . . . a little knowledge of what these conditions have actually been in the past will be of more value to the sociologist than many volumes of carefully elaborated theory based on abstract ideas.'   (Alice Clark, 1919)

The early modern period is sometimes seen as a watershed in the history of women's work in Europe, a period when women descended from the comparative 'paradise' or 'bon vieux temps' of the later middle ages.[1] In the first section, this hypothesis will be examined in order to provide a theoretical background to the empirical findings of the rest of the chapter.

i The Descent from Paradise

'England is a paradise for women, and hell for horses.'

The history of women in early modern Europe has been understood by the interaction of two explanatory themes, one a constant in human affairs and the other a product of the period under discussion. The constant theme is that of patriarchy, 'the system of male domination and female subjugation in any society'.[2] Despite its constancy, the particular form of patriarchy will reflect the changing nature of society and this is where the other main explanatory theme, the rise of capitalism, comes in.

No writers claim that the medieval paradise for women was perfect, since patriarchy and the misogynous ideology which justified and supported it were already in sway. Medieval women were thus subordinate to men who monopolized the government, military force, the church and the law, and were held to be the superior partners within marriage. There was also a marked gender division of labour, reflecting cultural preconceptions that men were strong and women weak and intellectually inferior, that men's destiny lay outside the home and in the world and women's within the home and with children. The outcome was that the division of labour favoured men with the most prestigious, most skilled and better paid jobs and ensured that women did most of the housework, the division of labour by gender tending to benefit men, as Heidi Hartmann has observed.[3] Nevertheless, compared with what was to come, such inequalities are seen as comparatively muted in the later middle ages.

The period is characterized in an idealistic way as one in which the dominant activity, agriculture, was a largely self-sufficient operation in which men and women worked together in harmony to provide the wherewithal for the family's survival. Men tended to do more work outside the house and women within, but the woman's role is thought to have been a satisfying one in which she was able to fulfil herself to the best of her talents. Although she concentrated on such tasks as the management of the dairy, the garden and the hen-house, no agricultural work was seen as beyond her competence, while she was particularly talented in buying and selling and so did much of the marketing for the farm, a role which enabled her to mix with and be well informed about the world beyond her household. All the same, it was within the household that her talents were most fully utilized – in the preparation of food and drink for the home, in the making and maintenance of textiles and furnishings, in the preparation and lore of medicine and, above all, in the bearing, nurture and education of children. There was, then, a clear sexual division of labour in this medieval countryside, but it was not one which demeaned or belittled women, the role of 'housewife' in the broadest sense being an honourable and fulfilling one despite what might seem an appalling work-load.

A similar system of partnership and harmony is seen to have existed in the towns, though here there were already clear signs of a shadow over paradise. The problem was that towns were by their very nature islands of specialization with a much stricter division of labour than in the countryside. This division of labour was determined by patriarchal ideology and power and so was biased in favour of men, although it is felt to have been less biased than it was to become later. Nevertheless, there is little doubt that in the middle ages, as in later centuries, most of the more skilled and prestigious crafts were monopolized by men, whose continuing monopoly was ensured by severely restricting or totally barring the entry of women to these trades.

Two factors mitigated the impact of this already fairly strict sexual division of labour. Crafts in late medieval cities were mainly conducted by the craftsman working for himself in his own workshop and, in these circumstances, there was clearly an advantage in making full use of the labour of the women (as well as that of the men and boys) of his own household. As a result, women despite their lack of formal training were able to play a part in their husbands' and fathers' work as helpmeets or assistants, either by actually helping to produce the particular goods or services of their trades or by providing such ancillary services as buying raw materials, selling finished goods or supervising apprentices and other members of the work force. Such experience meant that women became familiar with all aspects of the trade and were able to take over the running of the workshop in the event of their husbands' deaths, most crafts recognizing the right of widows to practise their former husbands' trades.

There was, then, an important role for women to play in the urban crafts, albeit normally a subordinate one to that of their fathers and husbands, and a rather less satisfactory situation than that of the separate but equal partnership of the idealized small farmer's wife. The urban woman also shared her country sister's role as 'housewife', though this again was not quite such a wide-ranging and fulfilling role as in the country, since more of the goods and services consumed in the town were bought on the market rather than produced in the household, a fact which might encourage the craftsman's wife to work harder in helping her husband swell the family income and spend less time in fulfilling her domestic role as housewife.

This then was the 'paradise' or 'bon vieux temps'. If the picture is true and not just a figment of historians' imagination, it was a paradise in which women must have worked remarkably hard for

low returns in a world of low productivity, but where they
certainly had an important role to play and were respected for it.
This small-scale harmonious world was to be undermined in the
sixteenth and seventeenth centuries by the development of a
more market-oriented economy in which capital and profit,
specialization and division of labour, became increasingly
apparent. Such developments were paralleled by and largely
motivated by a growth of towns and populations which, at least
until 1650, swamped any productivity gains which might have
been achieved by economic change. The result was a deterioration in the standard of living of most countries in Europe and an
increasing polarization between rich and poor.

These economic and demographic changes had a number of
effects on the economic and domestic role of women in society. In
the countryside, there was a tendency to polarization in the use of
land, with a growth in large market-oriented farms, a decline of
the middling self-sufficient farms which had been the ideal type
in the late medieval countryside and a rise in the numbers of very
small holdings which were insufficient to provide a living for a
household unless some of its members went out to work elsewhere for wages, either on a day-to-day basis or permanently by
migrating to the growing cities. These developments naturally
disrupted the previous partnership of self-sufficiency. Now, there
was less work to be done by both men and women on their own
holdings and, if standards of living were to be maintained, both
sexes would need to work for wages in order to pay for the
necessities they could no longer produce for themselves. This
might involve working on other larger farms or it might involve
industrial work done at home, for one result of growing specialization within the economy was a huge increase in demand for
rural domestic labour in such industries as textile manufacture.
Such changes led to a diminution in the time (and resources)
available for women to fulfil their previous role as 'housewife', a
role which was necessarily reduced in dignity and respect as it
became less all-embracing. The changes also meant that both
men and women had less control of their lives, since money
earned as farm labourers, spinners or weavers was at the mercy
of decisions made by farmers and clothiers who were in turn the
slaves of the market.

In the towns, the effects of economic change were more

complicated, but again tended to diminish the scope for partnership between husband and wife. The growth of capitalism and the accumulation of profits by capitalists meant that more people became rich enough to employ servants not only to work in their businesses but also to run their homes and do the work previously done by the housewife. Such developments relieved the wives of the rich from all work except supervision of domestic servants and encouraged them to be idle, a means of displaying the economic success of their husbands and a role model for lesser men and women, who learned the lesson that an idle wife was a sign of success and a working wife an indication of low status or failure.

Idleness was a luxury enjoyed only by a minority, but capitalism had other ways of undermining the working lives of women. In some trades, as was seen in the last chapter, technical change or the benefits of economies of scale encouraged the development of large workshops employing men unable to afford the cost of setting up for themselves, a change which restricted the opportunities for their wives to work in partnership with them. More commonly, capitalism affected the ways in which things were sold rather than how they were made. Craftsmen now made goods to be sold by the big masters or by specialist retailers rather than by their wives from the front of the shop. Such developments often involved a much more specialized type of production in which the craftsman only made a small range of objects or sometimes only parts of objects which were assembled by the big masters, changes which would again affect the possibility of his family helping him in production.

Increased specialization of another sort affected the types of work available to women and the nature of the partnership between husband and wife. Once women were forced to work for wages to help maintain the household, they had less time to act as housewives, thus encouraging the market to supply many goods previously produced within the home, such as bread, beer, textiles and clothing. Such developments went much further in the towns, where a whole range of tasks formerly undertaken by the housewife as part of her all-embracing duties were now commercialized and done for wages, usually by women. These changes produced a huge increase in demand for living-in domestic servants, but also for seamstresses, laundresses, char-

women, schoolteachers, nurses and medical practitioners. Such
people had existed before, but the early modern period was to see
a rapid increase in the numbers of such specialist workers, all
doing for wages or other payment part of what had once been
done by the non-specific housewife.

In both town and country, but particularly in the towns, there
was then a differentiation of the tasks formerly done by the
husband and wife partnership in the self-sufficient farm or
workshop. In the long run, economics would suggest that such
differentiation would be beneficial to all levels of society since
goods and services produced by specialists should be better in
quality and take less time to produce than those formerly
supplied by the non-differentiated housewife and her husband.
In other words, time spent by a wife earning wages should enable
more and better goods and services to be consumed than if she
had produced them herself. Such benefits of capitalism are not
automatic, however, since they depend on work being available
and real wages rising for their enjoyment. In fact, real wages
were falling and there was a high level of underemployment as
population rose rapidly in the sixteenth and early seventeenth
centuries. There were also social costs in that the wage-earner
had lower status than the independent producer and the wage-
earning wife had a lower status than the all-producing housewife.

Such costs of economic change were heightened for women by
a redefinition of the gender division of labour to suit the new
economic order. This was mainly a product of population growth
and the increased competition for jobs which it created. In such
circumstances, efforts were made to protect jobs from potential
competitors and the easiest way to do this was for men to use
patriarchal power (through guilds and government) and fraternal solidarity to exclude women. As a result, the sixteenth and
seventeenth centuries saw a reduction in the number of occupations open to women, whether they were spinsters seeking
training and apprenticeships, wives wishing to work alongside
their husbands or widows wishing to continue their husband's
trade after his death.

The results of such changes varied in detail from city to city,
but their overall effect was similar. In the now more specialized
and more capitalist economy, there was a tendency to reduce the
importance of women both as housewives and business partners

and to restrict the range of jobs in which they could earn wages to purchase the goods and services which housewives had previously supplied. Women had always been barred or discouraged from work which required strength or great skill and training, which necessitated regular absences from home or which was considered not to be 'feminine'. Now they were barred from still more tasks and were for the most part confined to work of low status which their male contemporaries considered to be both 'feminine' and trivial, such as the commercialized aspects of domestic work mentioned above, the least skilled aspects of the textiles and clothing industries and the lowest and least capitalized parts of distribution and catering. Such changes naturally diminished 'women's work' as a whole and encouraged women not to engage in paid work at all if they could afford to be unemployed, since such work tended to be both poorly remunerated and of low status.

ii The Structure of Women's Work

'Only a fool will take a wife whose bread must be earned by his labour and who will contribute nothing towards it herself.'
(Eliza Haywood, 1743)[4]

Most of the first section of this chapter was based either on 'theory', i.e. speculation, or on scattered titbits of information relating to the working lives of women. The sources for a detailed study of women's work do not exist for any period before the one considered in this book, when the depositions of witnesses in the Church courts provide a unique opportunity to discern how well theory reflects reality. The analysis which follows is based on the depositions of 1,436 London women who, between 1695 and 1725, answered a question relating to the means by which they were maintained or got their living.

The first subject that will be examined is the proportion of women who were engaged in gainful employment. This is set out in Table 4.1, where the heading 'wholly maintained by employment' means that no other means of support was mentioned by the deponent and 'partly maintained' indicates some other category of support, most commonly provided by a husband.

The table shows that a high proportion of women were wholly or partly dependent on their own earnings for their livelihood. Only thirty per cent of the whole sample and forty-two per cent of wives mentioned no gainful employment, a proportion which might be compared with the fifty-seven per cent of all London women aged twenty or over who were listed as being without occupation in the 1851 Census.[5]

There are a number of reasons why women might not engage in gainful employment – because they did not want to or need to work, because their family commitments were so time-consuming that they were unable to work even if they had wanted to, because they were old and in the contemporary phrase 'beyond their labour' or, as today, because there was no work to be had. All these reasons were in evidence, but there are many indications that what today is called voluntary unemployment was the most important. There is, for example, an association between female unemployment and high status, as the idleness thesis discussed in the last section would suggest. This can be illustrated by the comparative literacy of women with no paid employment, sixty-seven per cent of them signing their names compared with forty-five per cent of the employed.[6] It is also shown, in the majority of cases, by the occupations of husbands. No woman whose husband was described as a master said that she worked for her living and, in general, the occupations of those whose wives were without paid employment were more distinguished or better paid; most of the gentlemen come into this category, as do professionals, most of the middling people and the more skilled artisans, though there are many exceptions. The

TABLE 4.1 Proportion of Women Gainfully Employed

	Wholly maintained by employment		Partly maintained by employment		No paid employment	
	Nos	%	Nos	%	Nos	%
Spinsters	295	77.8	18	4.8	66	17.4
Wives	215	31.4	181	26.4	289	42.2
Widows	264	71.0	31	8.3	77	20.7
Total	774	53.9	230	16.0	432	30.1

Source: Female employment sample. For details, see Appendix, pp. 263–5.

wives of the less skilled and the poorly paid, on the other hand, normally needed paid employment to help keep the family going.

A further indication of which wives were or were not in paid employment can be seen in Table 4.2, which sets out the age structure of employment. The pattern is strikingly different from that of today, the level of employment rising through the family-raising years to a peak in the age-group thirty-five to forty-four and declining thereafter. The logic seems clear. Paid work was something done for the most part by poor women and most women were poor, but they got poorer as they struggled to raise their families, an inevitable condition of the poverty cycle.

Much work done by mothers, such as needlework and catering, was done at home so that it could be combined with childcare. Where this was not the case, a variety of arrangements existed for looking after children. Older children were often at school, while younger children might be looked after by a wet-nurse or by some other child-minder who could earn a few pence this way. Landladies, for instance, often looked after their lodgers' children. Older children, especially girls, also fulfilled this role, the very high incidence of child mortality often leading to large gaps in age between the surviving children of a family.

The types of work done by London women are analysed in Table 4.3. The main occupations will be discussed in some detail in the remaining sections of this chapter, but some general points can be made here. It can be seen that much the largest group of working women were the domestic servants, who account for over one-third of the total if the charwomen and washerwomen

---

TABLE 4.2 Age Structure of Gainfully Employed Wives

Age group	No. employed	Total	% employed
24 & under	27	62	43.5
25–34	143	241	59.3
35–44	136	220	61.8
45–54	65	116	56.0
55 & over	25	46	54.3
	396	685	

Source: Female employment sample.

who provided such domestic services but did not live in are added to the servants living in their employers' homes. Next come the women in the needle trades, the only major part of the city's manufacturing sector in which women played a dominant role. They are followed by another group providing personal services, the women who practised various forms of alternative medicine and, in much greater numbers, the nurses, who account for about ten per cent of the total of female employment and are a good example of the way in which personal services formerly provided by the housewife or other women of the household had become commercialized. Between them, these three largest groups of female workers account for almost exactly two-thirds of all women's employment, a proportion which foreshadows the even greater concentration of working women in these same occupations shown by the 1851 Census.[7]

Just over half of the remaining third of gainfully employed women in our period worked, normally for themselves, as small shopkeepers or in the catering and victualling trades, women chandlers or keepers of alehouses and dram-shops being the most numerous in this group. Another sizeable group is made up of the market women and those who hawked goods or carried them about the streets. Then there were the women engaged in

TABLE 4.3 Occupations of London Women

Occupations		Numbers employed			% of
	Spinsters	Wives	Widows	Total	total
Domestic service	203	25	25	253	25.2
Charring/laundry	12	54	32	98	9.7
Needle trades	51	86	50	187	18.6
Nursing/medicine	7	56	61	124	12.3
Catering/victualling	5	56	28	89	8.9
Shopkeeping	17	30	35	82	8.2
Hawking/carrying	2	41	19	62	6.2
Textile manufacture	9	20	19	48	4.8
Other manufacture	2	8	8	18	1.8
Other services	4	13	15	32	3.2
Hard labour/daywork	1	7	3	11	1.1
	313	396	295	1004	100.0

Source: Female employment sample.

manufacturing, most of them in the East End. The largest
numbers here were the silk-winders who prepared the raw silk
for the weavers in Spitalfields, an industry controlled mainly by
male master-throwsters who employed large numbers of women
and girls and especially the wives and daughters of sailors on the
mills in their workshops.[8] Much smaller numbers of women were
engaged in spinning cotton, flax and worsted, and in weaving
and in knitting, these last two industries being ones which had
been largely lost to men in the course of the seventeenth century
as a result of successful male exploitation of technical change.[9]
Finally, there was a wide variety of miscellaneous industries
which employed women, such as chair-caning, pottery and the
making of such marginal adjuncts to the city's consumption
needs as baskets, bellows, fans, flasks, pipes, sacks and sieves.
These were all small and poorly organized industries in which it
had not been seen to be worthwhile to invest patriarchal or
fraternal effort to exclude women.

Another group of women's occupations involved the provision
of miscellaneous services, the most important numerically being
the schoolteachers, followed by those who provided services for
the local church or parish as pew-opener, vestrywoman or
sextoness, the last occupation often being inherited from a
husband. Women also provided services for the sailor community, as was discussed in the last chapter, and for those in prison,
such as Anne Deal, the wife of a turnkey who ran errands for the
prisoners in the Savoy.[10] There were also entertainers, such as
actresses, acrobats or singers, not to mention the large numbers
of prostitutes who, not suprisingly, did not declare their occupations to the registrars of the Church courts.

Indeed, it seems probable that there was a fairly large
substratum of women not considered sufficiently respectable to
give evidence in the courts, for, despite the lowly nature of some
of the occupations discussed above, one finds others even more
lowly in other sources. Many of these are subsidiary to occupations already mentioned. Bridget Bingley, for instance, was
assistant to the pew-opener of St Clement Danes Church and
described herself as 'but a servant of servants', while other
women were employed to fetch water for washerwomen or to run
errands for virtually anyone. Some women could exploit the
skills of their country childhoods by engaging in agricultural

tasks on the edge of the city, such as Elizabeth Harwood, 'a strong robust woman who, not understanding women's work, had been constantly employ'd in gardening and hay-making'. There were also rag and cinder pickers, shoe-blacks and ballad singers, fortune-tellers and street sweepers, as well as women like Catherina Lutolph, 'a poor woman . . . who used to go a shoring (picking up what she could find upon the shores when the tide was down, for firing)', a forerunner of the Victorian mudlarks.[11]

There was very little formal training provided for women in London, female apprenticeship being common only in the needle trades, as can be seen from the registers of the tax paid on apprenticeship premiums from 1710. Occupations are not always clear in these registers but, where they are, they show that ninety-two per cent of female apprentices were in trades involving the making, maintenance or selling of clothes, the four commonest occupations being mantua-maker (i.e. dressmaker), milliner, coatmaker and seamstress, which between them accounted for seventy-one per cent of clearly identified occupations. Apprenticeship in these trades was seen as suitable for girls from genteel but not particularly wealthy backgrounds and there are many fathers listed in the registers as esquire, gentleman, clergyman or merchant. The premiums demanded reflect this high status and apprenticeship in the high-class needle trades was not for the poor, although median premiums indicate a clear hierarchy. This was headed by the milliners with £30, followed by coatmakers with £18, while the average for mantuamakers and seamstresses was only £10, though a few mistresses with a particularly high reputation could demand £30 or more, much the same as was paid by male apprentices to skilled crafts.[12] The training provided by an apprenticeship was however only available for a small minority of women, the great majority of whom received what training they did get as domestic servants in a private household.

Few women engaged in the same occupation throughout their working lives, a point which can be illustrated by the age-structure of occupations as shown in Table 4.4. Domestic service dominates the younger age-groups, only the needle trades providing much competition, but tails off very rapidly as servants get married. Many of the younger married women engaged in catering and shopkeeping or in the needle trades, the latter reaching a peak when women were in their mid-thirties, after which declining eyesight and arthritic fingers reduced the proportion of women capable of maintaining themselves 'by their needle'. The older age-groups found themselves increasingly confined to the generally low status occupations of nursing, charring, washing and hawking, and in this respect the very high proportion of 'other occupations' undertaken by those over fifty-five is significant since, although it contains a few high status occupations such as midwife and schoolteacher, most of the women in this group were engaged in a ragbag of very lowly occupations. Those who survived to old age were therefore likely to have been engaged in at least three occupations as they moved through the life-cycle of work, from service to needlework to washing clothes or some other combination. It needs hardly be said that most old women, like most old men, worked until they dropped.

Literacy provides a guide to the status of occupations, as can be seen in Table 4.5, which shows a clear hierarchy in the world of women's work, ranging from the total illiteracy of the East End silk-winders to the full marks of the schoolteachers. It is fitting that domestic servants should come halfway down the list since, as has been seen, most of those engaged in other occupations when they gave their evidence had previously been servants and

TABLE 4.4 Age Structure of Female Occupations (number in occupation as a percentage of all employed women in age-group)

Occupation	Age groups				
	24 & less %	25–34 %	35–44 %	45–54 %	55+ %
Domestic service	63.9	30.5	9.9	2.5	2.1
Needle trades	13.4	21.2	19.7	15.6	12.6
Catering/shopkeeping	6.8	15.4	20.6	23.8	13.8
Nursing	4.0	7.7	16.7	20.0	10.5
Charring/laundry	1.5	7.4	9.9	10.6	16.8
Hawking/carrying	2.5	5.3	6.0	10.0	10.5
Other occupations	7.9	12.5	17.2	17.5	33.7
	100.0	100.0	100.0	100.0	100.0

Source: Female employment sample.

the jobs that they did in later life reflected both their education as children and the training they had received in service. Former servants with little education whose work had been mainly manual were likely to end up as charwomen, washerwomen, hawkers or nurses. The better educated, which would normally mean the women from higher status homes, were likely to end up as shopkeepers or needleworkers, the latter form of 'work' being the staple of girls' education, as has been seen.[13]

A few general points can be made about the world of women's work as revealed by this analysis. First, it is clear that there was an extreme gender division of labour in London and that the work of women was almost entirely divorced from the men's work discussed in the last chapter. Even when there seems to be an overlap between the two spheres, as in domestic service and retailing, this is more apparent than real, since female servants did completely different work to male servants and female shopkeepers confined themselves mainly to goods which lay within the 'feminine' sphere. The marginalization of women's work discussed in the previous section had thus already happened. Women did 'women's work', which, with a few exceptions such as high quality needlework, was of low status and increasingly so as they grew older.

Most of this work was also casual, intermittent or seasonal. Few women except servants and those running shops or victualling outlets would have expected to be employed the whole year through, as was pointed out by the philanthropist Thomas

TABLE 4.5 Literacy of Selected Female Occupations

Occupation	Sign	Total	% sign
Winding silk	0	26	0
Char/washerwoman	12	87	14
Hawkers	13	62	21
Nursing	34	99	34
Domestic servants	121	253	48
Needle trades	129	175	74
Shopkeepers	68	82	83
Midwives	19	22	86
Schoolteachers	12	12	100

Source: Female employment sample. 'Sign' = ability to sign deposition.

Firmin, who wrote in 1678 of 'a poor woman that goes three dayes a week to wash or scoure abroad, or one that is employed in nurse-keeping three or four months in a year, or a poor market-woman who attends three or four mornings in a week with her basket, and all the rest of the time these folks have little or nothing to do'.[14] Women's work was also poorly paid compared to that of men, which is hardly suprising when so many women were chasing so few types of job, none of which were organized or protected by guilds or livery companies. Actual earnings are difficult to determine, as was seen in the last chapter, but the typical pay rate of a man in London ranged from about ten shillings a week or just under to a pound a week or more for the more skilled men. Typical women's pay was about half the lowest male rate, five shillings a week being about the norm, though many women got less.[15] Neither men nor women were likely to be able to earn such wages throughout the year but, in general, women's work was even more intermittent than that of men so that their potential annual income was likely to be considerably less than half of a typical male income. Despite this, it is clear from the depositions and other evidence that the great majority of women were able to support themselves and often their children on such wages and only a fairly small minority found themselves in such a desperate plight that they had to apply for assistance from charity or the parish.

It has been shown that the world of women's work in our period was very similar to that of Victorian times, though, as will be seen in later sections, it is possible that there was some deterioration in women's opportunities between 1700 and 1850, just as there had been in the knitting and weaving industries in the course of the seventeenth century. What is difficult to tell from the available evidence is whether the picture portrayed here is in any real sense different from the situation in later medieval times. Feminist theory suggests that things were better then and that there was a less strict gender division of labour. This may be true, but it is difficult to be certain on the basis of the evidence currently available to the historian. This rarely has much to say about the poorer women who made up the great majority of the female population of medieval cities and must have done most of the paid work, just as they did in early modern cities.

The other main theme of feminist theory has been to suggest

that there was at some time between 1500 and 1800 a decline in partnership between husband and wife in the world of work, a decline explained by the rise of capitalism which destroyed the family economy of the urban workshop. On this score, the evidence from the material in the Church courts is fairly clear. By 1700, there was very little partnership between husband and wife. There were 396 wives in the sample who said that they worked for their living, either supporting themselves entirely or supplementing their husband's income from his trade. Only forty-six of these women, or just under twelve per cent, could be said to be in partnership with their husband and most of these engaged in work belonging more to the feminine sphere than to that of men.

The commonest shared occupation was running a food and drink outlet, no less than twenty-two of the forty-six working in a tavern, victualling house, cook-shop, coffee-house or dram-shop, while another five were bakers or pastry-cooks. Six more were in the needle trades, three worked as servants alongside their husbands and the rest were in a variety of lowly industrial trades in which it could be said that men were engaged in women's work rather than the other way round. It is possible that other wives helped their husbands, as business partners as well as house-wives, but received no money for their help and so did not think that such work was relevant to the questions asked by the court. However, the jobs that wives actually said that they did provide little support for Alice Clark's claim that the majority of wives found scope for productive activity in their husbands' businesses in the late seventeenth century.[16]

In fact, most wives, far from being in partnership with their husbands, probably rarely saw them during the hours of day-light. Both men and women worked long hours (six in the morning to eight in the evening with a dinner break was common) and most men and women worked at different trades in different places. The world of women's work was in fact a very female world in which women worked with women, talked to women and amused themselves with women, and were even for the most part employed by women. This is a world of parallel spheres and not a world of economic partnership between the sexes.

Further support for the general observation that wives rarely shared their husband's occupation is given by the fact that few widows carried on their husband's trade after his death and that some who did gave up fairly quickly, such as Jane Wright who followed her husband's trade as a master tailor for two years after his death but then gave up the business and 'now works to a slop shop', a job description which meant that she worked at home making seamen's jackets and drawers.[17] Other widows were more successful in carrying on their husbands' businesses; there are two butchers, two linen-drapers, two goldsmiths, two corn dealers, a tallow-chandler, an engraver on stone, a parish clerk and a few others amongst the widows in the sample. However, at the most generous, there are only twenty working widows engaged in male trades out of a total of 295 and some of these are very marginal. The parish clerk could not write and carried out her duties by a male deputy; the engraver on stone seems unlikely to have been a great success since she could not even draw a straight line when she marked her deposition; while one of the goldsmiths had clearly feminized her former husband's business since she was selling linen and lace on the side.[18]

There were some very competent businesswomen in London, as will be seen in a later section. There were also some women engaged in male trades who were brutally effective at them, such as the murderess Ann Mudd who worked as a butcher alongside her victim husband in Carnaby Market. 'She liv'd by killing of beasts, in which way of trade she was very expert, understanding it better than her unfortunate husband.'[19] However, the Ann Mudds of early modern London were exceptional in more ways than one and it must be the conclusion of this section that women did women's work in the metropolis of our period, a city which was certainly no 'paradise for women'.

iii Domestic Service

'Women servants are now so scarce that from 30 and 40 shillings a year, their wages are increased of late to 6, 7, and 8 pounds per annum, and upwards; insomuch, that an ordinary tradesman cannot well keep one; but his wife, who might be useful in his shop, or business, must do the drudgery of household affairs: and all this, because our servant wenches are so puff'd up with pride, now a days, that they never think they go fine enough.'

(Defoe, 1725)

Domestic service provided, as has been seen, both the largest
sector of the female employment market and the one in which
most women got their first job. The number of servants
employed in London was growing quite rapidly, as increasing
wealth enabled more people to employ at least one servant and as
those who were better off began to think in terms of a staff rather
than a single maid. 'I believe nobody will deny', wrote Defoe in
1724, 'that people live more profusely, keep greater equipages
and more servants than ever was done before.'[20]

The servant population was becoming increasingly female as
time went on, as the ideals of middle-class cleanliness and
comfort became the norm. Many household chores were done by
male servants in the sixteenth and early seventeenth centuries
but, by our period, there was a clear gender division of labour
within the household. Male servants, as was seen in the last
chapter, were coachmen, butlers, footmen and occasionally
cooks; when they provided personal services, these were usually
for the master. Female servants cleaned the house and washed
and maintained the clothes, looked after children and the sick,
did most of the kitchen work and, in households with servants of
both sexes, provided personal services for the mistress.

Female servants far outnumbered men, as can be seen in
Table 4.6, which analyses the domestic servants in two wealthy
City parishes in the 1690s. The table shows that four out of five
servants were female and also that nearly eighty per cent of the
households had just one or two servants, usually female. Well
over half of the households had only one servant, 'the useful
housewifery servant, commonly called maids of all work', as Sir
John Fielding described them. Only when there was a staff of
three or four or more were there likely to be male servants, who
were a sign of considerable status but expensive and largely
confined to the richer households within the City and the gentry
households of the West End. Domestic service was to become
even more dominated by women after 1777 when a tax on male
servants made their cost even greater, and by 1851 about nine
out of ten servants were women.[21]

The growth in demand for female servants outran the increasing supply from the countryside and the period was generally a

good one for servants. This was reflected in a growth in pay from a typical £2 or £3 a year plus full board in the middle of the seventeenth century to £5 or £6 a year by 1750, enough to allow a careful young woman to accumulate a small dowry, especially when such perquisites as vails or tips from guests were added in. These modest wages seemed outrageous to contemporary employers, especially to foreigners like Battista Angeloni who thought that the cost of the tea demanded twice a day by London servants 'amounts to as much as the wages of servants in Italy'.[22]

There were many different forms of service but, at least in middle- and upper-class homes, the living conditions were comfortable enough, better than most servants had enjoyed before going into service and better than most would experience after leaving it. There was usually plenty of food served up three times a day, with a high cholesterol mid-day dinner providing most of the bulk. Most female servants enjoyed the privacy of their own bedrooms, which were reasonably well furnished, with a curtained bed (usually not shared), good bedding, a chest of drawers and often a looking-glass. They were also normally well dressed, either because that was what they chose to spend their wages on or because they were the recipients of their mistress's discarded clothing, which tended to be discarded quicker and quicker as fashion took a firmer grip in the early eighteenth century. Where a servant was unlikely to be comfortable was in

TABLE 4.6 Distribution of Domestic Servants

Size of staff	No. of households		No. of servants		%
	No.	*%*	*Female*	*Male*	*Female*
One servant	100	56.8	96	4	96
Two	37	21.0	62	12	84
Three	20	11.4	54	6	90
Four	7	4.0	16	12	57
Five	7	4.0	21	14	60
Six & over	5	2.8	22	17	56
Total	176	100.0	271	65	81

Source: CLRO Marriage Duties Assessments 62 and 73 (St Mary le Bow and St Michael Bassishaw). All households listed as having at least one domestic servant are included. The parishes were chosen because their assessments distinguish clearly between domestic servants and apprentices, clerks, journeymen, etc., who are excluded.

the homes of artisans who did not have much comfort themselves or in situations where service was combined with other work, such as small shops and victualling outlets where both the work and the living conditions were often very unpleasant compared with service in a middle-class house.[23]

Service may also have been becoming less demanding as a result of increased specialization of work and job specification, so that a smaller proportion of servants found themselves the only servant in the household. This was certainly the view of Defoe, who claimed in the 1720s that it took two servants to do the work previously done by one, illustrating his point by a story about a girl who made it clear to her prospective employers what she considered a proper work-load. 'If you wash at home, you should have a laundry-maid; if you give entertainments, you must have a cook-maid; if you have any needlework, you should have a chamber-maid; for such a house as this is enough for a house-maid in all conscience.' One certainly finds all these categories of servants in the sources, with a clear hierarchy amongst them, and sometimes their duties are spelled out in detail. Mary Cockerell, for instance, was chambermaid to Lady Calvert and 'her business was to wait upon her when she was dressing, take away her linnen, make or helpe make her bed and clean her rooms and it was her immediate businesse to attend upon her Ladyshipp's person in her chamber and to take care of her body linnen'.[24]

The phrase 'if you wash at home' is significant, since the increasing employment of living-out washerwomen and char-women was another sign of specialization within domestic service which reduced the drudgery of the most exhausting household tasks. Any added burden might lead to the employ-ment of such women but, once the example had been set, it was difficult to revert to the previous situation of one servant doing all the work. Elizabeth Davis, for instance, 'was hired as a servant . . . to doe the household worke as washing and dressing for the ministrant [i.e. defendant] and his family . . . After the ministrant tooke boarders into the house, the linnen was putt out to washing and charwomen sometimes hired to assist this respondent in her business, but before that all household affaires were done by this respondent.'[25]

The charwoman's work is adequately described by the contemporary phrase, 'a goeing out a washing and scowring'; it was hard labour done mainly by older women who often had to leave home very early to go to work.[26] Those who took in laundry to wash at home also worked hard, but were definitely in a higher status occupation, which had its pitfalls since washerwomen were responsible for the linen in their possession. This could be a worry, since linen was very expensive and washerwomen were particularly vulnerable to theft when they were drying clothes, so that they often appear as prosecutors in the criminal courts. On the other hand, possession of their employers' property put them in a stronger position than most servants in the only too common situation of being owed wages, since they were able to 'stop' the linen in lieu of payment. We have not yet reached the age of the great Victorian laundries, but some of these women ran sizeable businesses, employing other women to help them wash and iron.[27]

The hard work done by washerwomen and charwomen was also of course the lot of most living-in domestic servants and it should serve as a reminder that the relatively good times emphasized here did not mean that domestic service was an easy option. London houses were kept to a high standard, César de Saussure reporting that well-kept houses were washed twice a week 'and that from top to bottom; and even every morning most kitchens, staircases and entrances are scrubbed. All furniture, and especially kitchen utensils, are kept with the greatest cleanliness.' On top of this was the washing, ironing and mending of clothes, the arduous work of the kitchen, the making of beds, minding of children and close attention on the persons and clothes of the master and mistress, all of which was made more tiring and time-consuming by the layout of London houses, which meant endless going up and down stairs with coal, water, food and drink, warming-pans, close-stools and commodes.[28]

Hard work was, however, true of virtually all occupations carried out by women. What was most irksome about domestic service was almost certainly the continuous and all-pervading degree of subordination which the job involved, far more than in virtually any other type of occupation in the city. It was suggested earlier that an important motive for female migration was a desire for freedom from the restraints of a village life in which female subordination by males and by village elders of both sexes was a major theme. It was difficult to achieve this freedom as a domestic servant when master and mistress expected a continuous appearance of obedience, humility, piety, respect and gratitude. Many servants were of course independent; some were downright rude to their employers; but too much of such behaviour could lead to a blacklisting through the employers' grapevine, 'as no persons' fortunes depend more upon their reputation than those of servants, who have generally little else to depend upon'.[29]

How long did female servants spend with any one employer? The answers in depositions range from a few days to thirty years, and the general pattern was fairly volatile, as can be seen in Table 4.7. Some servants stayed in one household throughout that part of their life-cycle spent in service, often working their way up through the domestic hierarchy to become a well-trusted housekeeper or confidential lady's maid. Many others stayed several years in one household. On the other hand, many servants were constantly chopping and changing, a few months here, a few months there, bringing the median down to a single year. Such restlessness reflects a change from the early seventeenth century when the average length of service with one household was four years, with only 13.5 per cent of servants staying for less than a year.[30] High rates of turnover suggest that jobs were quite easy to get in the early eighteenth century, though there were always many servants 'out of place'.

It is difficult to generalize about the careers of female servants within London, since these were so varied. Some only worked in high status jobs in high-class houses, such as Judith Thompson who was successively 'woman' (lady's maid) to the Ladies Cuffs, Winch and Wentworth and the Countess of Huntingdon. Some only worked as skivvies in alehouses or worse, such as Mary Binney who was 'very poor and not worth five shillings in all ye world' and was employed as a servant for £1 a year in a cellar cook-shop. There were also specialist groups of servants, such as the women who acted as bedmakers and laundresses in the chambers of lawyers in the Inns of Court.[31]

However, most servants moved easily from one type of environment to another, from a peruke-maker to a brewer to a colonel to a tavern bar, to take one example. The same variety is true of the areas of London in which they worked. Some only

TABLE 4.7 Length of Time in One Place as a Domestic Servant		
Time	*Nos*	*%*
0–3 months	56	21.3
4–6 months	45	17.1
7–12 months	63	24.0
1–2 years	48	18.2
3–5 years	25	9.5
Over 5 years	26	9.9
	263	100.0

Lower quartile: 4 months
Median: 1 year
Upper quartile: 2 years

Source: Female employment sample, using those cases where length of service can be calculated.

worked within the City or the East End or in a particular, quite small part of Westminster. Others moved to and fro across the river, 'over the water' in contemporary parlance, from East End to West End, from town to country, often taking in a visit to their relations while they were there. Many servants did not even stay continuously in service, moving from a place as a domestic to lodgings where they supported themselves by needlework or some other means, to their parents, back to service and so on. There were apparently no fixed servant tactics, though many seem to have made an effort to spend over a year in at least one place so that they might have a parish settlement in London to fall back on in time of need. Most women seeking poor relief did so in the parish of their husband's or former husband's settlement, which he had normally gained by birth, apprenticeship, the paying of taxes or by renting a house for over £10 a year.[32] But it was wise to have obtained a settlement of one's own, in case of disaster or spinsterhood or both.

The majority of the women of the metropolis, the London-born as well as migrants, went through a period of service which normally ended at marriage and began some time between their mid-teens and early twenties. This was their only apprenticeship, when they acquired or honed the skills which would enable them to earn a living later in their lives, and also a period in which a dowry could be accumulated in anticipation of marriage. The circumstances of the time made service better paid, more comfortable and probably less arduous than it had been, though there were of course the countervailing disadvantages of being shut up in someone else's house in a very subordinate position. Most of the other occupations to be considered in this chapter gave women scope for greater personal freedom, but few enabled them to live so comfortably and securely as they had done during their years as a domestic servant.

iv Medicine and Nursing

'I imploy myself in the practise of physick and surgery by which I receive some advantages by presents by which and something I have of my own I am maintained.'
(Dorothy Warburton, widow, aged thirty)

'I have followed the employment of nurseing children either at home or abroad and by that meanes have and now do maintaine myselfe.' (Sara Wilkinson, wife of a fisherman)[33]

Healing and nursing were always part of women's sphere in that traditional division of labour which governed the operation of the household. It was women who helped to bring children into the world, who doctored and nursed them through the myriad illnesses and accidents of childhood and adulthood, and laid them out when they died. Social obligation on the part of the rich and particular skills on the part of the poor also meant that many women practised beyond the bounds of their own families and such practitioners provided much the most important source of medical services in rural society and probably in most towns. Preparation for such roles was an important aspect of education for girls, an education normally provided by mothers. This would involve early attendance and instruction at the sick-bed and practical initiation in medical care and in the gathering of plants with supposed healing or prophylactic powers and their making up into medicines for the household; such recipes provided a substantial contribution to the many manuscript 'cookery' and commonplace books which have survived from the early modern period. In a world where 'professional' medicine could do little for the sick, self-diagnosis and self-help were by far the commonest aspects of medicine and the women who provided the diagnosis and the help were respected for their skills and were as likely to be as successful as any professional in the curing of the sick or at least in the alleviation of their discomforts.

This female domination of medicine was to be challenged in the early modern period by an expansion in the numbers of male physicians, apothecaries and surgeons, who attempted, with some success, to impose an intellectual and legal authority on the practice of medicine which would provide them with a monopoly and leave to women what were seen as the lesser activities of providing first aid and nursing services. This development was, however, a very slow one and was far from complete even in the later nineteenth century when the distinction between male doctor and female nurse was probably at its greatest.

In our period, nurses were invariably female but medicine itself was by no means monopolized by men, despite the claims of such institutions as the Royal College of Physicians and the Society of Apothecaries. Indeed, the late seventeenth and early eighteenth centuries may well have been a period in which proportionally more women earned their living by medicine than ever before or since. This would be hard to prove, but there are good reasons to support such a hypothesis. First, as has been seen, the period was one which saw an increasing commercial-ization of services formerly provided within the household. Medicine and nursing were no exceptions to this and, since it was women who had always provided these services, they were the main commercial beneficiaries. The period was also one which saw an enormous increase in demand for medical services of any kind, partly because there was more money to pay for them and partly because of a decline in the former stoical acceptance of sickness and pain, which led to a frantic search for cure and comfort from medical practitioners be they men or women. Such a demand gave rise to a bountiful supply and the age is a heroic one in the history of quack medicine.[34]

Women in medicine are difficult to identify since they did not normally practise within the official bounds of contemporary medicine and so do not appear in official source material. There are no women, for instance, in the lists of apothecaries, surgeons and physicians of the period, although a few women can be found applying successfully for licences from the Church to practise 'physicke and chyrurgery'.[35] A variety of female quacks can also be identified from advertisements in contemporary newspapers, some competing in a general way with male quacks in selling medicines or particular medical services, such as bone-setting or the cure of venereal diseases, some specializing in services more directly aimed at women, such as cosmetics and the treatment of 'things relating to the Female Sex'.[36]

It seems unlikely that many female practitioners would have bothered either to apply for a licence (which was more than likely to be refused) or to go to the trouble and expense of advertising in newspapers, and those identified in such sources would be only a fairly small minority of the women providing medical services within the metropolis. How many there were altogether is anyone's guess, but a few can be identified from our sample, in which there were eight women who earned their living by practising medicine. These included three who said they practised 'physicke', one who practised surgery and one who practised both surgery and physick, an apothecary, a woman who 'cures cancers' and one who 'treats people for the pox'. The apothecary was a widow who had probably learned her trade from her husband, as did one of the physicians, Elizabeth Bleekey, who told the court that her husband had 'imparted his skill to her and ever since her husband's death she hath practised physick'.[37] The background of the others is unclear, but they give the impression of being poor women who had taught themselves – the wife of a sailor, the wife of a weaver and so on.

Male medical practitioners made very good incomes, but women probably did not do so well since they were legally not allowed to charge for medical advice and so relied on 'presents', which could of course have been substantial, and on the profits they could earn from the supply of medicines. These too could well be substantial, enormous claims being put forward for the profits made by apothecaries from their drugs and medicines. However, our one apothecary stated that she was worth between £300 and £400, quite a good fortune for a woman but not much compared to the male apothecaries of the early eighteenth century who were more likely to be worth £1,000 or £2,000. The other female medical practitioners do not seem to have been doing so well as the apothecary; one of those practising physick had given it up by the time she gave her deposition and was running a haberdasher's shop, presumably because it paid better; another claimed that her earnings from medicine amounted only to 'some advantages by presents', while a third would go no further than to say that 'sometimes by her ingenuity she gott a penny for herselfe by her practice in surgery'. Such statements might have been disingenuous, but they certainly suggest that females were little competition for such stars of the London medical world as Dr John Radcliffe, who made twenty guineas a day in his first year of practice and accumulated a fortune of £140,000 by his death.[38]

Nearly all the female healers so far considered were operating on the fringes of the law, either practising medicine illegally without a licence or operating within the terms of the so-called Quacks' Charter of 1542 which exempted from the monopoly of the physicians 'divers honest persons, as well men as women, whom God hath endowed with the knowledge of the nature, kind and operation of certain herbs, roots and waters, and the using and ministering of them to such as be pained with customable disease'.[39] There was, however, a much larger group of females who worked by licence of the Bishop of London. These were the midwives, most of whom would treat women's complaints as well as deliver their babies.

Women had an almost complete monopoly of midwifery in the seventeenth century, male surgeons only being called in when instrumental interference became necessary. However, from the last decades of the century, the female midwives faced a challenge from the man-midwives or accoucheurs, who first acquired a practice amongst the ladies of the court and were able to expand this considerably by a propaganda campaign aimed against their female competitors. Midwives were criticized for their ignorance, superstition and incompetence, and for the effects that these had on mother and child.

Maternal mortality rates were appallingly high in our period, the rate in London being 21 deaths per 1,000 births in the late seventeenth century and 14.5 per 1,000 in the first half of the eighteenth century; the rate in England today is 0.1 per 1,000.[40] Such figures suggest that contemporary criticism of midwives had some justification. However, it would be wrong to blame everything on the ignorance of the midwives. The physicians themselves were very ignorant of obstetrics and gynaecology until the first half of the eighteenth century, when considerable progress was made. In the meantime, even the best man-midwives might engage in some fairly questionable practices. When we learn that Sir David Hamilton, the most celebrated man-midwife of the reign of Queen Anne, tried to induce the child of the Countess of Westmorland by having her driven in a coach over some particularly rough roads, it becomes less of a surprise to discover that contemporary midwives used to toss pregnant women in a blanket for the same purpose.[41]

London midwives were normally considered the best by contemporary critics and were about the most respected and best rewarded of all working women in the metropolis, despite the occasional slur that some of them dabbled in sorcery or doubled as abortionists. They were unusual amongst English midwives in going through a formal period of training, as we are informed by the early man-midwife, Percival Willughby. 'The young midwives at London be trained seven years under the old midwives, before they be allowed to practise for themselves.' 'Young' in this context is presumably a relative term since only two of the twenty-two midwives in the sample were under forty, one of whom, the thirty-six-year-old widow Mary Browne, was 'learning to bee a midwife' from her mother. When their training was completed, the aspirant midwives would be examined by 'four or more other women, experienced in midwifery, [who] gave evidence before the bishop or the chancellor that the candidate had not only experience, but had been skilful in bringing a child into the world'.[42]

In principle, this sounds professional enough but in fact the bishop was more interested in the midwife's religion, morals and standing amongst her neighbours than in her professional competence, while a system by which ignorant or at least unlearned midwives taught other midwives allowed for no improvements in skill or knowledge, as critics pointed out. However, schemes for a more formal education of midwives in physiology and anatomy all came to naught, leaving them fairly easy prey to the inroads into their profession made by the university-educated man-midwives of the eighteenth century.

Female doctors and midwives were thus faced by increased

and increasingly effective competition from men in the eighteenth century, a development which by the nineteenth century was to eliminate female doctors almost completely and to restrict the practice of female midwives to the poor. No such competition was faced by nurses, who provided much the largest numbers of women employed in medicine in our period, with nearly a hundred in the sample, just under ten per cent of all employed women. General histories of nursing ignore these thousands of nurses who sought to ease the suffering of the sick throughout the seventeenth and eighteenth centuries, a period written off as 'the dark ages of nursing', a historical blank between the dissolution of the nunneries and the rise of Florence Nightingale.[43]

There were several different types of nurse. Best known to the modern student are the wet-nurses, who have attracted considerable attention mainly because of recent historical interest in fertility. The practice of employing a wet-nurse was widespread in the seventeenth and early eighteenth centuries, though it declined after 1750 as a result of medical and moral criticism, causing many more mothers of the upper and middle classes to nurse their own babies. Whether the practice was also common amongst working mothers, as it was in France, is not clear; there are certainly criminal cases where mothers attempted to excuse theft by saying they needed the money to pay their children's nurses, but it would be difficult to say from such evidence whether this was a widespread practice.[44]

Research has tended to concentrate on the wet-nurses who lived in the villages around London, since the burial registers of such places often note the death of 'nurse-children', sometimes naming their London parents. The air in these villages was considered to be much healthier for babies than the smoke-polluted air of London and in some villages the wet-nursing of London children was so prevalent that it has been described as a well-paid cottage industry, so much so that in villages where there were other cottage industries employing women, such as lacemaking or straw-plaiting, there were few or no wet-nurses.[45]

This emphasis on London children being nursed a long way from home in the country is somewhat misleading since it ignores the many babies who were wet-nursed at home or by neighbouring London women, a practice which cannot be documented from burial registers where such children would be described as the sons and daughters of their parents rather than as nurse-children. Several of the London women in the sample named wet-nursing as one of the means by which they earned a living, such as Susan Eldridge, the wife of a Clerkenwell carpenter who kept a small alehouse and took in nurse children, or Margaret Overy, the Huguenot wife of a weaver, who maintained herself by keeping a shop and by wet-nursing the babies first of a wine merchant and then of a sugar merchant.[46] Another source of demand for London wet-nurses came from the parishes, most of which had a fairly regular supply of babies which they wanted to get off their hands – either because their mothers had died or more commonly because they had been abandoned. Such children were often kept by the parish nurses for years until they were sent into domestic service or apprenticed. This work was quite well paid; a flat annual fee of £6 a year was paid to the nurses by the parish of St Katherine Coleman, which would have been a very useful supplement to the income of a poor family, who might have been able to handle two or even more children. Wealthy parents would normally have paid considerably more than this, making the practice of wet-nursing as valuable to the nurse as it was convenient to the natural mother.[47]

It is often difficult to tell from depositions whether a woman who said she earned her living by nursing children was in fact a wet-nurse or what we would call a nanny and contemporaries often called a dry-nurse. The latter was certainly a common occupation for women, especially in large households. Many women of course did both, starting as a wet-nurse and then continuing to look after the child after it had been weaned. Mary Prince, for instance, had been wet-nurse and then dry-nurse to the daughter of Lady Bellomont until she was taken over by a governess, and even then she was called in regularly to nurse the girl through the many diseases of childhood.[48]

Nursing other women's children provided employment for a considerable number of London women, but far more earned their living by nursing the sick, an occupation normally described as 'nursekeeping' or 'goeing out a nursekeeping' in contemporary parlance. Nearly all these women were employed in private houses, the numbers employed in hospitals being necessarily small since there was only a handful of hospitals before the end of our period and these rarely employed more than ten or a dozen nurses. Hospitals existed for the treatment of the poor, and the pay and conditions of nurses working in them were accordingly indifferent. Such women have had a poor press from historians of nursing, who tend to assume that hospital nurses were the only nurses, except for high-born and well-respected amateurs, and so run down the occupation as a whole.[49]

Nurses were certainly untrained in the modern sense of the word and would have acquired what expertise they had through experience and from the usual education of women. Nevertheless, it is probable that the occupation became rather more important and more highly regarded from the late seventeenth century onwards. This period saw changes in medical practice brought about by such famous doctors as Thomas Sydenham and John Radcliffe, both of whom emphasized improved conditions in the sick-room as a means of restoring their patients to health. Such an emphasis would seem to require an improvement in nursing and some modern writers have in fact suggested this in attempts to explain the undoubted decline in both infant and general mortality rates amongst the English upper and middle classes during the eighteenth century, such wealthy people being the only ones likely to employ nurses in the sick-room.[50]

Little direct evidence on nursing practice exists, but the rules for sisters at St Bartholomew's Hospital in the sixteenth century probably sum up the general expectation as well as anything. Here the emphasis was on keeping the patients and their beds and bedclothes 'sweet and clean' and also on such tender loving care as 'using unto them good and honest talk, such as may comfort and amend them'. The physician Thomas Fuller, who wrote 'Of a Nurse' in 1730, went rather further than this. The good nurse should be 'of a middle age', fit, healthy, quick of hearing and observant of changes in the patient, quiet and still. She should be handy and nimble, clean and sober, 'well-tempered, to humour and please the sick as much as she can; chearful and pleasant to make the best of every thing'. She should also be 'observant to follow the physician's orders duly; and not to be so conceited of her own skill as to give her own medicines privately'. One suspects from this last comment that many nurses were indeed conceited of their own skill and that many of their patients would have been happy to rely on their nurses' medical advice. Whatever the truth, such a bundle of qualities was not easy to find and good nurses got paid well and all nurses got paid more than ordinary servants, the few figures so far encountered suggesting rates of eight or ten shillings a week all found.[51]

One specialist group of nurses who played an important part in the lives of London women were those who 'looked to women in their lyeings in'. Such women would arrive some time before the birth, assist the midwife and then spend a few weeks helping the mother with the new baby, work which was in fairly constant demand in a high fertility city.[52] Other nurses specialized in looking after sick women or sick children. Most nurse-keepers, however, were non-specialists who would attend anyone who called for them, though a few were perhaps understandably fussy, such as Ellen Birch, the wife of a Chelsea pensioner, who told the court that she 'doth use nurse keeping but not to attend on pocky folkes'.[53] Some of these nurses spent months looking after patients in someone else's house, a way of life which must have been very inconvenient for the many wives who earned their living this way. However, one suspects that the majority of nurses were called in at the last moment, most people being reluctant to involve themselves in the extra expense unless it seemed absolutely necessary. Such work might involve watching over a dying man, laying him out and no more, a few days' work at the most and an intermittent form of employment which forced many nurse-keepers to engage in the meantime in other less well-paid jobs in order to maintain themselves. Elizabeth Paine, for example, a widow from Stepney, 'goes out nursekeeping and when at home winds silk and sometimes goes out a charring'.[54]

The medical profession relied not only on nurses but also on a group of women who earned their living in what may be called the medical supply industry. Contemporary medicine was turning increasingly to chemical compounds and to drugs, such as opium, which were imported from overseas. However, the great majority of people still looked to the herbs and roots of the countryside for the raw materials of their medicines and ointments. The collection and supply of such products to the metropolitan market was a business largely undertaken by women, whose skills in such matters were recognized in the town as they were in the country. Rebecca Baker, for instance, a widow from Ratcliffe in the East End, gave evidence in 1698 relating to her supply of poppy heads which were brewed up for a man who was constantly 'distracted by drink', presumably on the basis that he would be better off being distracted by something else. She told the court that she earned her living by 'gathering physic herbs, seeds and roots and other such things which shee sells to the apothecaries and others that have occasion for them'. A rather bigger business was run by Mary Langton of Newington Butts, who entrusted a former servant with her 'trade of selling herbs, flowers and rootes to apothecaries, chyrurgeons and chymists', the profits of which were to be used 'for the benefitt of her grandchildren to helpe to bring them up'.[55] These examples serve to show that the tentacles of the London medical world stretched well out into the surrounding countryside and they also suggest how dependent that medicine remained on the ancient country lore of herbs and plants, a lore traditionally handed down from woman to woman. Men might be invading the sick-room, but it still remained very much within the sphere of women.

v The Needle Trades

'Though a young woman can work neatly in all manner of needle work, yet she cannot earn more than five or six shillings a week, out of which she is to find herself in board and lodging.'
(R. Campbell, 1747)

The needle trades in the widest sense were the most important occupation for London women outside domestic service and they were also those which probably grew most rapidly between 1650 and 1750. There were two main reasons for this. The century after 1650 was the first to see ready-made clothes play a major part in metropolitan and, to a lesser extent, provincial demand, so that by 1700 it was quite common (for the lower classes at least) to buy complete outfits ready-made. Outerwear would be bought from dealers called salesmen or saleswomen, while shirts, shifts, underwear and the various embellishments to clothing were bought at haberdashers and milliners. Such developments created a rapidly growing demand for outworkers, most of whom were women.[56]

The second development started in the 1670s and 1680s when major changes in women's fashion, in particular the wearing of unboned and looser fitting dresses such as mantuas, brought to an end the situation in which mainly male tailors made outer-wear for both women and men. Male tailors continued to dominate the business of making men's outerwear, though the challenge of cheap female labour was to remain a threat throughout the eighteenth century, but most other items of men's apparel, such as shirts, cravats, bands and other accessories, were made by women. Women also made virtually all women's clothing after the rise of the mantua, except for such 'tailored' items as riding-habits and the boned stays, normally called 'a pair of bodies', which defined a woman's shape under her petticoats and mantua. Stay-making was in fact one of the few London trades where women worked alongside men, women doing the stitching part of the work and men cutting out the canvas and manipulating the whalebone stiffening.[57]

These changes, together with the vagaries of fashion which saw the appearance of such specialist trades as hooped petticoat-making, gave rise to a wide variety of occupations and methods of economic organization within the needle trades. The com-monest occupation was what we would call a seamstress, though this word was rarely used by deponents, who said instead that they did plainwork or simply 'worked at their needle', these and similar descriptions accounting for about forty per cent of those who gave their main occupation as some form of needlework, while many more supplemented their earnings in other occu-pations by seamstress work. Such women engaged in many different types of work, but the commonest was working with linen to produce shirts, shifts, cravats and bands, bed and table linen and so on.

The second main group, accounting for about a quarter of needleworkers, were the mantua-makers, who were the benefici-aries of the fashion changes mentioned above and were to become dressmakers later in the eighteenth century. Mantua-making was the most prestigious branch of the needle trades and the one to which girls were most often apprenticed, many mantua-makers being very skilled workwomen engaged in making fashionable creations for the ladies of the West End. Mantuas were not, however, only worn by ladies and there was a middling and lower part of thi; trade, the lesser mantua-makers often doubling as seamstresses.

The remainder of the needleworkers used similar skills in a bewildering variety of specialist trades. There were those who made up ready-made clothes for shops or prepared furnishing materials for upholsterers, many of these simply describing themselves as 'working to the shops' or 'to the milliners', one large group in this category being women in the East End 'working to the slopp shops', making drawers and jackets and other clothes for the seafaring community, a lowly trade but one step above 'making souldiers breaches for four pence a day', which was so low that it could serve as an insult.[58] Then there were the women who made particular items of clothes either for individuals or again for the shops. The bodice- or stay-makers and the hooped petticoat-makers have already been mentioned, but there were also in the sample women who made frocks and gowns, scarves, feather muffs, children's coats and various types of headwear. Finally, there were a number of specialist trades which can be placed under the general heading of needlework, such as quilters who worked on petticoats and bed-quilts, glovers, lace-makers, embroiderers and flourishers who embroidered muslin and gauze.

Determining the economic organization of these needle-workers is not easy, since it was a subject of little interest to most contemporaries. It is possible, however, to piece together scraps of information from such vignettes as Church court depositions or evidence given in the criminal courts. Such material suggests that the commonest type of organization was for an individual woman working at home to contract directly with her customers for such work as making mantuas or shirts, such small businesses sometimes developing into rather larger ones by a mother working with her daughters or by the regular or occasional employment of apprentices and journeywomen.

The livelihood of a mantua-maker or seamstress rested on her reputation, which in turn depended on her professional competence, reliability and honesty, since the silks and linen with which she worked were by no means cheap. She also had to have

the ability to find customers, a much more commercial skill
which required the development of a network of friends, satisfied
customers and professional intermediaries who could recommend her to other potential employers. Such networks might be
easy to develop for someone who had previously been 'woman' to
the Duchess of Gordon or had worked as apprentice to a skilled
mantua-maker whose reputation was widespread. Other women
needed to work harder to build up and retain a clientele, ideally
amongst 'friends and acquaintances' in the immediate neighbourhood but if necessary wherever they could be found; Sarah
Davis of St Giles drew on former customers living as far away as
Rotherhithe to vouch for her honesty at her 1745 trial for theft.
Indeed, much of the work in the London needle trades came from
customers not normally resident in the city at all, people like Mrs
Wilkins who 'generally came to town twice a year to be clothed',
and had to be caught when they were there.[59]

Such people tended to arrive in the spring, in the peak months
of the social season, during which most women in the needle
trades were stretched to the limit, working all night to produce
the elaborate clothes which their customers were always
demanding to be ready immediately; they were maybe earning
good money but were only too well aware that the work would
soon vanish in the dead months of summer when the fashionable
had all left town once again. Many of course never did build up a
clientele and followed an only too common downward path, such
as Susan Perry who 'at first learnt to make manteaus: but when
she was out of her apprenticeship, not being able to find work in
that calling for her maintenance, she then went to live with a
seamstress, with whom she staid but a little while; and then
betook her self to cry, sometimes news-papers, and at other times
fruit etc. about the streets'. Such a downfall, which in her case
ended on the gallows, might be the result of incompetence,
idleness, dishonesty or drink, or it might be just bad luck or 'lack
of trade', for even in a good year there were too many mantua-
makers and seamstresses for them all to make even a moderate
living.[60]

The market might be somewhat against those dealing directly
with their customers, but it was at least a free market in which
they were able to bargain as individuals. This was less true of

those working for the shops, where there was a far greater possibility of collusion and price-cutting amongst the employers. However, such work was not as yet subject to the extreme forms of sweating characteristic of the later eighteenth and nineteenth centuries, when a huge influx of country and Irish labour turned the scales very heavily against both the outworker and those working in the small workshops of garret- and chamber-masters.[61] Nevertheless, 'working to the shops' was lower in status and probably less well paid than working for individual customers. Shop work was organized in three main ways: by individuals working as journeywomen in the shops, which was not very common except in the millinery trade; by women working in their own homes for the shops on a piece-work basis; and by the means of intermediaries, both men and women, who employed women as outworkers or in small workshops to produce goods either for bespoke clients or for the shops.

There is only very scattered evidence on the rewards which women could earn in the needle trades, most of which suggests that these were meagre considering the skills and training that were necessary. The most comprehensive comes from Campbell's *London Tradesman* right at the end of our period, though he was rather prejudiced against women workers and may not be reliable. For what it is worth, he suggests that living-in workers would get about three or four shillings a week on top of their board, which at £7 to £10 a year was considerably more than they would have got as servants, but not as much as a nurse. The wages of outworkers ranged from about five shillings to a high of about twelve shillings a week, the latter being very good pay for a woman in London. Really skilled dressmakers employing several women or the other types of entrepreneur mentioned above would make considerably more than this, though all women in the needle trades were subject to a haemorrhage of their annual income as a result of the seasonal nature of their trade.[62]

Earning even five shillings a week depended of course on finding work and the unlucky, unwell or incompetent might find it necessary to put away their needles and descend from the garret to the street, there to join the hawkers and basket women who will be considered in the next section.

vi Women of the Streets and Markets

'I have known her twelve or fourteen years. She has been a hard
working girl all that time: nay I may say twenty years, selling in
the morning livers and lights, and in the evening sheeps-heads.
And, as I have been a Beadle five years I must have known if she
had been upon the loose order.'
        (Character witness for Elizabeth Williamson, who was
                acquitted of assault and theft in 1744)

The women engaged in the occupations so far discussed were
hidden away indoors most of the time. We now come to a group
who were both visible and audible, the women who worked in the
markets and hawked or cried goods about the streets. Such
women, burdened with their baskets, are familiar from the
fanciful depictions of the 'Cries of London' series, from the vogue
for paintings of markets, especially Covent Garden, and from
such word pictures of London as John Gay's *Trivia* whose
descriptions were not very flattering. 'You'll see a draggled
damsel here and there, from Billingsgate her fishy traffic bear;
on doors the sallow milk-maid chalks her gains.'[63]

These trades were dominated far more by women in the early
eighteenth century than they were to be in Victorian times.
Mayhew, for instance, emphasized the dominance of men in the
street trades and asserted that the great majority of the women
were the wives, daughters or widows of male street traders.[64]
This was not true in our period; none of the female hawkers in
the sample was married or had been married to a male hawker or
market trader and there were far fewer men trading in the streets
than in later years. Husbands and wives working together in the
markets can be found in other sources, but nevertheless it would
seem that, poor and marginal as most of the female hawkers
were, their occupations must have suffered considerable
encroachment by men in the century after our period.

The hawkers tended to be middle-aged or even elderly, the
wives or widows of men in the most poorly paid of occupations.
They can be found all over the metropolis, but most lived in such
poor areas as the East End or St Giles, quite often a long way
from their source of supply. They dealt in a very wide range of
goods, of which the commonest were fruit and vegetables, fish,

meat, bread and old clothes, but a living could be made from all sorts of other things: from the food of the poor, such as pease porridge and sheep's heads, tripe and sausages, liver and lights, from the food of the rich, such as oranges and lemons, coffee and chocolate, butter and eggs, as well as from such non-food items as linen and haberdashery, china and earthenware and even such essentials as water.

Many different forms of economic organization can be seen amongst these thousands of women of the streets and markets. Some carried baskets or cried goods through the streets simply as the agents of others, such as the fishwives of Southwark who took their husbands' catch to Billingsgate market, the women who distributed the products of pipe-makers and earthenware dealers or those who engaged in the messy business of selling meat for the butchers; Dorothy Walloe, for example, was employed 'to carry out severall ded sheep cut out in joynts to sell for 3 pence a pound'. Others sold food for the bakers: bread of course but also such things as puddings, pies and gingerbread, some of which were made by the seller herself, such as Sarah Delagree, the wife of a Lambeth waterman who brought her over the water each day to sell baked puddings at a stall in Covent Garden.[65]

Other women were petty capitalists who bought the goods they sold, at the markets or from market gardeners or from dealers in such things as tea and haberdashery. Some of these women sold from a market stall or from a fixed point of sale such as a street stall or a cellar; some traded with cook-shops or coffee-houses or sold direct to the wealthier households; but most of them cried the goods through the streets till they had disposed of them. Much of the fish, fruit and vegetable trade was conducted like this, the women (often two in partnership) walking to the markets early each day to purchase the day's stock, as did Mary Marson, who was asked in court what she was doing walking in the streets of Soho at four in the morning. 'I belong to Billingsgate,' she replied. 'I was going there for fish.'[66] Even more capitalist were the milkwomen, since they often had a fixed investment in their cow; a cowman would look after a small herd owned by several milkwomen who arrived each day to fill their pails for the morning round.

The main problem for these women operating on the margins of the capitalist economy was to find the money to buy their daily stock in trade, since it was rare for a basket-woman to be given credit. Profit margins were low and some of the stock purchased might prove to be unsaleable, even to the poor, so that to earn the typical five shillings a week of the London workwoman required considerable capital. Money might be borrowed from friends or landladies, but the main recourse was to pawnbrokers, who took in the hawkers' best clothes every Monday for redemption 'at the weeks end, to wear on Sunday'.[67]

Hawking tended to be a poor woman's living, sometimes close to begging, and was often a seasonal or very part-time trade, taken up and then abandoned in a search for something better, as in the case of Mary Risebrook, a young widow from Shadwell who 'has sold . . . butter and eggs and has wound silk for throwsters and has washed linnen and nursed a child. She has left off one employment and taken up another in hopes to get a better livelihood.' Some, however, made it a much more permanent occupation, such as Jane Poole, who claimed in 1743 to have been a fruiterer in Covent Garden market for over sixty years.[68] Women like her, with a good business nose and a bit of luck or an adequate starting capital to avoid the huge interest of the pawnbrokers, could do well, just as well if not better than the majority of the businesswomen considered in the next section.

vii Women in Business

'Elizabeth and Judith Yale at the Blue Ball in the Long Walk, milliners, for their household goods and stock in trade in their dwelling house – £500.'

'Elizabeth Leaper at the Coffin and Saw at the corner of Fleet Lane in the Old Bayley, coffin-maker, for her household goods and stock in trade in her dwelling house – £350, and for her stock in her yard and workshop – £150.'
                 (From the policy registers of the Sun Fire Office)[69]

It should be clear from preceding sections that a large number of London women ran a business in the widest sense of the word. The keeper of an apple stall or a milkwoman both needed a modicum of fixed equipment and some working capital and so in a sense belonged to the business world of profit and (possibly)

1. Faces in the crowd at Billingsgate.
Detail from 'The Wonders of the Deep'
by Arnold Vanhaecken, 1736.

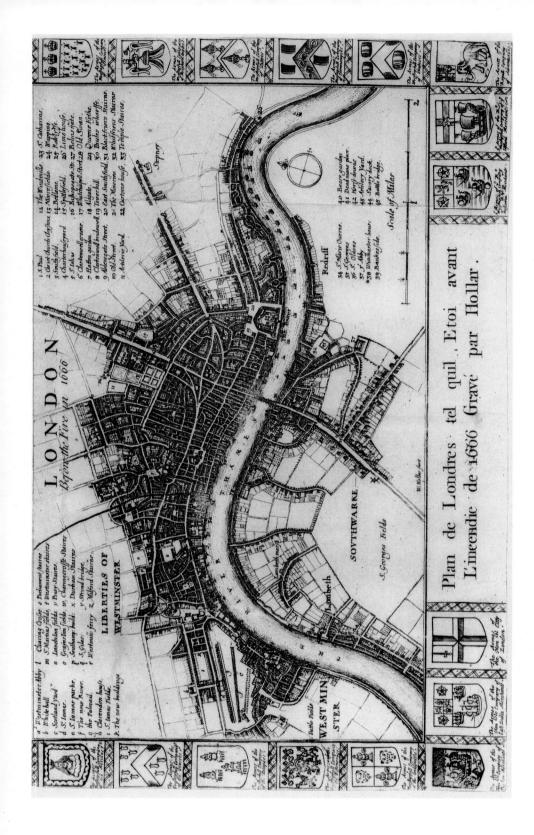

Plan de Londres, tel qu'il, Etoi avant L'incendie de 1666 Gravé par Hollar.

2 & 3. The growth of the metropolis can be seen by comparing these two contemporary maps, of 1666 and 1733. The later map shows clearly the new building in the East and West Ends and the expansion of the built-up area south of the Thames.

4. (*left*) The emphasis in female education was on needlework, much of which reached a high standard, as can be seen from this sampler of 1661.

5. (*below*) London boys and girls at school; frontispiece of *The Complete English-Man, or, the New London School* (1685).

6. (*top opposite*) A fate worse than death lies ahead of this young countrywoman arriving at a London inn and being tricked into prostitution by a bawd. 'Innocence betrayed, or the journey to London' (1731), the first in Hogarth's series 'The Harlot's Progress'.

7. (*below opposite*) The gallows at Tyburn was part of the mental furniture of all Londoners, a dreadful reminder of the savagery of the law. This striking late seventeenth-century composition is by Marcellus Laroon II.

8 & 9. (*this page*) Working women: 'Maidservant with a broom' by Charles Beale, c.1680. Frontispiece of *The Queene-like Closet* (1681), a cookery book by Hannah Wolley.

10. (*top opposite*) Signatures are used as a rough and ready indication of literacy. In this sample all but Mary Dadycote and Ralph Arnfeild would be considered literate. The signatures are:

Mary Dadycote, servant (mark); Barbara Holman, apprentice to a mantua-maker; Ellen Busse, widow; Alice Smith, glove-washer; Mary Dancy (sic), washerwoman; Karen (Catherine) Startup, servant; Sara Blowitt, distiller; Elizabeth Burbridge, nurse; Lucretia Cony, lodging-house-keeper; Sarah Goble, midwife; Elizabeth Smith, nurse; Hannah Margots, publican; Sarah French, housekeeper; Mary Godwyn, gentlewoman; Katherine Hickman, button-maker; Ralph Arnfeild, victualler (mark); John Bryan, bricklayer; David Hunter, publican; Clement Knapp, tailor; John Jones, bricklayer; Robert Higgins, goldbeater; Roger Tucketts, surgeon; Marmaduke Jenkinson, gardener; Richard Shirley, haberdasher; John Thomas, public notary; George Washington, apothecary; Robert Gilder, innkeeper; Joseph Wells, victualler; Solomon Beaumont, scrivener.

Sample from the Guildhall Library (9065A/10–11) and the Public Record Office (PROB 24/48–49).

11. Working men. Detail from 'The different degrees and occupations of men' from p.40 of the third book of Randle Holme, *An Accademie of Armory* (1688), a marvellous compilation of fascinating trivia.

Urban occupations illustrated here include baker (30), butcher (32), smith (33), saddler (34), tailor (35), shoemaker (36), embroiderer (37), joiner (38–9), candlemaker (40), water-carrier (44), weaver (49), cooper (50), carpenter (51), mason (52), labourer (53), potter (54), ropemaker (55), printer (56), porter (63), and beggar (68).

THE
QUEENE-LIKE CLOSET
Or
RICH CABINET

Printed for Rich: Chiswell
And Tho: Sawbridge 1681.

The mark of Mary ✗ Dadycote

Peter holmon

Jon Hage

Als Smith

Mary ganes

buron fravupp

Sam Blovitt

E burbidge

Lucrese Corg

Sarah Goble

Elizabeth Smeth

Hannah Margots

Sarah ffrench

Mary Godwyn

Katherine Hickman

The Marke of Ralph R Infild

John Bryan

David Hunter

the marke

John Jones

Robert Higgins

Roger Pockett

Marmaduke Jenkinson

Rich Shirley

Ja Thomas

G Washington

Robt Gildon

Joseph Wells

Solomon Beaumont

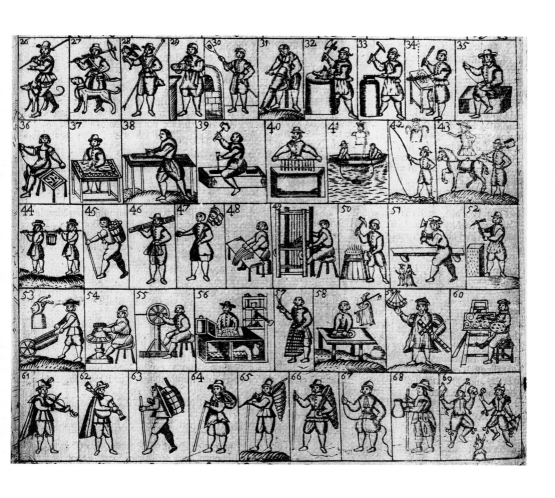

12. 'The chiefest emporium, or town of trade in the world.' Sheets 5 and 6 of Wenceslas Hollar's 'Long View of London' (1647).

accumulation. The businesswomen considered in this section are distinguished from such petty capitalists only by the fact that most of them operated on a rather larger scale.

A good overview of the types of business run by women is provided by the policy registers of the Sun Fire Office, which become fairly detailed by the 1720s and give a valuable panoramic view of the world of London property. The types of business insured by women are set out in Table 4.8. These businesses were all fairly substantial since it was rare for anyone to insure goods worth less than £300 with the Sun, a fact which means that many types of small business, such as mantua-making and the smaller catering outlets, are under-represented. Despite this bias, it can be seen that for the most part women running businesses adhered to that gender division of work which has been the main thrust of this chapter. Women can be found running virtually any kind of business in the city, as merchants, coal-sellers, metal-workers, coopers or whatever. There were even women in the armaments industry, two women's fire insurance policies covering a saltpetre refinery and a sword-cutler's business, while, for a few years, the entire supply of gunpowder to the Ordnance was provided by a partnership of two women.[70] However, such enterprises are more interesting than typical and, as can be seen from the table, most women concentrated their activities within the usual sphere of women's work – running a catering establishment selling food and drink, or a shop selling food, textiles, clothing or such fancy goods as toys, glass, china or perfumes, while pawnbroking was another occupation with a fairly high proportion of female participants, as is confirmed in criminal records where female pawnbrokers as receivers of stolen goods play a prominent part. Only in the group of businesses headed 'miscellaneous trades' are there many 'male' trades and these were nearly all run by widows who had taken over their former husband's business after his death.

These 'male' trades are only a small proportion of the total, perhaps fifteen per cent if one includes some of the more male occupations entered under other heads, such as bookseller, dyer, clothworker and butcher. But in fact such a figure exaggerates the proportion of women engaged in such trades, since the fire insurance policies distort the analysis of women in business in two ways. First, as has been seen, they relate only to fairly big

TABLE 4.8 Occupations of Businesswomen

Occupation	No.	%
Food, drink and entertainment	76	37.6
Textiles and clothing	62	30.7
Pawnbroking	23	11.4
Other retailing	14	6.9
Miscellaneous trades	22	10.9
Unspecified trade	5	2.5
	202	100.0

Food, drink and entertainment: victualler (14), distiller (14), tavern-, inn- or alehouse-keeper (11), tallow-chandler (5), grocer (5), butcher (3), baker (3), coffee-house-keeper (3), cheesemonger (3), dealer in spirits, dealer in tea and chinaware, pastrycook, tobacconist, bagnio (2 each), gingerbread-baker, soap-seller, sutler, poulterer, show-woman (1 each).
Textiles and clothing: linen-draper (11), milliner (10), child's coat-maker (4), haberdasher (4), hosier (4), shoemaker (3), coatseller, weaver, woollen-draper, mercer, glover, mantua-maker, slop-seller (2 each), skinner, dyer, pinker, clothdrawer, indigo-maker, cap-maker, gown- and habit-maker, packer, throwster, seamstress, hat-seller, robe-maker (1 each).
Other retailing: glass-seller (4), shopkeeper (4), colour shop, oilshop, bookseller, perfumer, toywoman, dealer in musical instruments (1 each).
Miscellaneous trades: merchant, apothecary, coachmaker, coal-seller, upholsterer (2 each), pewterer, cutler, clock-maker, farrier, warehouse-keeper, coffin-maker, ironmonger, potter, chemist, turner, cork-cutter, wheelwright (1 each).

Source: GHMS 11936/23–29 (1726–9). The table is reproduced from Table 6.2 on p. 170 of Earle (1989a).

businesses and most male types of business were bigger than most female ones. They also relate almost entirely to businesses run by widows and spinsters and so ignore the very large number of businesses run by married women. The reason for this was the legal situation in which married women were not normally able to own property or indeed anything else, even their wages being technically the property of their husbands.[71] This being so, it was necessary for the husband to insure in his name the utensils and stock in trade belonging to his wife's business.

It is clear from depositions, however, that, whatever the law might be, wives did in fact run their own businesses and considered that business and its profits to be their own, as indeed they usually seem to have considered their wages their own and not part of some joint family income. When these businesses run by wives are analysed, it can be seen from Table 4.9 that, although they reflect the general pattern of women's businesses seen in Table 4.8, there is far greater concentration on small businesses supplying food and drink, which account for nearly three-quarters of the total. There are also, not too surprisingly, virtually no 'male' types of business, since these would have been run by their husbands.

TABLE 4.9 Businesses Run by Wives

Occupation	No.	%
Food, drink and entertainment	69	73.4
Textiles and clothing	14	14.9
Pawnbroking	1	1.1
Other retailing	7	7.4
Miscellaneous	3	3.2
	94	100.0

Food, drink and entertainment: victualler/public house (30), chandler (13), brandy/strongwater-shop (7), tavern-, inn- or alehouse-keeper (5), baker (4), cook-shop (3), dealer in tea, dealer in spirits (2 each), coffee-house, cheesemonger, pastry-cook (1 each).
Textiles and clothing: linen-draper (3), milliner (3), haberdasher (3), glovemaker, lace-seller, throwster, patten shop, selling quiltings (1 each).
Other retailing: potter's shop (2), shopkeeper (2), toyshop, picture shop, trunk-seller (1 each).
Miscellaneous: coal-seller, pipe-maker, dealer in seamen's tickets.

Source: Female employment sample. Hawkers have been omitted, as have tailors, mantua-makers etc., since it is often difficult to tell if they are running their own business.

Running a business was therefore an option for those women in the metropolis with access to the necessary capital. It was an option taken up by something like a fifth of all working women and a larger proportion of working wives, some of whom did well and could be numbered at least in the middling ranks of the city's capitalists. About one in eight of the sample of women drawn

from the records of the Sun insured their goods for at least
£1,000, the two biggest being Sarah Saul, a Westminster
pawnbroker, and Theodocia Fear, a mercer, who insured for
£3,000 and £2,000 respectively.[72] Many other women failed to
make a go of their businesses and had to revert to something else,
like Elizabeth Hickox, a coal-merchant who got into debt and
was earning her living when she gave her deposition by 'selling
coffee, tea and chocolate to her freinds', or Anne Heath, wife of a
cavalry officer who 'for about three-quarters of a year kept a
milliner's shop at her house in Pell Mell but did not get any thing
thereby' and settled for filling her house with lodgers.[73] Some
women, especially widows, were nominally running a business,
but relied very heavily on the assistance of a man, very often their
former husband's apprentice. Such women were not likely to stay
in business long, just long enough to wind the business up or
until their son was old enough to take it over. Most female
businesswomen fell between these extremes, running modest
chandler's or haberdasher's shops or victualling houses and
doing modestly well, earning enough to maintain themselves in
some comfort.

Small businesses were the norm for women, because women
with sufficient capital to run a large business usually preferred
not to. Business might be profitable, it might even be challenging
or fun, but it was not in our period a very genteel activity for a
woman to engage in. Richer women chose therefore to invest
their money to provide themselves with a rentier income on
which to lead the life of a lady of leisure, an attractive option in a
world of drudgery and hard work, and one which will be
examined in the concluding section of this chapter.

viii Women without Gainful Employment

'I now receive alms of ye parish of St Martins in the Fields.'
> (Dorothy Thompson, widow, aged seventy-four)

'I live in Berkley Street and maintain myself with my fortune.'
> (Anne Berkley, spinster, aged thirty)[74]

It may seem illogical to include women who did not work for a
living in a chapter called 'Women's Work', but this survey of

London women would not be complete if we did not discuss those with no gainful employment. Such women cover the whole gamut of metropolitan experience, from very wealthy women of independent means living in the West End to very poor widows living on the meagre pensions provided by parishes. Altogether, this group makes up a sizeable minority of all women, as was seen in Table 4.1 above (p. 114), where it was shown that thirty per cent of women had no paid employment and a further sixteen per cent had some other source of support apart from what they earned by their work. As one might expect, these two groups were dominated by wives, who constituted about two-thirds of those without paid employment, but about one-fifth of all widows and a rather smaller proportion of spinsters were also in this position.

In Table 4.10, the means by which these women were maintained is set out, and this provides no surprises. Most unemployed wives were supported by their husbands, as might be expected, spinsters were supported mainly by relatives, usually their parents, and most unemployed widows were maintained by the fortunes they had received either from their parents or their former husband (or husbands). It is unfortunate that the income provided by lodgers is under-recorded in the Church court depositions, since this was definitely more important than is shown in the table. It is probable, too, that those receiving relief from their parishes are under-represented, since it is clear from the questions put to some deponents that the receipt of alms was likely to discredit a witness. The ten parish pensioners in the table represent less than one per cent of the whole sample. What the true proportion would be is difficult to say, but it was certainly much higher.[75]

The depositions do not, unfortunately, throw much light on the financial arrangements between husband and wife. Most wives simply said that they were 'maintained by their husband' or by their husband's trade or fortune, though a few were a little more specific. Bridget Wood, for instance, received 'from her husband sometimes five shillings per week and sometimes more or less as she can get it for ye support of her self and her four children' – the same amount as the typical wages of a working woman. Anne Haynes, possibly a deserted wife, had 'an allowance of £15 per annum paid her, by which she lives', a sum which

TABLE 4.10 Maintenance of Women without Gainful Employment

1. Partly maintained by gainful employment

Maintained also by	Wives	Widows	Spinsters
Husband	169	0	0
Relatives/friends	9	7	14
Lodgers	2	6	2
Own means	0	14	1
Parish	1	3	1
Crown pension	0	1	0
	181	31	18

2. No gainful employment

Maintained also by	Wives	Widows	Spinsters
Husband	273	0	0
Relatives/friends	7	12	46
Lodgers	2	4	0
Own means	5	55	19
Parish	0	5	0
Crown pension	2	1	1
	289	77	66

Source: Female employment sample. In several cases, more than one of the above sources of maintenance were mentioned; only what seemed the major source of income has been tabulated here. Crown pensions were paid to some of the Huguenot women and to the widows of army officers.

works out at 5s.9d. a week.[76] One can hardly generalize on the evidence of two cases, but it is implied in many depositions that the wife was responsible for maintaining herself and her children and that she either earned a living or received money from her husband for that purpose. Husbands might well have considered that what they gave as 'housekeeping' should be about the same as a working woman's wages, five or six shillings a week.[77]

    Relatives and friends were the main source of financial support for those with no husband and no fortune or property of their own. Children or other relatives were, for example, the support of many widows, but not as many as one might expect in a society sometimes thought to have been more caring than our

own. Some wives were also supported wholly or partly by
relatives, such as Mary Booth, the wife of a schoolmaster who
was maintained 'by working at her needle and by some moneys
she hath sent her yearly by her father'.[78]

Most of the women supported by relatives were, however,
spinsters from reasonably well-off families. Such girls normally
stayed at home with parents or other relatives until they got
married or became financially independent, like Elizabeth Holt,
an eighteen-year-old from Westminster who 'lives with her father
and mother from whome shee expects a provision [i.e. a portion
or dowry]'. Some of these young women no doubt lived in
idleness, but many were expected to work hard for their keep,
such as Elizabeth Jackson, aged twenty-four, who was her
uncle's housekeeper 'without any wages . . . and hee maintaines
her', the position of course of most of the wives who have been
described as being 'without gainful employment'. Parents might
also subsidize their daughters, paying their rent for instance or
giving them a small allowance to supplement their wages.
Normally, these wages seem to have been regarded as the
daughter's property, to spend as she liked, but there are cases
where a daughter's paid work was seen as a supplement to her
father's income. Marie Batteaux, for instance, was maintained
by her father, a weaver who 'receives what shee earns by
twineing of silke, having a small allowance hee makes this
respondent thereout to find her in clothes'.[79]

Finally, there were many London women who were financially
independent, able to live without paid work on the income from
property or investments. This was sometimes a very large
income but was usually a fairly modest one, incomes of £20 or
£30 a year being common in those depositions which mention an
actual sum. Legacies to daughters were commonly paid at the
age of twenty-one or at marriage, whichever came first, so many
spinsters in their twenties can be found living on their own
means, such as Jane Arbuthnot who had 'noe trade, profession or
employment [and was] maintained by what her father left her
. . . Her father was Sheriff of the County of Angus and a
gentleman.'[80] One also finds a few wives living on their own
private income, examples of the doctrine of 'separate estate'
which circumvented the common law doctrine that a wife's
property became the property of her husband. Rose Birkhead,

for example, lived 'by cappmaking and an estate of thirty pounds a yeare left her by her first husband', while Mary Bolland, who was married to her third husband when she gave her deposition, lived on £50 a year, 'a separate estate from her husband'.[81]

Most women of independent means were, however, widows, though it should be emphasized that the rich and merry widow was far rarer in reality than in legend. Most widows, however independent they might be, suffered a considerable fall in income and life-style from what they had been used to in marriage. Elizabeth Gee, for example, 'lives upon what she has of her own' but had had to move into lodgings and reduce her establishment from three maidservants to one after the death of her husband. Such descents into genteel poverty often led to a rapid reduction of the widow's capital and a need to find some other means of livelihood, the fate of Elizabeth Green, who 'liveth upon what her husband left her and by needle worke and lived entirely upon what her said husband left . . . untill about a yeare and a halfe since'.[82]

A wide range of investments was available for financially independent women and a number of these are mentioned in depositions. Anne Overton, for example, lived 'by a small estate and house and land in the country and money in the government'. Philadelphia Jones, a spinster aged twenty-six who was worth £2,000, employed a scrivener 'to place out moneys for her on government securities' and also owned a substantial estate in the East End called 'King Harry's Yard'. Elizabeth Herbert had an estate in land and 'some hundreds of pounds out at interest'. Dorothy Overy lived as a servant with her brother-in-law, but also drew an income of £25 per annum from her ownership of a lighter which was worked for her by a man with whom she shared the profits.[83]

The two most important sources of income were, however, the ownership of London houses and money-lending.[84] Houses might provide a rental income or they might be divided up into lodgings – a very common source of income which comprised not just rent, but also payments for services such as the provision of 'dyett', washing clothes and child-minding. Money-lenders would include the female pawnbrokers who were discussed with the other businesswomen in the previous section. It was far commoner, however, for a woman to realize her former husband's estate and then place it all out at interest, often using a scrivener as an intermediary, and this was an important source of capital for the London business community. Women were also important as investors in the government debt, once this had been made 'gilt-edged' by the Financial Revolution which started in the 1690s.[85]

Women may have been barred from government and from almost the whole gamut of male employment, but no one minded borrowing their money. Nor did those women who had money mind lending it and few women kept their savings under their mattress, preferring to receive the five or six per cent interest which was the usual return on loans in this period. However, at such rates, it required a capital of some £250 to provide an income equivalent to the five shillings a week earned by a typical working woman. Few women had such a capital and so London was a place where most women worked for their living, a task which became harder as the eighteenth century continued and the world of 'women's work' became increasingly squeezed by male competition.

5   Londoners at Home

'Home is home, though it be never so homely.'
(John Clarke, 1639)

In the last two chapters, men and women have been treated separately. Here they will be brought together in a discussion of marriage, family, home and neighbourhood life. Not that this togetherness should be exaggerated since, as will be seen, marriage did not often last very long and men and women tended to play rather different roles in the life of the neighbourhood. Those separate spheres so characteristic of work in London were not absent from other aspects of metropolitan life.

i   Marriage and Family

'What is it then to be married? Why, 'tis to chuse with circumspection and deliberation, by inclination, and not by interest, such a woman as will chuse you after the same manner.'
(Thomas Brown)

'There is so great a diversity of temperaments and degrees of understanding, that there are scarce any two persons in the world, but there is some unsuitableness between them, some crossness there will be of opinion, or disposition, or interest, or will, by nature, or by custome and education, which will stir up frequent discontents.'
(Richard Baxter).[1]

Marriage in early modern England has attracted a huge amount of historical interest in recent years, though this literature has not much to say about the ordinary Londoners who are the subject of this book. Historians with strongly opposed views have debated the emotional basis of the institution. Were relations between partners becoming more affectionate and mutually supportive? Was love replacing money or dynastic ambition as the motive for the choice of partners? Or did very little change across the period? The debate has been lively and illuminating, even if more light has been thrown on the endless variety of human experience than on the resolution of the questions asked. Emphasis has been mainly on those members of the upper and middle classes who kept diaries or whose correspondence has survived, a group whose experience was likely to have been very different from that of the typical Londoner. Love in Stepney or St Giles has yet to find its historian.

Other historians have pondered the canonical and legal basis of marriage during the period and have once again demonstrated the variety of experience, in this case the variety of ways in which one could get married. This work has thrown some interesting light on the marriage customs of Londoners by showing that they were very fond of 'private marryings', marriages that avoided the calling of banns in church and the public ceremony of a Sunday wedding before the whole parish. This could be done by purchasing a licence, followed by a private wedding in church, a favoured practice of the middling and upper ranks in London society. Poorer people tended to opt instead for 'clandestine' marriages, which, by the early eighteenth century, took place mainly in the area round the Fleet Prison known as the Rules. Here, in a 'marriage house', often a tavern, they would be married in an abbreviated form of the church service by a Fleet parson, sometimes a man who was not a clergyman at all but usually one who had lost his living or been imprisoned for debt. These rather sordid ceremonies required no banns, no parental consent nor any other interference from outsiders.[2]

Several thousand men and women each year were persuaded to join together in these cheap and private Fleet marriages until they were made illegal in 1751, but just what such furtive weddings tell us about Londoners is difficult to say. The cheapness was obviously an attraction, though one that could soon be eroded when the Fleet tavern bill was presented. Privacy would also have been an unusual luxury in the lives of the poor, as will be seen. It is possible too that the popularity of Fleet weddings provides an indication of attitudes towards the

Church. Many witnesses in the Church courts were asked when they last took Holy Communion and it is striking how many had never done so or had not taken it for several years before they gave their depositions. And yet Easter communion, like a church wedding, had once been an almost universal experience. Could a Fleet marriage, like the modern Registry Office ceremony, be an indication of religious indifference?

Many Londoners did not even bother with the slack requirements of a clandestine marriage. A verbal contract before witnesses, followed by consummation in a 'bedding' ceremony, was considered a legal and indissoluble marriage by canon law, though not by the common law, and it is clear from cases in the Church courts that such 'contract' marriages were quite common in London. Nor did Londoners accept that these or other marriages were as indissoluble as canon law dictated. Many people either disregarded or were ignorant of the law relating to divorce, which made a legal remarriage while one's spouse was still alive almost impossible. Popular opinion would not accept this and many broken marriages were followed by one or both parties remarrying either by contract or clandestinely in a Fleet tavern. Such unions were of course technically bigamous, though they seem to have been generally accepted and very few people were prosecuted for bigamy in our period.

London marriages were, then, often legally dubious and most were celebrated with the minimum of publicity. Such conduct was for most brides and grooms a matter of deliberate choice, since provision for an open marriage in church was easily available at a cost which was within the means of the great majority of Londoners. But what such behaviour tells us about the mental make-up of the men and women of the metropolis remains a puzzle. Secrecy and self-effacement were by no means the normal conditions of London life, which was typically conducted more as a spectator sport than as something to be carried out quietly and furtively behind closed doors.

The third main strand of historical writing on marriage, and the most prolific, has been the work of historical demographers, who see marriage and nuptiality as a central feature determining the rate of growth of the English population. The evidence available suggests that both illegitimacy and birth control were at fairly low levels during the early modern period, with the result that the level of fertility was largely controlled by the age at which women first got married and the proportion of all women who did marry. In both these respects, the late seventeenth and early eighteenth centuries would seem to have been a period of crisis in English marriage, with very high numbers of people never marrying at all and those who did marrying at later ages than usual. Wrigley and Schofield, in their path-breaking study of English population, estimate that around a quarter of English adults never married in the later decades of the seventeenth century, a proportion that falls quite rapidly in the eighteenth century. Most of their evidence is drawn from outside London and it needs to be considered whether the metropolis shared the national taste for celibacy.[3] Was London a city with large numbers of permanent bachelors and spinsters?

Two general and contradictory points may be made at the outset. London was well known as a marriage market which attracted people of all classes, especially women, who were set on making a better marriage in the material sense than they might hope to make in their place of origin. It was marriage as well as wages which attracted female domestic servants, for instance, and this may well have made the level of nuptiality in London higher than elsewhere in the country. However, this very attraction had led to a serious imbalance between the sexes, as has been seen. If Gregory King's estimates are correct, there were only ten males to every thirteen females in London, a fact which might well have led to large numbers of permanent spinsters in the city, though the marriages of widowers to spinsters would have reduced this imbalance somewhat.[4]

The only way to test such hypotheses is to discover the proportion of spinsters to all women in the higher age-groups, on the assumption that those who had not married by the age of, say, forty-five would never do so. If this exercise is done for the women in the female employment sample used for this book, the result shows a very low proportion of permanent spinsters, just eleven out of a total of 358 female witnesses aged forty-five or more, or about three per cent, figures which hardly suggest a crisis of marriage within the city. It is possible that there was some prejudice against using elderly spinsters as witnesses before the Church courts, though why this should be is difficult to say and there is no evidence that there was such a bias.

It seems probable, then, that a much higher proportion of women got married in London than in the rest of the country, despite the shortfall in numbers between women and men. The market may have been 'against our sex just now', as Moll Flanders is often quoted as saying, but their poor bargaining position does not seem to have prevented the great majority of London women from marrying. And since it takes two to make a marriage, this presumably means that a high proportion of men got married as well. Contemporary fears that men in London were abandoning marriage because of the financial benefits of bachelorhood and the ready availability of prostitutes and paid housekeepers would seem to have been exaggerated.[5]

Marriage not only seems to have been a more universal experience for Londoners than in the rest of the country, it also seems to have taken place at a rather earlier age than elsewhere, at least for those women actually born in the metropolis. Age at marriage in the past is usually calculated from parish registers by family reconstitution, a technique not very suitable for London since it requires sufficient people to remain in the same parish from birth to marriage to provide a representative sample. Londoners were mobile people, especially the poorer members of the population, constantly changing their jobs, their lodgings and, since most parishes were very small, their parish of residence. As a result, the only reconstitution study done for London parishes has to rely for its analysis of age at marriage on a very small and probably unrepresentative sample.[6]

The ages of bride and groom were, however, recorded in applications for marriage licences and this has enabled Vivien Brodsky to make some interesting observations on the pattern of age at marriage in London in the early seventeenth century. She found that the average age at first marriage of London-born women married by licence was only 20.5, nearly four years younger than women who were immigrants to the city and six years younger than the average of country and small town women whose age at marriage has been recovered from family reconstitutions. She also discovered that, generally speaking, the higher the social status of the groom, the younger was his bride and the greater the difference in age between bride and groom. This pattern suggests that middling- and upper-class men married quite old and chose young brides, most of whom were born in London, while artisans and labouring men tended to marry in their mid-twenties and choose immigrant women of roughly their own age.[7]

The pattern discovered by Brodsky persisted into the eighteenth century.[8] Female witnesses in the Church courts were often asked how long they had been married and, since they were also asked their age, it is possible to calculate their age at marriage, though this will be subject to errors as a result of either age or length of marriage being reported incorrectly. The results for those witnesses who also gave their place of birth are analysed in Table 5.1, which shows almost exactly the same pattern of age at marriage as discovered by Brodsky. There seems little doubt that London-born women married very young by the standards of the day. Immigrants, too, married rather younger than was typical in England as a whole. No evidence exists to show why this should have been the case, though one suspects that it has something to do with the comparative freedom and prosperity of Londoners. Restraints which could be imposed on young people by parents, friends and elders generally in the village were largely absent, while the earnings of young adults of both sexes were sufficiently high or at least seemed sufficiently high to enable them to contemplate early marriage with few qualms about its viability. The arrival of children or a stop of work could of course soon make such calculations seem absurdly optimistic, with the result that the desertion of wives by their husbands seems to have been a distressingly common experience.

TABLE 5.1 Age of Women at First Marriage from Depositions

Age at marriage	London-born		Immigrants	
	No.	%	No.	%
19 & under	25	29.4	40	18.3
20–24	30	35.3	64	29.4
25–29	16	18.8	59	27.1
30 & over	14	16.5	55	25.2
	85	100.0	218	100.0
	Median = 21		Median = 25	

Source: All cases in female employment sample which provide this information.

Londoners may have married younger and have been more
inclined to marry at all than people in the rest of England, but
their marriages did not tend to last very long as a result of the
high rates of mortality among young adults. Once again, this has
been demonstrated by the work of Vivien Brodsky, who analysed
104 marriages in the late sixteenth and early seventeenth
centuries, of which more than half only lasted ten years or less
before they were broken by the death of one of the partners.
Many of the surviving partners remarried, often several times,
producing a pattern similar to that created by divorce today,
with a confusion of 'mixed' families containing step-parents and
half-siblings, as well of course as many single parents and
orphans.[9]

This pattern of broken families was still the norm a hundred
years after the period studied by Brodsky, as can be seen by
analysing a data set collected for my book on the London middle
class.[10] The median age at marriage of a group of 224 brides was
twenty-two and over a quarter of these women were widows
before they were thirty. The median age at widowhood was
thirty-five, an average marriage length of just thirteen years.
These, it should be noted, were 'middle-class' marriages where
the chances of survival were almost certainly higher than in the
marriages of artisans and the poor. The analysis also takes
account only of marriages broken by the death of husbands, since
there is not sufficient information to include marriages ended by
the death of wives. Overall, it seems probable that the typical
marriage only lasted some ten years in 1700, just as it had in
1600.

Many widowers remarried and so did more widows than is
sometimes thought, especially the widows of craftsmen and
tradesmen, these often marrying their former husbands' apprentices or other younger men. Remarriage was, however, less
common amongst the widows of the poor and was not common in
any class for older women, with the result that London was a city
with very large numbers of widows, sometimes living alone,
sometimes heading households comprising their children and
servants. Gregory King estimated that there were nearly a
quarter of a million widows in London in the 1690s, just under
five per cent of the total population.[11] High mortality ensured
that these widows were of all ages, some being only in their teens.

TABLE 5.2 Age Structure of Widows and Wives			
Age-group	No. wives	No. widows	Total	Wives as % of total
15–24	62	7	69	90
25–34	241	64	305	79
35–44	220	102	322	68
45–54	116	100	216	54
55–64	41	61	102	40
65 & over	4	36	40	10
	684	370	1054	

Source: Female employment sample.

However, widows completely dominated the older age-groups of the female population as is shown in Table 5.2, suggesting that remarriage was not all that common an experience.

Short marriages and the high mortality of the young also ensured that London families did not teem with children, despite a lack of birth control and evidence that fertility in the city was exceptionally high. Gregory King estimated that in the 1690s there were 2.6 children in London for every married couple, while Vivien Brodsky found an average of two surviving children per marriage in her study of the period a hundred years earlier.[12] Table 5.3 confirms that somewhere between two and three children per marriage was the typical family size in London. The table is based on material drawn from the Orphans' Court, which lists the children of recently deceased citizens. The families reflected in the table were those of mainly middling or wealthy people who were likely to have higher fertility rates and lower infant and child mortality than the population as a whole. The sample in the table also includes no childless families since it is based on data derived from orphans' records. The picture for London as a whole would therefore be of families considerably smaller than those shown here.

Family structure in London was therefore rather similar to that of today, though for very different reasons. The average marriage lasted about ten years and, despite many births, produced only about two surviving children. These children might be brought up in a variety of mixed households, together

TABLE 5.3 Surviving Children per Year of Marriage			
Years married	Ave. number surviving children	Surviving children per year of marriage	No. of marriages
1–5	1.26	0.39	35
6–10	2.41	0.31	54
11–15	2.94	0.22	35
16–20	3.22	0.18	27

Source: Numbers of surviving children from Common Serjeants' Books in CLRO; dates of marriage and death of father from Boyd's Index of London Citizens; drawn from sample described in Earle (1989a), pp. 394–404.

with step- and half-siblings, and might experience a bewildering succession of step-parents as death removed natural parents at frequent intervals. Despite all this, most children seem to have been well brought up, as was shown in Chapter 2. Parents, step-parents and guardians knew their duty and normally did it. Most children went to school and those parents who could afford it ensured that both boys and girls were placed out in the world to their best advantage.

What we cannot tell is just what psychological effect this continuing loss of siblings and parents had on young children, though one feels that it must have been substantial. Nor do we know much about the relations between husbands and wives, despite the literature referred to at the beginning of this section. The evidence of the Church courts makes marriage seem a cruel and savage battleground in which kindness, consideration and harmony were rarely to be found. But such evidence is drawn mainly from cases of marital dispute in which husband and wife sought separation from each other. Happy marriages, then as now, do not make the news. Nevertheless, the demographic data outlined above suggest that one should not be too optimistic about the impact of the family on the individual. Keith Wright-son has written that 'within the family, individuals found security and identity and the satisfaction of both physical and emotional needs not catered for by other social institutions. The family was fundamental.' Vivien Brodsky feels, with some justification, that such an optimistic assessment 'has a strictly limited application to the familial experiences of most Londoners'.[13] One can only agree with her. The family might still be fundamental in early eighteenth-century London, but it was a very fragile institution.

ii Living Space

'First then in order of all those who occupy only parts of houses stand the tenants of stalls, sheds and cellars, from which we take our flight to the top of the house in order to arrange in the next class the residents in garrets; from thence we gradually descend to the second and first floor, the dignity of each being in the inverse ratio of its altitude, it being always remembered that those dwelling in the fore part of the house take the *pas* of the inhabitants of the back rooms, and the ground floor, if not a shop and warehouse, ranks with the second story. Situations of houses I conceive to rank in the following order, passages, yards, alleys, courts, lanes, streets, rows, places and squares.'

(Francis Grose)[14]

London was a densely populated city in which filth, fleas, lice, poor water, open sewers and other environmental problems made a major contribution to the high rates of mortality. It also had a continuous inflow of young adult migrants searching for accommodation. It does not, however, seem to have been like a modern Third World city where similar conditions have led to a ring of shanty towns round the outskirts of the city. Visitors recorded, often with horror, the uncivilized mess round the edges of the great city, a wasteland of brick-fields with smoking kilns, stagnant ponds, dunghills and ditches cluttered with rotting refuse on which fed the hogs which provided London's bacon. Such distasteful catalogues do not, however, make much mention of sheds and shacks and other makeshift accommodation for the poor.

Some people did sleep rough, of course; the brick-kilns themselves were notorious as a warm refuge for beggars. One remembers too Defoe's description of the 'street bred' beggar boys in *Colonel Jack*. 'And as for lodging, we lay in the summer-time about the watch-houses, and on bulk-heads, and shop-doors, where we were known; . . . and in winter we got into the ash-holes, and nealing arches in the glass-houses.' Defoe's

realism is confirmed by evidence given to the Church courts by
Benjamin Bynes, a vagrant who admitted creeping in to sleep in
the warmth of the glass-house on Salt Peter Bank in the East
End. Criminal records produce similar examples, such as
Susanna Jones who slept out on the wharves and was accused in
1742 of stealing tobacco from a hogshead. However, it seems
clear from the infrequency with which one comes across this sort
of comment that the great majority of Londoners had a roof over
their heads and lived in a house or part of a house.[15]

This suggests that the building industry was usually able to
keep up with population growth and to build houses cheap
enough to yield a profit from the rents of the poor. Many of these
houses were very shoddily built, especially those run up in the
first half of the seventeenth century when the population was
rising very fast.[16] But, after 1660, fear of fire was to improve the
quality of houses considerably, even in poor areas, with the
general use of brick and tile in place of the timber, lath and
plaster, and thatch which had been the usual building materials
in the past. Naturally, the quality of houses varied enormously
from area to area, depending on the wealth and social status of
the inhabitants. The fine town houses of the gentry and aristoc-
racy in the West End and the merchants' houses in the City were
often on four or five storeys, with high-ceilinged and well-
proportioned rooms, wide frontages and ample space for yard or
garden at the back. The typical houses in the East End were very
different. Here, streets were often as narrow as fifteen feet wide
and houses were densely packed together, with frontages of
twelve feet or even less and very little space outside. The houses
were usually on two storeys with a total of three or four rooms
and sometimes even less, just one room up and one room down.
Similar houses were the norm in other poor areas, in Southwark,
in St Giles and in the densely populated areas to the north of the
city such as Shoreditch and Clerkenwell. As more people
crowded into these areas, the open spaces belonging to the larger
properties of the past were built over and more and more alleys
and courts, rents and closes were set up to house the poor. Living
in such dark, airless and smelly tenements can hardly have been
very pleasant, though one has to be careful not to exaggerate the
horrors of low-cost housing. In a world with no council housing
the poor could not have afforded anything better and it seems

probable that both the quality and the density of housing were no worse than they were to be in Victorian London.[17]

What sort of accommodation did Londoners occupy within these houses? We can start with what was an important distinction to contemporaries, that between housekeepers and lodgers, boarders or inmates, a distinction which was one of status as well as house-room, even if the house was only a small and rather squalid one in the East End. Most houses in London were rented or held on long leases and housekeepers were people who rented or held the lease of a whole house, sometimes occupying the whole property themselves with their family and servants, sometimes letting off rooms or floors to lodgers. Housekeepers, males and females, were people of some permanence in a neighbourhood, many indeed remaining in the same house for decades.[18] Male housekeepers were likely to play a part in the management of local affairs, through membership of the parish vestry and other organs of local government. Women were normally denied this role, but they were still proud to be a housekeeper, such pride being manifest in their declaration of housekeeper status in depositions and in the regret with which they informed the court that, though once a housekeeper, they were now a lodger, a common fate of widows.

The down side of housekeeping was that the privileges and respect that went with the status were paid for by contributions to national taxation and to local taxes collected for the upkeep of the church, the cleaning of the streets and the maintenance of the poor, lodgers normally being exempt from such taxation.[19] Exemption was also granted to the poorer housekeepers and local taxes provide a rather good indication of the social and economic hierarchy in a neighbourhood. At the top were those who paid central government taxes and all local taxes. Then come those who paid no national taxes, but paid local taxes to both church and poor. The next level comprises those paying only the church rate, while at the bottom were those housekeepers who paid no taxes at all. People moved up and down the hierarchy, sometimes moving down to the lowest stage of all and being in receipt of poor relief. Such hierarchies can be graduated even more finely by considering not just which taxes were paid, but how much was paid by individuals. In 1727–8, for instance, contributions to the poor rate throughout the metropolis averaged out at around one pound per year per house but individuals paid widely differing rates, from several pounds down to a few shillings, while many were not rated at all despite being housekeepers, people like Samuel Miller, an elderly retired tallow-chandler of Shadwell, or John Lee, a poor waterman living south of the Strand.[20]

Rents varied even more than rates. Several hundred pounds a year might be necessary to rent a house fit for an aristocrat in the West End and well over £100 for the best merchants' houses in the City, while the average rent for all merchants in the early 1690s was £56 a year. Similar rents were paid by the richer shopkeepers and wholesalers. But these were the elite and the average rent for all housekeepers in the City was much lower, £25 for male housekeepers and £19 for females, with the cheapest houses being rented for around £10.[21] The City, even its poorer parts, was a high rent area and £10 would rent a quite good house in the East End or Southwark. Typical rents here were between £3 and £5 a year, the lowest from our depositions being £2 10s. for a two-room house in Five Bell Alley, Whitechapel, paid by Catherine Bradhurst, an elderly widow who let off one of the rooms and earned her living by weeding in the summer and spinning in the winter.[22]

An expensive house might therefore cost a hundred times as much to rent as the cheapest slum houses in the East End. However, the majority of people in London were not house-keepers but lodgers and there was a similar, though smaller, disparity in the cost of lodgings. César de Saussure told his readers that weekly rates for lodgings in London ranged from 'sixpence to half a guinea a head' and, judging from the information on rents which can be obtained from depositions and other sources, this was remarkably accurate. The most expensive lodgings were between £20 and £30 a year, which is about half a guinea a week. Such places would normally comprise a floor with two or three rooms in the pleasanter parts of the metropolis and would be occupied by gentlemen or ladies visiting town or by well-heeled residents. The attorney John Harrison, for instance, paid £22 a year for his chambers in the Inner Temple, while Jonathan Swift paid eight shillings a week or £20 a year for two rooms in Bury Street in 1710, a rent which he thought 'plaguy deep'.[23]

Such rents were clearly well beyond the pockets of poor or relatively poor people, most of whom paid one or two shillings a week or between £2 and £5 a year for their lodgings of one or two rooms, with rather higher rents to the west of the City and rather lower rents to the east. About £2 a year would get you a couple of rooms in Stepney, but only one in Holborn or Covent Garden, for instance.[24] It is not always clear whether rents quoted by deponents were for furnished or unfurnished accommodation, but the latter was obviously much cheaper. Jeremy Bagshaw, for instance, was a book-keeper who rented a room on the second floor of a house in Bloomsbury. He paid eighteen pence a week for the room furnished, but later decided to furnish the room himself, on which the landlady agreed to reduce the rent to £2 a year or about ninepence a week. Many lodgers would also be paying more because they received board as well as lodging. The sailor Thomas Askew gave evidence in 1701 that it was 'usuall for seamen to allow to their landlords or landladyes for lodging and dyett six and seven shillings a week', a figure similar to the board wages given to servants. The 'dyett' element in such a rate would have been about four or five shillings a week and the lodging about two or three shillings.[25]

De Saussure's bottom figure for lodging was sixpence a week, say a penny a night. This is the rate often quoted for common lodging houses and it is also the very cheapest accommodation that has been found in the sources used, not counting such special arrangements as sons or daughters renting a room in the house of their parents. The examples found in the depositions were all poor widows, people like Elizabeth Morgan, who cleaned shoes and went on errands for a living and lodged at a pewterer's in Fetter Lane for six shillings a quarter, or Susanna Chiswell, a char who paid sixpence a week for lodgings in Chick Lane, West Smithfield, an area with a very unsavoury reputation. These were the real poor, often renting part of a room from someone equally poor, like Sarah Main, who lodged 'with a single woman – a poor woman, she blacks shoes. My landlady, and a woman big with child, and a boy was in the room, – 'twas a ground room, where the woman, the boy and I used to lie for a penny a night.'[26]

There was, then, as one would expect, a huge disparity in the cost, quality and size of domestic space enjoyed by Londoners, a disparity which was also of course reflected in income, wealth and the quality and cost of furniture and other domestic possessions. Overall, rents seem to have borne a realistic relationship to likely earnings. A wealthy merchant would be paying his rent of £50 or £100 a year out of an income of at least £500 and probably much more. Artisans paying £10 or £20 for one of the lesser houses in the City or one of the better houses in the East End would be lucky to earn twice that in a year, an arithmetic which made imperative the letting of much of the house to lodgers and so provided space for the poor. A shoemaker or tailor might expect to rent a room or rooms for a shilling or two out of earnings of perhaps ten shillings a week, not too bad if his wife was bringing in money as well. A spinster or widow, earning her living by needlework, could rent a moderately genteel room for perhaps a shilling out of her earnings of five shillings or so a week, perhaps a little less if she was prepared to share with someone else, like Mary Booth, a needlewoman who lodged in Round Court off the Strand and 'now lyes with another gentle-woman and payes her eightpence a weeke for her lodging'. And if it came to the worst, it was always possible to get a room for nothing if you could persuade the parish of your need, as had Mary Johnson, the wife of a sailor. She dwelled in a parish house in Tuttle Fields, Westminster, and scraped a living together by keeping a chandler's shop and making bodices, 'shee troubling the parish for nothing more than her rent'.[27]

Two rooms, one room, sometimes only part of a room, were thus the living space of a large proportion of the population of London. This is not much space by modern standards and one can imagine that life was cramped and not very private and that there was neither room nor money available for many possessions. Small families helped a little, even if they were caused by high infant mortality, and the vagaries of such mortality often meant that survivors were widely spaced in age, providing ready-made baby-sitters for mothers who needed to go out to work. Many women of course worked at home, as indeed did many men, and then the space must have been cramped indeed, as in the room rented in Petticoat Lane by the weaver Josiah Roberts and his wife Margaret, a spinner of hair. She deposed that they were worth little, their 'effects consisting of a roome furnished, her husband's loom and other utensills for their respective trades'.[28] She had been married for only eighteen months when she gave her deposition, and so would have had only a baby if she had any children at all, but even so it must have been good to get out of this small room in the East End. It is evidence like this that makes one realize why so much of London life was lived in spacious taverns and alehouses or in the streets and alleys and why cook-shops and itinerant sellers of food flourished in the metropolis. Few people can have had the space or equipment to do much cooking for themselves.

iii Neighbourhood

'What is thy duty towards thy Neighbour?'

'My duty towards my Neighbour, is to love him as myself, and to do to all men, as I would they should do unto me . . . To hurt no body by word nor deed: To be true and just in all my dealing: To bear no malice nor hatred in my heart: To keep my hands from picking and stealing, and my tongue from evil-speaking, lying, and slandering.' (*Book of Common Prayer*)

Most Londoners were immigrants and most of them, once they had arrived in the metropolis, moved around from service to service, job to job and lodging to lodging. Despite this mobility, there was a very strong sense of neighbourhood in the city, as is made abundantly clear in depositions where the opinions and behaviour of neighbours form a recurring theme. Just what a neighbourhood consisted of is never spelt out, but one's impression is that most of them were very small areas, often a single street with the alleys and courts leading off it, sometimes rather bigger, but rarely as big as a parish, which particularly in the City was itself likely to be very small. These neighbourhoods reflected to some extent the country background of the majority of their adult inhabitants. They were a collection of small villages in which residents took an extremely inquisitive interest in each other and disapproved of deviations from what were considered the norms of social and personal behaviour. London was not yet the place of anonymity and anomie that it is supposed to be in the twentieth century.[29]

Neighbourhood was first and foremost experienced through the eyes and ears of residents, who watched each other and, when they could not see each other, listened to each other with a persistence scarcely credible to the modern city-dweller.[30] Everybody knew everybody else's business, information which could easily be acquired by watching the street through windows and from commanding positions at doorways, by looking into other people's houses and lodgings and by listening in yards and alleys or out of one's bedroom window. What one could not find out for oneself could be learned through gossip in the kitchens of neighbours, in the street or in the alehouses, dram-shops and taverns that formed a focus for neighbourhood activity, both for men and women.

Some people operated as more or less full-time gossips; shopkeepers and the owners of catering establishments, street traders and stall-holders were in a particularly good position to see or learn what was going on, and porters' work was often based on regular 'standings' from which they were able to survey the street. To this should be added the gossip of servants, whose lives were largely spent, if depositions can be believed, with their eyes glued to cracks in partitions, crevices in walls and the inevitable keyhole. Gossip about the master and mistress and their family was the most heinous servant crime in the eyes of employers, but watching and talking about the lives of so-called superiors was much too attractive a recreation to be eschewed.[31]

Much of this close neighbourly attention was simply a matter of intense interest in other people's affairs, a cheap and fairly universal form of entertainment. There was, however, more to it than that. Neighbours saw it as their duty to impose moral standards on each other and many sanctions were available to bring those found wanting into line. These standards reflected the duality and, to modern minds, hypocrisy which characterized the norms of reputation in the period.[32] A good reputation for a woman depended principally on her maintenance of chastity both before marriage and within it, though attributes such as scolding and shrewishness were also strongly disapproved of and if possible curbed. A good reputation for a man was rather different. Sexual misbehaviour was not approved of but was likely to be condoned. Much more important was the maintenance of a reputation for honesty, business probity, sound credit and reliability, what contemporaries described as 'bottom'. A man who had no bottom or provided any hint of dishonesty, criminal activity or criminal associations was subject to very strong disapproval by his neighbours, whose gossip might very quickly dry up his credit and run him out of business or into a debtors' prison. Men who abused their power, strength or position of authority were also likely to be restrained or at least rebuked if this was at all possible. Neighbours might cry shame at a master who mistreated his apprentices or servants, a moral disapproval which might well cause him to change his behaviour or else lose business. Neighbours were also willing to intervene if husbands beat or otherwise mistreated their wives more than seemed reasonable, either calling on the watch or a constable to retrain the husband or going into his house and doing the job themselves.[33] It was the duty of neighbours to maintain the harmony and quiet of the street as well as the moral standards of those who dwelt in it.

The maintenance of character or reputation was an essential safeguard against times of trouble when the opinion of one's neighbours could be literally the difference between life and death. Many a defendant at the Old Bailey won a not guilty verdict from a jury or relative mercy from a judge by the willingness of neighbours to come and speak in court for his or her character. George Snell of Shadwell, for instance, was acquitted of burglary after he 'call'd a great many of the neighbourhood who gave him a very good character'.[34] Reputation was equally important in less dramatic circumstances. It could make the difference between a job and no job, tick or no tick at the local chandler's shop or alehouse, a pension or free accommodation at the expense of the parish rather than a spell in the workhouse or eviction from the parish for the destitute. Neighbours looked after their own, but they only looked after those of whom they approved.

The sanctions available to neighbours were very considerable. Gossip itself was a powerful weapon of control which could destroy a small businessman, as noted above. It could prevent those thought idle or dissolute from getting a job in the neighbourhood. It could effectively prevent an 'unchaste' woman from making a 'good' marriage and it could ruin the work chances of a supposed adulteress. Few people would have their house cleaned or their needlework done by a woman labelled 'whore' by her neighbours.

One step up from casual gossip was the ritual abuse known as defamation. The abuser would select his or more commonly her moment when the street or alley was crowded and the maximum number of people could bear witness to the accusation of unchastity or dishonesty laid against the victim.[35] Clapping her hands to hold the attention of the crowd, she would cry 'whore', 'bitch', 'thief' or 'rogue' as the case dictated, normally with much circumstantial detail. Many a victim sought to defend herself against such defamation in the Church or civil courts, seeking to disprove the slander and recover damages or a public apology from her defamer. Other victims, especially those who were relatively well off, had their defamers bound over to keep the peace, a threatening procedure which could cause them to make a public apology or pay compensation rather than leave themselves open to further expensive litigation.[36] Such defensive action was often successful, but the harm to reputation done by the initial public abuse was very hard to reverse.

Most defamation cases were brought by a victim against a single defamer, but much of this type of activity was group action against a person or persons who had offended against the neighbourhood norms, some of this being little more than the prosecution of a local vendetta. In some cases, this took the form of such seemingly rural rituals as a charivari or a skimmington ride, a piece of crude street theatre designed to ridicule the offender and provide a moral lesson to bystanders. More often, it consisted of calling a crowd before the offender's house to shriek abuse and sometimes to take such physical action as breaking windows or throwing excrement or mud at the victim, a type of mob action which Robert Shoemaker has shown to be the commonest type of riot prosecuted at the Middlesex Quarter Sessions in the early eighteenth century.[37] The historian only gets to learn about such behaviour if the victim was prepared to defend him or herself in the Church courts or if a riot was prosecuted, such cases presumably only representing a minority of those that actually took place. Since prosecuted cases were themselves common enough, one gets the impression that London's streets and alleys must have rung very frequently indeed with the 'hot words' of abuse and that it would have been a fortunate offender who could avoid for long the censure of neighbours.

One of the most striking aspects of both defamation and local riots of the type described above was the role played by women. Women were normally both the victims and the defamers and they predominated in the mobs taking part in street theatre. It was women then who provided the moral police of the neighbourhood, or at least of that half of the neighbourhood who were themselves women, a self-confident if somewhat censorious role. Not that this was the only role played by women. There was a kinder side to the social life of the neighbourhood, in which women borrowed food, clothes and money from each other, gave comfort and assistance in sickness and childbirth and generally provided mutual support for each other. Mutual entertainment was also sought by women, who gathered together in each other's kitchens or more publicly in alehouses and dram-shops, whose clientele was by no means confined to men, as was the case in the cabarets of contemporary Paris.[38] Women certainly did not conform to any 'Victorian' standards of domestic behaviour by confining themselves to the privacy of their own homes; they were people of the streets and very visible.

The role of men in neighbourhood life was different, though it overlapped with that of women to some extent. There were male victims of defamation and there were male defamers. Men also played a prominent part in such vigilante bodies as the Societies for the Reformation of Manners which flourished in early eighteenth-century London and brought prosecutions against such moral offences as sabbath-breaking, swearing and drunkenness, though much the commonest prosecutions were of those engaged in 'lewd and disorderly practices', these normally turning out to be prostitutes, in other words public whores rather than the private whores condemned by female defamers.[39] However, a more common role for a man was to monitor the behaviour, especially the economic behaviour, of other men by keeping an eye on their business affairs and their credit, and reporting any dereliction to male drinking partners in the tavern.

Men, particularly middling men, also monopolized the official organs of local government, such as the parish vestry, and they provided the great majority of local office-holders, such as churchwardens, constables and bailiffs, as well as making up the numbers of the watch whose function was to police the streets at night. Men therefore were responsible for the public order of neighbourhoods and of the parishes of which they formed part, though in carrying out these duties they often had the assistance of women as informers, character witnesses and indeed as potential catchers of criminals in a world where the victims of crime and their neighbours were expected both to arrest the criminal and to prosecute him or her.

Male control of local government also meant that it was men who ran the parish systems of poor relief and, since it was poor women and their children who were the major applicants for relief, this gave men an important weapon with which to reward those women deemed virtuous or respectable and to punish those of bad reputation. The same sanctions existed of course to maintain control over the poor men of the parish, to determine who were the deserving and who the undeserving poor and to treat them accordingly.

Finally, it should be apparent that men controlled the parish church, once the main arbiter of neighbourhood life. Minister, curate, churchwardens and sidesmen, all were men and usually men of some social standing. What significance this had is difficult to evaluate. The church held views on gender and class supportive of a system of patriarchy and subordination, and such views were reflected in sermons, but how many people came to hear them? This is one of the great imponderables of the period. The early eighteenth century was clearly a time when religious belief was very much stronger than it is today, but the degree of this strength is impossible to establish. Children were certainly imbued with religion at school, if not by their parents, and some beliefs no doubt remained in the minds of even the least religious adults. Witnesses in the Church courts were often asked if they knew the punishment for perjury in the next world and, without exception, they all claimed that they did. 'She believes shee shall bee punished by hell fire hereafter for any perjury shee shall committ in this world.'[40] Such evidence might have been the result of coaching, though the wording varies sufficiently in the depositions of different witnesses to suggest that these are real beliefs and that most people accepted the concept of an afterlife in which there would be divine rewards and punishments. Such a belief did not of course prevent perjury, but its existence was an essential element in social control since the very idea of hell was the best moral deterrent that existed, far better than the gallows, as noted by the nonconformist preacher Timothy Cruso in 1697. 'Death hath really no sting, and if it may be called an enemy, is a very harmless one, if there be no hell to follow it.'[41]

In theory, a reminder of hell should have been more effective than the threat of defamation in maintaining the moral standards of the neighbourhood, but it is doubtful if more than a minority of Londoners were sufficiently regular attenders at church or meeting to get the full benefit of the message. Some were, of course, people like the widow Elizabeth Hallet who 'went dayly to Covent Garden church to prayers and for the most part twice every day'. Many other deponents gave evidence of going to church at least once a week, this being as much a social as a religious duty for those who sought to gain a reputation for respectability.[42] Nevertheless, it is clear that not everyone went to church on a regular basis; if they had, there would simply not have been room for them, especially in the huge parishes of Middlesex and Westminster where the great majority of poor Londoners lived. So one suspects that most people's piety was about on the level of Elizabeth Hewet's, the wife of a Westminster painter, who told the court that she 'was last at church about two or three months since'.[43]

She also said that she had 'never received the sacrament of the Lord's Supper', despite being thirty years old, a common enough admission, as has been noted above, but one that was in striking contrast to early seventeenth-century Southwark where attendance at least at Easter communion was virtually universal amongst adults. There were still many regular communicants in the early eighteenth century but their numbers were probably balanced by those who had either never received the sacrament or had last received it a very long time ago, often at some moment of crisis, such as the eve of their departure to London or during a serious illness.[44]

The Church then was losing its power to control and influence the poorer members of the urban community by the early eighteenth century. This was noted by contemporaries and was a major reason for the great efforts made by the promoters of charity schools and especially by the Society for Promoting Christian Knowledge (founded in 1698) to try to correct the situation. If the poor could be brought back into the religious fold, it would serve not only to save their souls but also to make them useful members of society, for the SPCK believed with some justification that 'no one could be both devout and lazy'.[45] Such efforts certainly had some success, though many feared that what was taught to charity school children by day was forgotten at night in the company of their irreligious parents. Nevertheless, the London of our period was becoming overall a more secular society where virtue was more likely to be instilled by fear of a neighbour's tongue than by fear of the wrath of God.

Two

Voices of
Londoners

Introduction

A famous historian once advised his students and colleagues to keep on reading documents until they could hear the people of the past talking. This is admirable advice but difficult to follow. Most historical documents are couched in language far removed from the tones and nuances of everyday vernacular speech. Many are written in Latin, in legal jargon or in the stilted prose of the professional clerk. Many are abstract records, such as land surveys, parish registers, churchwardens' accounts or muster rolls. These may often tell us much about the economy and society of a period, may even enlighten us on the lives of individuals, but they rarely enable us to hear the people of the past actually talking.

The documents which have been most important in the writing of this book are, however, unusual in that, on occasion, they do allow us to hear the voices of the past. These include depositions from the Church courts and the Mayor's court, verbatim reports of witnesses from trials at the Old Bailey and biographies of convicts from the *Accounts* of the Ordinary of Newgate. These and other records have been used in the first part of this book to provide a structural analysis of such subjects as migration and work. In this second part, the same sources have been mined in a different manner to illustrate a number of themes in the lives of Londoners, using as evidence the language of the Londoners themselves. What the Londoners have to say is often entertaining and amusing, but it also serves to convey a number of insights into the values, beliefs, sensibilities and prejudices of the age.

Editorial comment has been kept to a minimum and nearly all of this second part of the book consists of quotations from documents, some very short, some longer, arranged under various loose headings such as 'People', 'Work', 'Neighbourhood and Home', 'Eating and Drinking' and 'Entertainment'. Most of the quotations are from statements originally made by deponents who were questioned in court or elsewhere, and their language reflects the vernacular idiom and vocabulary of the period. This testimony often appears in the original as recorded speech interspersed with legal jargon and formulae. Editing has therefore sometimes been necessary to recover the original speech of the witnesses. Recorded speech has been changed to direct speech, actual names have been substituted for such legal terms as 'the ministrant' or 'the producent', and legal jargon such as 'the said' has usually been omitted. The resulting quotations are thus as near as possible to what the witness actually said when examined in court. There has also been some discreet editing of spelling and punctuation where this seemed necessary to assist the modern reader.

1 People

Most of the following extracts are from evidence given in the Church courts. Witnesses were often partisan but, true or false, these depositions reflect the prejudices and attitudes of the age.

John Cart is a jolly fatt man with a red face and hath two moles on the left side of his face. He is a middle sized man and weares a faire wigg.[1]

Holcraft Blood is Colonell of Her Majestie's Train of Artillery in Holland . . . He is a gentleman, a man of honour, courteous and civil in his carriage, peaceable and quiet in his humour and conversation and obliging to all persons so far as ever I observed.[2] (Evidence of Edward Gibbon, paymaster to the Train of Artillery)

Elizabeth Bayley is a person that has been well educated, and of a genteel carriage, and of a modest and vertuous life and conversation, and of a beautifull complexion, well proportioned shape, young and as such is generally accounted among her neighbours and acquaintance.[3] (Evidence of Rebecca Bayley, Elizabeth's sister)

I have known Francis Gotobed three or four years. He gets his living by selling milk. He is a poor man but has the character of an honest man. He is sometimes called Shitten Dick, but for what reason I have not heard.[4]

Ann Eade sells oysters at the Globe Tavern in Hatton Garden. Her father James Ellis drives a hackney coach and hath been gone from them since Christmas last and where he now is I cannot tell and her mother is now in Newgate and is to be transported to morrow.[5]

I have known Robert Haynes for about ten years who is by profession a porter. He has been frequently employed by me and severall others . . . [and] hath behaved him self very honestly, diligently and soberly in his calling and business, and getts his livelihood and maintains his family by his diligence and care in his calling.[6] (Evidence of James Chaundler, servant in the household where Haynes was once employed)

> Sarah Gaines was noe servant . . . but a sort of an idle wench who used there to wash up their dishes and look after the jack and weed in the garden and fetch water from the Thames for the use of the house . . . an idle wench who would often sweare, talk bawdy and take the Lord's name in vain.[7]

John Hughes is a married man and I believe he has been so for ten years past. He is a housekeeper and has served the offices of scavenger and headborough and is a person of sober life and conversation for ought I know and is reputed a substantial man and of a good trade or business.[8]

> Lavinia [Gentry] is soe outrageious and turbulent in her carriage towards her husband [whom she had left] and hath within six months past frequently come to his house and abused him with base language and without any cause hath used horrid oaths and imprecations and thereby caused a mobb to come about his house to his great disgrace and the disturbance of the neighbourhood.[9] (Evidence of Margaret Williams. John Gentry was a fringe-maker and parish clerk of St Peter's, Cornhill.)

I became very well acquainted with the humour temper and disposition of Lady Charlott Calvert and did always observe dureing the time of my service [with her] that shee was a very obedient dutyfull and oblidgeing wife to her husband and a fond and tender mother to her children, generally spending the most part of her time in their company, and shee always appeared to bee . . . a person of a very sweet mild and affable temper and humour.[10] (Evidence of Mary Thompson, cook and housekeeper)

> Terence MacMahon [a trooper] said that he had in her the best of wives who maintained him like a man.[11]

Catherine Conduit hath carried herself very modestly and dutifully towards Daniel her husband and cutt the hair of her head and sold it to buy shoes and other necessaries for the said Daniel . . . She hath maintained herself by her labour but I believe that now she is reduced to a poor condition and ready to want.[12] (Evidence of Elizabeth Raitt. Daniel, a sailor at the time of this deposition, had taken a second wife.)

> I have heard Frances Deye praise and extol Charles Stanley and saye hee was an eternall charme and talked the finest of any man in the world.

Another woman reputed of loose character and goeing by the name of the Figure of Eight.

> The Rev. Dr Barry was very well knowne about Drury Lane and hee came very often there a mistress hunting.

One called Mr Fielding commonly called Handsome Fielding very much frequented the company and conversation of the said Lady.

> 'What is her character?'
>   'She has the character of a washerwoman, and one that takes a great deal of pains for her living.'[13]
> (Character witness for Eleanor Young, acquitted of receiving)

Good women

A very sober and regular person and using to work much at
her needle . . . a poor but honest woman and workes hard for
what shee getts . . . as honest a woman as ever stept upon
English ground . . . if she was a bad character she would
hardly work so hard . . . a sober and discreet woman of good
credit and reputation amongst her neighbours . . . a loveing
dutyfull and obedient wife to her husband . . . a sober,
vertuous, prudent, carefull and frugall woman . . . a carefull
industrious and saveing person . . . just, honest and dutiful to
her parents . . . as good a character as any young woman in
the parish . . . of unspotted life and conversation . . . as good
humour'd a woman as ever lived in the world.

Bad women

 A lewd and debauched woman of an ill life and
conversation . . . soe rampant and full of lust that
shee could not tell what to do with herselfe . . . a
company keeper . . . a woman of a wicked loose
scandalous and debauched life . . . reputed to be kept
as a Miss or a woman for pleasure . . . she made
herself the Town talk . . . a very hasty, rash and
unadvised woman . . . a woman of a violent and
vexatious spiritt and humour . . . a very morose and
troublesome person who frequently abuses and gives
very provoking language to many of her neighbours
. . . she did not shew, carry or behave herself with
that duty, love and respect to her husband as shee
ought to doe.

Good men

He bears a good reputation in the world . . . a man of good
reputation and very faire and just in his dealeings . . . a very
cautious wary person and very exact and punctual in his
affairs . . . an honest man and a rich and wealthy man . . . a
man of good understanding . . . a person of considerable
quality . . . a man of a pious and sober life and conversation
. . . a frugall saveing man . . . a loveing and kind husband . . .
he constantly carried himselfe towards her with all the respects

love and kindnesse that a tender and good husband should
. . . as honest a gentleman as ever lived by God's bread.

Bad men

A disgrace to his family . . . a person of a loose,
debauched and vitious life and conversation . . .
much addicted to the unlawfull conversation of
women . . . a man of indifferent character and of a
saucy behaviour . . . an extravagant man in his
expenses and much addicted to drinking . . . a
contentious man and an oppressor of the poor . . . a
man who was seldom or never any wayes loving or
tender to his wife . . . a person of a cruel barbarous
and inhumane temper and disposition . . . a man of
weak capacity and easily imposed on . . . as
impudent and vile a fellow as ever I knew . . . I have
frequently heard him to curse and sweare at his owne
mother.

2 Lives

Thomas Wright was born in Black Fryars, was put to
nurse at three quarters old to the wife of one Wright,
a carman, liv'd with them as their own child, called
them Father and Mother, and went by their name,
and was put to school by them to Mr Haydon in
Scallop-Court where he went four or five years and
made a pretty good proficiency in his learning . . .
When he grew a little up, his foster parents put him
to Mr Clendon, a distiller in Bishopsgate Street as an
errand-boy with whom he lived about three years, till
his master died, and he behaved very well. He
afterwards lived with Mr Penny, a printer, where he
likewise behaved well; from thence he went to Mr
Cooke, a pamphlet shop at the Royal Exchange, with
whom he lived about a year and an half; and the last
place he lived at was Mr Larrat's, a distiller in
Black-Fryars. Being discharged from thence and
going home to his foster father, he bid him go about
his business and would not take him in; he never
went to any place after, but worked with the carmen
in Black Fryars, backing coals, got acquainted there
with several idle boys, and went picking of pockets
and doing other disorderly acts.[14] (Thomas Wright
was hanged in 1744 at the age of seventeen for
assault and theft.)

I have heard and believe that my father and mothers names
were Thomas and Dorothy Way and that they lived over
against St Andrews Church in Holbourn and that I was born
there and that they dyed in my infancy and that by the care of

my aunt Sarah Pauling I was nursed and put to [the Charity] School in the parish . . . About sixteen years since Jane Lillingston took me out of the Charity School in order to be a servant to her and Henry Rhodes . . . I lived with them for ten years without any wages and from that time I have had four pounds per annum.[15] (Evidence of Ann Way, aged twenty-seven. Jane Lillingston kept house for Henry Rhodes.)

> I was bred a seedsman, but now followe noe calling or profession but that of goeing to service . . . About eight or nine yeares since I was butler to the Lord Jersey with whome I lived about a yeare and voluntarily left his service because the steward claimed part of the card money. Then I went to Sir Godfrey Kneller in Great Queen Street with whome I lived eight months as his valet de chambre and voluntarily quitted the same because I gott little perquisites. From thence I went to John Smith Esq. in Bond Street with whom I lived about two yeares as butler and voluntarily left that service. I then lived with the Lord Mohun first as butler afterwards as his gentleman for about nine months, then was turned away for disobligeing the steward. I then became servant to Lieutenant Generall Churchill with whome I lived about a yeare and was turned away for rideing at too farr a distance from his coach on Bagshott Heath. From thence I became a servant to the Duke of Buckingham with whom I lived halfe a yeare as Groome of the Chamber and left the same because my Lord Duke struck me. From thence I became valet de chambre to John Dormer Esq. by whom I was turned out at the instigation of his wife as I verily beleive. From thence removeing I became a servant to Charles Caesar Esq with whom I lived as butler for about a twelvemonth and was turned out of such service but for what I knowe not and then came to live with the Earle of Northampton as his butler with whome I now live.[16] (Evidence of Richard Morris, aged thirty-two, born at Wimborne, Dorset)

I am of noe profession or calling and have maintained myselfe
for these seven years by goeing to service and makeing of
mantuas when out of place. About seven yeares since I lived
and was a servant to the Lady How in Dover Street in whose
family I was a servant for seven or eight yeares but lived with
her as her owne proper servant for about a twelvemonth and
then voluntarily quitted that service as intending not to bee a
servant anymore. I went and lived with my father Francis
Cotton at Ailesholt in Hampshire, with whom I lived about
two yeares maintaining myselfe there by mantua makeing, and
then coming up to London became a servant to Diana Dormer
whose service I quitted by reason of my having the small pox.
I then removed to one Mrs Wells in Pickadilly where I stayed
about seventeen weekes and then removed to one Mrs Holt's,
a widdow in Pickadilly, where I lodged until I was well, being
last Michaelmas, following the employment of plaine worke
and from thence removeing became a servant to Mr Charles
de La Fay at Mr Taylor's a brazier in Pickadilly with whom I
now live.[17] (Evidence of Elizabeth Cotton, aged twenty-eight,
born Binstead, Hampshire)

> For about three months last past I have worked with
> Mr Dimbleby an oil lether dresser living in Barnaby
> Street in Southwark and, before that, I worked with
> Stephen Hall of the same trade living near Old
> Bedlam for about three months and, before that, with
> Mr Permy in Cherry Tree Ally in White Cross Street
> about three months and, before that, was out of work
> for about three months and before that worked with
> one Port in Grub Street about a year and, before
> that, I worked as a Ticket Porter upon the Customs
> House Keys about a year and, before that, I worked
> at my own trade for myselfe about two years and,
> before that, I looked after a shop kept by myselfe and
> my wife in Chick Lane near Smithfield for the buying
> and selling new and old cloaths for many years, and
> served an apprenticeship of seven years at my own
> trade to David Dennis then living at the Cross Keyes
> in Chick Lane . . . I never was at sea.[18] (Evidence of
> John Loyd, aged forty-five)

I am a married woman and was married to my present
husband Mr Holman [a soldier currently in Flanders] about
nine years since at the Chappell at Knightsbridge . . . I have
lived in an apartment of a house in Long Acre about nine
months and, before that, was servant to one William Collett a
lifeguardsman near St Giles about two years and, before that,
I kept a cellar and sold drink underneath a watchmakers near
Charing Cross about nine or ten months and, before that, I
lived and kept house in Hills Alley in Long Acre for about four
years. I formerly worked at the glovers trade till I lived at the
cellar near Charing Cross . . . where I sold drink and since
that time I have maintained myself by daywork and by
nursekeeping, and by workeing as a charwoman.[19] (Evidence
of Elizabeth Holman, born in St Sepulcre, aged forty-five)

> I was born in the parish of St Mary Overy's
> [Southwark], and was 48 years old the 27th day of
> May last. I liv'd in St Olaves Street most part of my
> life, and maintain'd my family there in a very
> tollerable manner. My wife was a very honest
> industrious woman, by whom I had five children;
> but she has been dead eleven years, and all my
> children are likewise dead except one who is now a
> shoemaker, and is about 24 years of age, and
> maintains himself by his labour in a very sober
> honest manner. When I was young, I was apprentice
> to Mr Matthew Bird, a shoemaker, at the corner of
> Lambeth-Hill in Thames Street . . . and served out
> my time to the satisfaction of my master. When my
> apprenticeship was expir'd, I married and kept a
> stall in Tooley Street, where I had good business,
> and took fifteen or twenty shillings a week for
> second-hand shoes and for mending jobbs; but when
> my wife died, I came to decay and then I took to
> coney-wool cutting [i.e. rabbit hair for the hatters]
> with my father's own brother; but this business not
> answering my expectation I went out, and being
> lame I asked charity, and in my way of begging I
> always used a great many Scripture words with good
> success; I went different ways because it was not

> convenient to be always about one place, and at what
> part soever of the town I happened to be at night,
> there I used to seek out for a cheap lodging-house.[20]
> (Account of Samuel Badham by himself. He was
> hanged in 1740 for strangling Susannah Hart whom
> he had met in a lodging house.)

I was born at New Towne in the County of Downe in the
Kingdom of Ireland. About eight yeares since I left the said
towne and came to Dublin and there lived as a servant with
several persons . . . I was a servant to Mr Nicholas
Southerden, an upholder in Cable Street in Dublin, and
thence removed and was a servant to Mr Charles Cao at the
Indian Queen on Essex Bridge in Dublin and then removed
and was a servant to Mr Dugan, a taylor in Michaels Lane in
Dublin, and there marrying I came for London and tooke a
lodging in Eagle Court in the Strand and thence removed and
tooke a cellar of Mrs Drake in Whitehart Yard in Drury Lane
and thence removed and took a cellar in Drury Lane of one
Mr Jenkins at the Three Pidgeons and Rabbitt in Drury Lane
where I now live. I sell fruite in a cellar for my livelihood.[21]
(Evidence of Jane MacDaniel, aged thirty. Her husband
Arthur was a tailor.)

> I was bred up to ye sea and have belonged to it from
> my youth. Ye last ship I sailed in was ye Arcana
> Galley . . . [I have also] sailed in ye England, Capt.
> Piggit commander, and also in ye Elizabeth a King's
> man of warr . . . and, before that, in ye Happy
> Returne a fourth rate and, before that, in a pinke,
> one Coleman master and, before that, in ye
> Coronation, Bennet master. I was about two or three
> yeares a buckaneering and sailed sometimes in a
> canoa, sometimes in a Spannish bottome and
> sometimes in a Dutch ship called ye Batchelours
> Delight. William Knights was there captain in ye
> Spanish ship and Capt. Davis in ye Dutch ship and
> tooke what they could from ye Spaniards. I have
> been pardoned for ye same by King James who sent
> me again to ye West Indies to carry pardons for

others.[22] (Evidence of William Hunt of Tower Street, sailor, aged thirty-nine)

I am a winder of silk for ye weavers and was born in Nightingale Lane [Limehouse] and lived there till I was about eleven years of age and then went to service in Bishopsgate Street and lived there thirteen years and from thence went to Waltham Stow and lived there above two years and then marryed [a weaver] and lived in Lamb Ally in Bishopsgate Street about five years [until the death of her husband] and from that time I have lived in Pettycote Lane and have lived by winding of silk.[23] (Evidence of Anne Ramsbottom, widow, aged thirty-seven)

> I was about eight or nine when I went to live with John Richards [as his servant in Dorset]. At first, I waited at the table and, afterwards, took care of his horses. I then lived as a footman or coachman in London from the time of leaving John Richards' service till about two years since and from that time I have lived at Greenwich and have maintained myself by being employed as a labourer.[24] (Evidence of John Pymer, aged forty-three)

I am a married woman and never was married to any other man than my present husband Edward Barrett who was formerly a gentleman's servant but now is a drummer in the first regiment of the Queen's Guards. About seven years since I was cooke maid to Collonell Anderson at Hammersmith, at which time my husband was a servant to Collonell James then Captain of the Queen's Guards and, removeing from our places, we tooke a victualling cellar in the Pell Mell at the Shoulder of Mutton and Sausages. Haveing lived there about halfe a yeare, I tooke a cellar in a house next doore to one Mr Taylor's a locksmith's in a Court in Duke Street in St James's Westminster where I lived for about two yeares and followed the employment of washing soweing or other businesse that I could gett to doe, during which time Edward my husband lived as a groome with one Sir Richard Sandys near Deale in Kent and afterwards went and lived with one Esquire Vachell

neare Reading as his footman. I quitting my cellar went and
lived as a cooke maid with one Esquire Pitt then liveing in
Golden Square with whome I lived a twelvemonth, for most
part of which time my husband continued to live as a servant
with Esquire Vachell and I quitting Esquire Pitt's service
became a servant to Lady Calvert [in Stretton Street] for
about three months [as a cookmaid] at which time my
husband was a footman to one Esquire Ratcliffe in Bow Street,
Covent Garden. Quitting the said Lady's service, I became a
cookemaid to one Sir Fuller Schipper then and now liveing at
Newbury Hall in Warwickshire where I lived about two
months, and quitting such service I came to London and
lodged at one Mr Taylor's a potter's in Pickadilly, where I
lodged about two months, and then became a cooke maid to
the Lady Anna Statia Holman then and now liveing at
Warksworth neare Banbury, where I lived about a quarter of
a yeare, and then comeing to London lived with my husband
at one Mrs Lunn's in Long Ditch neare Westminster Abbey,
at which time my husband was a drummer in the Queen's
Guards and he hath been ever since. I and my husband from
thence removed to one Mr Perry's the meeting house in Dirty
Lane neare Long Acre where I have lived ever since and now
live, save onely that I sometimes live with my brother
Timothy Collins at the signe of the Fox and Doggs and the
White Perewigg at Chiswick in Middlesex. I and my husband
have for all the last seven yeares lived either by the said
services, his being of the Guards, and by my own industry in
whatever I cann gett an honest penny by in washing, ironing,
makeing of heads or mending of cloathes or such like.[25]
(Evidence of Penelope Barrett, aged thirty-five, born Co.
Galway, Ireland. She had been married to her husband for
fourteen years.)

> William Farendine . . . said he was 23 years of age,
> born at Coventry: that, while in the country he
> follow'd the plough. About nine years ago he came
> up to London where he first got into service at an
> alehouse near Holborn-bridge. Some time after he
> went from that service to a tripe-shop in Fee-lane.
> Leaving this occupation, he turn'd a driver of small

cattle [i.e. sheep, etc.] and, last of all, ply'd as a
porter on a wharf near the Custom-house, carrying
goods out of ships, lighters etc.[26] (He was hanged for
breaking into the Angel Inn at Islington.)

3 Work

By what means do you live? How are you maintained?

I endeavour to maintaine myself and my family by winding of silke.[27] (Sailor's wife)

I live by my employment as a gardiner to Lady Russell and by keeping a public house in King Street.[28]

I am chiefly maintained by my husband but gett part of my living by nursing of children and winding of silk.[29] (Cowkeeper's wife)

I live by my trade of a fanmaker and the blessing of God.[30]

I live by goeing to service when my husband is at sea and absent from me.[31]

I am a twister of wyer and my wife makes commodes.[32]

I am by trade a mantua maker and my husband is an upholsterer by which my family consisting of myselfe my husband and two children are maintained.[33]

I deal in buying and selling of poultry and rabbetts and go abroad to markets to buy goods.[34]

I gett my livelihood by selling drinckes and makeing pyes and by my husbands assistance by being a musitian.[35]

I have lived by my service on shipboard . . . at the West Indies and other places beyond the seas.[36]

> My father gives me lodging and victualls and I maintain myself in cloathes by my owne industry in clear starching and selling muslins.[37] (Spinster, aged twenty-five)

I am a prisoner in the Fleet [debtors' prison] and have there supported myself as well as I could.[38]

> The business which I do now followe is that of buying and selling haire and I am also mistress of a company of comedians under the Duke of Richmond.[39]

I keep above twenty shee asses and sell their milk by which I live.[40]

> I have maintained myselfe by carrying a baskett at markett and receiving eighteenpence weekely from the parish. I owe no money and am worth the furniture of my roome.[41] (Widow, aged fifty-five)

I keep a slop shop and collect the Thames Water Rent in St George's Southwark.[42]

> I gett my livelihood by being a tubwoman and selling water or other day labour.[43] (Shipwright's wife)

I live by my trade as a woolcomber and by writing and have taken money for resolving lawful questions by the figures of the twelve houses or signs in astrology.[44]

> I keep a school . . . and my husband is a banckers man by which we maintain ourselves.[45]

I get my living by gathering in rents for gentlemen and persons of estates.[46]

I followe noe other trade or employment than
keeping of a coffee house as a mistresse . . . saveing
that sometimes I lett out lodgings.[47] (Widow, aged
fifty-eight)

I follow the imployment or businesse of killing ratts and other
vermine in her Majesties pallaces and in persons of qualityes
houses.[48]

I followe the employment of a washerwoman for
abroad and at home and have followed the same for
these fifteene or sixteen years.[49]

I am Steward of the Horse and Clerk of the Kitchen to the
Duke of Leeds.[50]

I followe the employment of a strongwater shopp and
of selling whipps and thongs to coachmen.[51]
(Coachman's wife)

I trade in snuff and other things.[52]

I followe noe calling buisnesse or employment
saveing that accidentally now and then I may gett a
small matter by mending of lace but in the generall
am maintained by my husband who followes the
employment of a coachman and letts out coaches to
hire.[53]

I have a share in the glass house of Lambeth.[54]

I followe noe employment and am now a pentioner of
the parish of St Martins in the Fields but before I
was soe I used to take in washing and kept an
herbshopp.[55] (Widow, aged sixty-six)

I am not now able to work and have expended what I was
worth in sickness and am now maintained by my wife (who is
a sizer of silk stockings) and by charity.[56] (Former journeyman
dyer, aged fifty-two)

I maintaine myself by keeping a milliners shopp and the taxes thereof and the house are paid by my mother.[57] (Spinster, aged eighteen)

I maintain myself and family by being assistant to the curates of St Giles in the Fields and schoolmaster of the Charity School there.[58]

My husband is a brickmaker by trade and in summertime I assist in brickmaking and in winter I sell fish and fruite about the street and by such means gett my livelyhood.[59]

For twenty years I have kept a bankers shop in partnership with my brother Joseph at the corner of York Buildings.[60]

I have maintained myself by making hoopt pettycotes for six years and before that by wet nursing.[61] (Widow, aged thirty-five)

I live by my trade of a taylor, by being clerke to a tabernacle in Pettycoate Lane and by teaching to sing. I have some skill and judgment in singing and especially in psalmes hymnes and spiritual songs and have for several yeares last past taught and instructed severall persons in the art of singing and have made the same part of my livelyhood.[62]

I gett my liveing by coming to markett and buying goods and selling them again.[63] (Spinster, aged twenty-seven)

I am a prisoner in Wood Street Counter and am maintained by the prison allowance and my friends.[64]

I live in a cellar under the house of Mr Hawkins in Queen Street in Bloomsbury and sell fruite and herbes being an employment generally called by the name of a greengrocer.[65] (Widow, aged eighty-six)

I maintain myself by my carts and horses and by the business of a carman in Trotter Alley.[66]

> For about six yeares last past I have been forced to maintaine myself by nursekeeping, my husband ever since ye Revolution being with ye late King James to whom hee was messenger.[67] (Jane Daniell, wife of John, 1695)

I ride in the Duke of Northumberland's Regiment of Horse.[68]

> I have nursed a child and worked at my needle and gone out an ironing by which I have maintained my self.[69] (Spinster, thirty-eight)

I sometimes play for my divertion, as other gentlemen doe, but not to gett a livelyhood thereby, neither do I gett my livelyhood by gaming, but live upon the interest of my money.[70]

> Now and for about two months, being past my labour, I live by the kindness of my freinds.[71] (Widow, aged seventy)

I get my living by carrying and delivering letters from ye Penny Post Office.[72]

> I have worked in making up slop cloaths to Mrs Williams of New Gravel Lane [Shadwell] but now knitt stockings, Mrs Williams having no worke for me at present.[73]

I have lived by my art of drawing faces for these seven years last past.[74]

> I kept the cellar and the place of turnkey in the Kings Bench Prison for twenty years . . . and now maintain myself by attending people as a nurse and by knitting and sowing and by my debts as I can get them in.[75] (Widow, aged forty)

I am a periwig maker and work at the same trade in my chamber.[76]

I am at present wett nurse in Dr Hambleton's house in Bow Lane and have been soe nurse there to the said doctor's child for about nine months.[77] (Widow, aged twenty-four)

I keep a sale shopp and lend out money upon pledges.[78]

I sell knives, scissors, combs, buckles and other such small things by which I live.[79] (Currier's wife)

I follow no employment save onely that sometimes I make pattens and cloggs and collect money for one Mrs Andrews for which I have an allowance and by that and by brewing fine ale and a small estate I have supported myself.[80] (Gentleman, aged sixty)

I make chocolett cakes for persons of quality and gentlemens houses, and lett lodgings by which I gett my living.[81]

I was a Captain of a shippe but am now a prisoner of warre, and am maintained by remittances from my relations in France.[82] (Toussaint Blanc, born Marseilles)

In the absence of my husband (who is at sea) I sell bisketts by which and other work as of sewing . . . I get a living.[83]

I am maintained by my practice of a fencing master.[84]

I live with Sarah Featherstone, widow, my sister, who keepes a publique house . . . and I take care of her house and manage and looke after her buisness for her, she being antient.[85] (Spinster, aged forty-eight)

I follow the employment of a porter and sometimes sell
gingerbread.[86]

> My husband is a framework knitter or stockin weaver
> and I seame stockins by which we live.[87]

I am a student in physick and maintain myself by what I have
gott in being tutor to Richard Newcourt and other
gentlemen.[88]

> I am supported by several good freinds who are
> sensible of my low circumstances and misfortunes.[89]
> (Widow, aged forty)

I am a foreman of a shoemakers shopp commonly called a
clicker.[90]

> My husband is a porter and chairman and I sell
> oysters by which I and my family are maintained.[91]

For the last three years I have followed the employment of
grinding razors, scissors and knives.[92]

> I maintain myself by making sweetmeats to ye Ladys
> at the Court.[93] (Widow, aged sixty)

I get my living by being a scavenger and watchman in Bolton
Street, being a hired servant to the inhabitants thereof for that
purpose.[94]

> I have maintained myself by opening and shutting
> the pews in Shadwell Church for many years.[95]
> (Widow, aged eighty)

I have lived by my trade in undertaking of funeralls . . . at the
sign of the Foure Coffins over against Somersett House.[96]

> I am one of the searchers belonging to the parish of
> St Botolph Aldgate . . . and I wind silke by which I
> live.[97] (Widow, aged fifty-nine. Searchers viewed
> corpses to determine the cause of death.)

4   Making Money

William Tilcome is a carman by trade and hath now
two carts and five horses and hireth men to worke
them . . . I knowe him to have very good buisness in
his way or employ as a carman and getts or takes, as
I verily believe, thereby foure pounds one weeke with
another, out of which I doe believe hee the said
William may cleare one weeke with another the
summe of twenty shillings at least.[98] (Evidence of
John Jervas, carman of St Sepulcre. This sort of
evidence needs to be taken with a pinch of salt, since
it was often given in cases relating to the
maintenance of separated wives. Jervas was giving
evidence for Tilcome's wife and would therefore be
likely to exaggerate her husband's ability to support
her. Other witnesses would do the opposite.
Similarly, the wife's ability to support herself would
be exaggerated or minimized.)

I knowe Jane Roberts to bee a lusty young woman and beleive
her to be about the age of thirty five yeares. She does keep a
shopp or stall in Ragg Faire and there followes the trade of
buying and selling of old clothes. I verily beleive shee hath very
considerable buisnesse in such her trade. Shee commonly kept
three and alwayes two women under her to worke for her and I
verily beleive that by such her trade shee may well maintaine and provide for herselfe and her husband. I beleive that
shee does gett and gaine twenty shillings a week at least . . .
having often heard her say that shee had a very good trade
and that shee used to sell to country chapps [i.e. chapmen]
who used to sell them againe and that of some of them shee
hath taken foure or five pounds at a time.[99] (Evidence

of Susan Burchell, a hostile witness who was the sister of
Jane's husband, a tailor)

> Ayliffe White is by trade a pastry cook . . . and if he
> takes by his trade the sume of two hundred pounds
> yearly, I verily believe the proffitts of such takeings
> does not amount to above one fourth part of the said
> sume . . . Fruit, sugar, flower and other things
> belonging to the trade of a pastry cook have for some
> yeares past and at present are at such dear rates that
> there is little gott by the trade and I and severall
> others of the trade with whom I am well acquainted
> cannot gett by their trade as it now is wherewith to
> maintain their families.[100] (Evidence of Joshua
> Hoare, pastry-cook, 30 June 1697)

I mett with one Mrs Reading who told me that a friend of hers
had a child to putt out to nurse and asked me what I should
have a month to nurse it and I told her that I would have
twenty shillings a month and expected dozens, being a dozen
of soape, a dozen pound of sugar and a dozen of candles,
whereto the said Mrs Reading agreed.[101] (Evidence of Susan
Eldridge, who nursed the child for five months before it died)

> Thomas Cole [formerly a hosier] now keeps a
> victualling house and . . . has a very good custome
> and trade and I have heard him say that one day
> with another he took 40 or 50 shillings a day in his
> trade and I verily believe Thomas could not gett less
> than a hundred pounds a year.[102] (Evidence of John
> Tippetts. Another witness said Thomas 'could spend
> with a man of £200 a yeare'.)

Frances Colcott was and is able by her needle to gett twelve
shillings a week and Frances hath severall times since her
intermarriage . . . told me that she thanked God that whatever
misfortune should happen she could gett her living by her
work.[103] (Evidence of Anne Harrison, her former teacher. If
true, these are very good earnings for a needlewoman.)

Frances Colcott about a fortnight before she eloped
and went away from her husband [William, a hosier]
came into my shop which was next dore to her
husband's shop, and told me that she could have
three or four hundred pounds a year to be a
gentleman's mistress whereupon I used arguments to
persuade her against such thoughts, telling her the
heinousness of the crime, but Frances would not
hearken thereto.[104] (Evidence of Mary King, wife of a
skinner)

Knowing the said Rowland Friend to be an extravagant man
in his expenses and much addicted to drinking and staying out
whole nights drinking, I did then ask him how he could afford
to spend so much money. To which the said Rowland replyed
that his prick was his plough, that he used to fuck Mrs Ross
and that shee gave him money for doing it.[105] (Evidence of
Antony Buckmaster in the case of Anne Ross v. Rowland
Friend, 22 July 1703)

I first knew and became acquainted with Thomas
Byfield by useing him as a pawnebroker. Within
these twelve months last past or thereabouts, I have
been frequent and often at his house in Eagle Court
in the Strand, sometimes two or three dayes in a
weeke, sometimes once a weeke or once a month or
once in two months as I had occasion to make use of
him. I know hee getts six shillings in the pound per
annum, haveing constantly paid him after that
rate.[106] (Evidence of Hanna Davis, wife of a tailor
and a tailor herself. Another witness said that Byfield
had given up his pawnbroking business and now
'deales onely in lending out money upon bond to bee
paid weekly at the rate of two shillings in the pound
per weeke'.)

Mrs Shaw brought Mary Kirkwood five pounds of money to
clipp and she was to have had eighteen pence in the pound for
clipping the same and she only gave her half a crown for
clipping it all . . . and she said her husband when he was alive

us'd to have eighteen pence in the pound for clipping.[107]
(Information of Sarah Cross, wife of Smith Cross, sailor of
Wapping, 8 April 1696. Clipping the coinage, a capital felony,
was a major business until the recoinage of 1696.)

> Joseph Merideth is by trade a weaver and hee now
> lives with his father in Halfe Moone Alley in the
> parish of St Buttolph Bishopsgate. He may gett tenn
> shillings a weeke by his trade of a weaver if hee will
> stick to it and mind it.[108] (Evidence of John
> Fothergill, weaver)

Edmund Roberts is by trade a taylour and I verily believe in
my conscience that the said Edmund if he will work by such
his trade of a taylor may gett tenn shillings a weeke in the
winter and twelve shillings a weeke in the summer and I have
often heard him say that hee could in summertime gett twelve
shillings a week and his breakfast.[109] (Evidence of Mary
Jackson. Other witnesses said that Edmund's eyesight was so
bad that he could only get twopence a week.)

> Jenny Wademan and Margaret Norman deposed
> that the girl used to lie out o'nights frequently in
> Drury Lane and Covent Garden and that she told
> them that gentlemen used to give her sixpence and a
> dram.[110] (Evidence re Ann Williams, aged twelve)

I was Mr John Powell's barber and went to shave him and cut
his corns and wash his feet . . . I have shaved him some times
thrice some times twice and at other times but once in a week
and at different times of the day and he paid me six pence
each time according to an agreement made by him with me.[111]
(Evidence of Robert Phillipps, barber and peruke-maker of St
Margaret Westminster. Most men of any quality would be
shaved by the barber at home, as in this case.)

> Mary Scarth for above eighteen years before and at
> her death had been one of the scavengers or rakers of
> the parish of St Giles in ye Feilds . . . by agreement
> with ye Justices of the Peace and had four hundred

pounds a year to provide horses carts labourers and
all other necessary materials and servants to clear
and carry away the durt rubbish and soil out of the
upper division of the parish . . . She always had four
or five carts and 19 or 20 horses and five men at
eight shillings a week to each of them for their
wages.[112] (Evidence of Mary Barker, Mary Scarth's
niece, 1 July 1723)

David Duncan hath kept a grammar school where hee now
has about five or three and twenty scholars, by teaching of
which I beleive he may gett between thirty and fourty pounds
a year and noe more.[113] (Evidence of James Hilton, writing-
master)

Bodenham Rouse now is . . . deputy or head turnkey
under Mr Pitts the present Master Goalekeeper of
Newgate . . . and this deponent saith that the said
place is reputed a place of great proffit and
advantage and further saith the said Bodenham
being sick about three yeares since and being
apprehensive that he should die of such sicknesse did
then pretend to sell the said place and this deponent
being then with him heard a youngman offer the said
Bodenham two hundred and fifty pounds for the
same, and the said Bodenham then told such man
. . . that hee (the said Bodenham) gave Mr Fell three
hundred guineas for the place, and that hee [i.e. the
potential buyer] must immediately make fourscore
pounds a yeare of his place, but hee (speaking of
himselfe) made more of it or otherwise he could not
live, and that if there came to bee a peace it would
bee a glorious place and well worth this money.[114]
(Evidence of Mary Redding, 22 October 1715. The
Master Keeper also gave evidence and explained that
'what they gett by such their places ariseth out of a
part of fees payable to this deponent upon the
entrance into or discharge of prisoners from the said
goale besides some small gratuities sometimes given
them for their extraordinary attendances and services

to some of the prisoners'. He declined to state an
annual income, the profits being 'soe very
uncertaine', and emphasized that turnkeys were
'liable to the escapes of prisoners', one escape having
cost Bodenham Rouse over £40.)

The very sexton pretends to outvie us in point of income, and
is not afraid to tell us that any common footman, with seven
pounds yearly and seven shillings a week board-wages, with a
good entire livery, his master's cast-off cloaths, and now and
then some accidental vails and private advantages, is in a
more prosperous and thriving condition of life than the highest
stipendiary curate among us.[115]

> For severall years I have gotten my living by goeing
> to sea in the King's service. I have £6 and a marke
> [13s.4d.] yearely pention from the King for the losse
> of my legg and otherwise am worth nothing.[116]
> (Evidence of Charles Roche, gentleman, aged nineteen)

I first came to Mr John Andrews' house to attend his wife as
her nurse on the 15th of June 1721 at eight shillings per week
and was afterwards hyred to attend Mr John Powell [lodger in
the same house] at the rate of £20 per annum and from his
death have served Mr Andrews and his family at the same
wages and am now kept there to work at my needle for them
and to help to dress his wife and daughter and to nurse any of
the family if they should happen to be sick.[117] (Evidence of
Isabella Ditcher, wife of a shoemaker)

> William Colcott is a hosier and keeps a small shop at
> the sign of the 3 Kings in the Strand, having been
> sett up about two years at ye trade, and paying
> upwards of forty pounds per annum for rent besides
> ye expenses of housekeeping, servants wages cloaths
> taxes and other necessary expenses which I beleive in
> the whole amounts to £200 a yeare at least . . . Since
> his intermarriage with Frances, his trade is very
> much fallen off and his proffitts much less than
> usuall and I have often heard him complain for want

of trade and have likewise heard him say that he has lost upwards of £300 since his intermarriage and I likewise heard Frances say that had it not been for her portion [which was £500], he must have gon to prison for what he had before was in bad debts.[118] (Evidence of Francis King, skinner)

Mary Chum grew very extravagant and was very expensive and shee would and did frequently sell and pawne his [her husband George's] goods and run him into debt, insomuch that hee was forced to leave his imployment in the Generall Post Office London and which place as hee severall times told me was worth threescore pounds per annum to him and hee went to Guinney a souldier in the service of the Royall African Company.[119] (Evidence of William Perkins, brother-in-law of George Chum)

5 Neighbourhood and Home

Witnesses were usually asked where they lived, a task made difficult by the fact that the numbering of houses only began in the 1720s and was not common till much later. The following excerpts give some idea of the variety of homes, as well as illustrating the colourful nomenclature of streets and of the signs that swung dangerously above them.

Where do you live?

In a bedchamber and dining room . . . in a garret . . . in part of a cellar . . . in one room in Shoe Lane which I furnish myself . . . in chambers . . . in an almshouse . . . in an alehouse . . . in one of the parish rooms . . . in a bagnio in Brownlow Street . . . in the Palace of St James . . . in a sort of ragg shed . . . on the pipes that belong to the Water-house at the Bridge.

At my own house next door to the Earl of Tankerville . . . with my uncle in Grub Street . . . at Mr Richards, a fencing master, except now and then when I go into the country for my diversion . . . at a milliner's next door to the Wax Work . . . at Mrs Lindsay's boarding school at Austin Friars . . . at a gravedigger's in Garish Street . . . in severall places as my attendance on the Queen required . . . in a tubbwoman's house near Puddle Dock . . . in a house called Heaven in the Old Palace Yard.

In Reddalls Rents . . . Artichoak Lane . . . Eagle and Child Court . . . Souldier and Trumpett Alley . . . Little Whalebone Court . . . Pelican Stairs . . . Flying Horse Yard . . . Fryingpan Alley . . . Dancing Bridge

Stairs . . . Dunghill Mews . . . Honey Suckle Court
. . . Labour in Vain Hill . . . Blunderbuss Alley . . .
Plumb-pudding Square . . . Theiving Lane . . .
Parrot Alley . . . Execution Dock.

At the sign of the Harp and Hautboy . . . the Hercules Pillars
. . . the Gentleman and Porter . . . the Three Pigeons and
Rabbitt . . . the Valiant Seaman . . . the Catt . . . the
Buffaloes Head . . . the Why not Beat Dragon . . . the Indian
Queen . . . the Jackanapes on Horseback . . . the Elephant
and Castle . . . the South Sea Monster . . . the Wandering
Sheppard . . . the Holy Lamb in Barnaby Street.

Witnesses were often required to state where they were or what they were
doing when they saw some illegal activity or heard someone being defamed.
This evidence provides a vivid impression of the dense living conditions and
lack of privacy in London life, particularly in the courts and alleys and
yards, and suggests that Tom Jones must have been unique in enjoying the
advantage of solitude in the metropolis.

I hastened therefore back to London, the best
retirement of either grief or shame, unless for persons
of a very public character; for here you have the
advantage of solitude without its disadvantage, since
you may be alone and in company at the same time;
and while you walk or sit unobserved, noise, hurry,
and a constant succession of objects entertain the
mind.[120] (Henry Fielding, *Tom Jones*)

I told her not to suffer her prentice to be so impudent as to
peep in at my window and make game of every person that
comes into my room.

She frequently affronts and reflects upon her
neighbours as they pass by her and is of a very
abusive temper.

There was a greate crowd of people about, occasioned by the falling out or scolding.

> There happened a quarrell between Ann Goss and Margaret Jones as they were standing at or near each others' doors.

I did alsoe see Mary Langley take Sarah Earbery by the arme and pushing her endeavoured to putt her amongst the rabble, the said Mary sayeing to the rabble take her for she is a whore.

> 'The young one over the way,' she said, nodding towards a window of a house opposite where Anne Sandys was sitting at worke with two other women.

I observed Mary Jones to walk to and fro by Anne Commins' dore and talk to her in an angry manner, as she was leaning on her shop board.

> I was sitting and winding silk in my house in Clarks Alley near Whitechapel Church when I observed Margaret Whittington come into the alley.

As I was standing at the doore of my Mistress the Lady Windhams house in Dover Street, I heard a quarrell.

> I was sitting on a bench outside my door when I saw . . .

As I came out of my owne house to goe to a cock of water which stands in the court, I did see Hannah Smith then goeing backwards and forwards between her own house and another cock of water in the court giving very grosse and abusive language to Joanna Banhill then standing and trundling a mopp.

> I was washing a sallad at the cock near Mrs Volaw's doore when I heard . . .

I was sitting by the fire in my mother's house about six doors off and hearing a noise came out into the alley.

> One may see out of one house into ye other very
> plainly especially if there be a candle in the roome
> into which he looks.

They sate in the kitchen and the doore thereof being open to the yard could plainly see and heare every thing that was said or done in the yard.

> About seven of ye clock in ye morning as I lay in bed
> in my house in Brick Lane, I heard a noise and
> people scolding in the street just under my chamber
> window, and listening very attentively did heare . . .

Neighbours did not just watch each other. They also imposed and attempted to maintain moral and sexual standards, the object of the public ritual abuse of defamation. They provided comfort and support in times of trouble for those of whom they approved and they were prepared to intervene when the harmony of the neighbourhood was disturbed.

> I believe hee soe spoake the said words with an
> intent to defame and take away the good name and
> reputation of Mary Roberts and I believe shee hath
> suffered thereby because since then I have observed
> Mary not to have soe good a trade among her
> neighbours as she had before the speaking of them.[121]

Thereupon William Burden fell abuseing Margaret Harding and said she was a whore and a bitch and likewise said that he would give a boy a penny to fetch the cryer to cry her, to lett Three Colt Street [Limehouse] know what a whore and a bitch shee was.[122]

> A quarrel happened, occasion'd by Anne White's
> telling ye musick or fidlers that were going round the
> neighbourhood that if they did not go and call Mary

Bowne bitch she would give them nothing at
Christmas.[123]

We have been most basely and vilely abused, scandalized and
disturbed by Margaret Langstaffe who makes it her business
to villify all her neighbourhood, leading them unquiet lives,
setting man and wife at difference and neighbour and
neighbour at difference.[124] (Petition signed by three men and
three women to the Middlesex Sessions)

> I was neare neighbour to Bodenham and Thomazine
> Rouse in Swann Yard [and] about twelve of the clock
> of a night . . . me and my husband . . . were gone to
> bed and was awaked out of our sleep by the voice of
> Thomazine and her sonns cryeing out 'Murder and
> helpe for God's sake', upon which my husband arose
> and went downe staires into the yard and I arose and
> went to the window and soone afterwards the
> neighbours called the watch to the house. I heard
> Thomazine then cry out that her husband had runn
> a sword into the crevice of the doore and he would
> kill her for shee could hold the doore noe longer.
> Some time after such watch came, the noise ceased,
> but I heard Bodenham curse and sweare at
> Thomazine for some time after the departure of such
> watch.[125] (Evidence of Anna Whistler, wife of
> Thomas, a porter)

Did not the defendant [a tinplate-worker] usually beat the
complainant [an apprentice] with wyre that he used in his
trade and was it not in your judgment an unlawfull weapon
and hath not people that passed to and fro in the streets cryed
out shame of the defendant in his immoderate correction of the
complainant and called the defendant rogue or rascall or some
other ill names for that reason?[126] (Question asked of
witnesses in the case between Thomas Yeings, an apprentice,
and his master, James Mew)

> I was intimately acquainted with Edward
> Greenberry, my neighbour and landlord. He came

often to my shop and sate and talked with me and
would often tell me if any thing troubled or went
amisse with him or if hee ailed any thing, or were
pleased at any thing.[127] (Evidence of Hannah
Catterill, widow)

Henry and Hannah Hollyday keep a coffee house . . . they
have been reputed to be a very poor shuffling and spunging
sort of people and to have borrowed their neighbours' goods
and pawned them at several times till very few of their
neighbours would lend them any thing more.[128]

We have bin soe disturbed with theifs that we have
not bin suffer'd to lay in our bedd after 1 a clock this
three nights. They have attempted Mr Slaughters
house twice and once Mrs Bells but have not carried
aney thing away with them as yet. Though they can't
be taken, I wish it don't prove some of our
neighbours when taken.[129] (Mrs Harbin to Mr
Ashton, 10 June 1704)

I found that I had been robbed. Upon which some of my
neighbours advis'd me to go to the cunning woman, and so I
did, and the cunning woman told me that I should find the
thief in a weeks time. The prisoner was a neighbours child,
and several had told her where I had been, and what the
cunning women had said to me, at which she appeared to be
very much concern'd, and this gave them such a suspicion of
her that they acquainted me with it, and I was resolved to
examine her my self. So I takes her into my room and begins
to catechise her. 'Hannah', says I, 'the Conjuring Woman has
told me that you was the thief that robb'd me, for she has
describ'd you so exactly.' She fell upon her knees and
protested that she was innocent, but I told her that it signified
nothing to deny it when the cunning woman had found her
out; and so I brought her to confess it.[130] (Evidence of Jane
Jordan at the trial of Hannah Clough of St Giles for stealing
two gowns, five shirts and an apron. She was transported.)

I have heard and believe that one Nell Caton who
was bred and born in Ann Phillis's neighbourhood

was executed for a crime the neighbours believed her falsly accused of and Ann Phillis gave or lent her a hood and drawers to be executed in.[131]

I do verily beleive that Agnes Harrison hath very much suffered in her trade and reputation among her neighbours by the reason of Sarah King speakeing the words predisposed, in respect that I knowe that severall of her neighbours who were customers to her before the speaking of the words have since left her shopp and become customers at other places and I have heard them say they did soe because shee was an ill woman which I never heard any person say of her before the time of speaking the said words.[132] (Evidence of Rebecca Wood. Sarah King had said that Agnes Harrison's 'goods were not good and that shee was a cheating bitch and a whore, a bawd and a procurer'. Agnes dealt in grocery goods such as coffee and pepper.)

6 Abuse

The colourful language of abuse is found mainly in defamation and divorce cases in the Consistory Court. Most defamation cases were brought by women against other women, the slander normally relating to their supposed lack of chastity, 'whore' being much the commonest epithet of abuse.

There was a quarrell or falling out between the parties . . . I heard some hott words . . . high words . . . grosse and abusive language . . . scurrilous and base language . . . she fell into a passion and . . . she did follow her up the street and clapping her hands at her said . . . spitting in her face she called her . . .

Whore . . . bitch . . . jade . . . carrion . . . slut . . . beast . . . puss . . . sow . . . toad . . . catt . . . catamaran . . . hussey . . . harlott . . . strumpett . . . trollop . . . shitt . . . turd . . . trull . . . drab . . . beggars brat . . . bawd . . . moll . . . procurer . . . sauce box . . . bold face . . . Mrs Impudence . . . Mrs Bitchington.

Fortunately for the researcher, the most common epiphet, 'whore', was often qualified.

Nasty whore . . . saucy whore . . . vagabond whore . . . painted whore . . . pocky whore . . . trolloping whore . . . brimstone whore . . . fat arse whore . . . hott ars'd whore . . . bawdy house whore . . . Bridewell whore . . . Jews whore . . . Irish whore . . . blackamores whore . . . Parliament mans whore . . .

churchwardens whore . . . my father's whore . . .
eternall whore . . . everybodies whore.

*The adjective 'common' was also often incorporated into abuse, implying
promiscuity and public as opposed to private whoredom, as well as
vulgarity.*

Blanckett arse Pegg you are a common whore by
God . . . common campaign [i.e. soldiers'] whore . . .
common Hackney whore [i.e. plying like a coach for
hire] . . . as common as the highway . . . as common
as ye kennell dirt . . . as common as a barber's chaire
. . . you are a common shoare and have lain with a
hundred men in a night . . . you shewed your arse as
common as your face to all the ships company . . .
you are a common nightwalker and your walk is from
Charing Cross to White Hall . . . such private
whores as you spoyle the common whore's trade.

Sometimes the abuse carried a story or at least a hint of one.

One stallion won't serve your turn, you must have
two . . . you've had the pox and you have not paid
your doctor . . . everyone knows who you are, for you
stand at the gate and lett all the fellers in the lane
ride you, and if they will not ride you, you will ride
them . . . there goes the young woman that sold her
maiden head for tenn guineas . . . there goes Jenny
Gladman who hath been in the country to lie in of a
bastard . . . you impudent bitch, you were married
out of a musick house . . . how long was you married
before you were brought to bed . . . you have
followed Will Crawford a twelve month because your
husband cannot knock you enough . . . you putt your
hand into Brownes cod peice and pulled out what he
had there . . . you played the whore in old Lee's

house of office [i.e. privy] . . . you'll turne up your
arse to any body for a pinte of two penny . . . you
would turn up your tayl to every dogg you mett in
the street.

*Abuse of men is feeble by comparison, the commonest epithets being 'rogue'
and 'rascal'.*

You rogue, you lay with Frances Browne, the
fiddler's wife . . . damn you for a fatt gutted dog . . .
you are a beast of a man and you are not fit for a
woman . . . you informing pimp, kiss my breech, you
shan't make me hold my tongue . . . kisse cunt . . .
pitifull sorry fellow . . . chuckleheaded fool . . . pocky
old dogg . . . letcher dogg . . . bastard . . . villain . . .
knave . . . thick scull'd, num scull'd, double squire
. . . bracketface . . . hatchet fac'd old rogue . . . white
livered rogue . . . son of a whore . . . cock bawd and
pimp . . . cuckold . . . cuckoo . . . you poore
cuckoldy dogg, you goe about with your egg baskett
while the Captaine knocks your wife . . . go home to
that whore your wife that has been lain with and
fucked by all the footmen and chairmen in town . . .
Sirrah, did you make a whore of my sister.

Mary Sermon replyed, holding out her hand and stretching
out two of her fingers, Hussy or Impudence, don't speak to
me, but speak to your companions in Bridewell, I don't mean
the Masters but the drunken crew. I was never found drunk at
two of ye clock in ye morning with my coates over my head.[133]

She called her husband rogue, dogg and severall
other opprobrious names and has wisht God rot him
and swore that she would murder him and doe what
she pleased and that she would ruin him and make
him rot in a jayl.[134]

Henry Leonard did often abuse and call Jane his wife bitch,
old whore and bawd and said he hoped to see her hang by the
tongue in hell and wished God's aeternall judgments to fall
upon her and follow her and swore he would give her a gallon
of brandy to drink if it would kill her.[135]

> James [an apprentice] did thereupon abuse me [his
> master's mother] bidding a pox on me for an old
> Devill and his master bee hanged and the shop fired
> and he did not care a turd for his master nor the
> shop . . . and he did not care a turd for the
> Chamberlain.[136] (Evidence of Martha Drury. It was
> part of the City Chamberlain's job to discipline
> unruly apprentices.)

'How now hussey, I know you to be a chambermaid.'
   'It's better to be a chambermaid than a kitchen wench as
your mother and grandmother are.'[137]

> 'You bitch, you have been knocking.'
>   'Why, how otherwise could I maintaine such a
> pimpe as you?'[138]

'Wee [i.e. my mother and I] never made souldiers breaches for
fourpence a day.'
   'That is better than goeing a whoring as your mother
does.'[139]

> I have heard and believe that Mary Reading did do
> penance in ye vestry of St James Westminster before
> the minister, churchwardens and severall of the
> inhabitants of the parish for calling Jane Saviere
> whore above a year agoe and did ask pardon of God
> and of Jane Saviere for ye same.[140] (Evidence of
> Anne Scot, 14 June 1706)

Immediately after morning prayer and sermon ended on
Sunday last was three weekes in the parish church of St
Dunstan Stepney . . . this deponent at the request of Rebecca
Bowen went into the vestry of the church there to see a woman

performe penance for defameing Catherine Homer the
daughter of Rebecca . . . Immediately upon their comeing into
the vestry, this deponent heard a woman till then a stranger to
this deponent [Elizabeth Allen] . . . who was then standing in
the vestry thus expresse herself. 'I am come to aske
forgivenesse of an impudent brazen faced whore to an honest
womans husband, and there stands the old bawd her mother',
directing her discourse to Rebecca Bowen. She the said
Elizabeth immediately afterwards performed penance in the
vestry . . . in the presence and heareing of this deponent, the
curate of the parish and Mr Wingfield one of the
churchwardens and severall other persons strangers to this
deponent.[41] (Evidence of Mary Fosse, 16 December 1715.
Penance and apology was a common punishment of persons
found guilty of defamation.)

7   In the Streets

In the winter indeed, the Town is not altogether so
pleasant in it self: the thick air, proceeding from the
moisture of the weather and the smoak . . . The
nights are incommodious by the rattling of coaches,
hurry of chairs and the great croud of people, and
the streets being not so well lighted as so great a City
ought, and still more troublesome are they by the
readiness of pick-pockets.[142] (*Foreigners Guide to
London*, 1729)

As I was coming thro' Cripplegate, I heard a cry of 'Stop-
Thief'. I saw the prisoner and no body else near him, upon
which I struck at him with my stick; I miss'd his head, but hit
his hand, and then he dropped the bundle.[143]

On the 4th of October in Oxenden-street about 7 at
night (having a lanthorn in her hand) the prisoner
knocked her down, snatch'd her pocket, and run
away.[144] (Trial of John Quin found guilty of
assaulting and robbing Rebecca Cater)

Between 12 and 1 at noon, I lost my watch in a crowd at the
corner of Exchange-Alley, where I stood to see a man in the
pillory.[145]

As I was standing with my shop-mates by the
pastrycook's shop at the end of Cheapside to see my
Lord Mayor's Show, a crowd of men came thrusting
along. Says my mate, 'That tall fellow there in a cape
coat looks like a pick-pocket.'[146] (Evidence of William
Beck, cabinet-maker)

Crossing the alley, I brush'd smoothly but closely by the man, with my hand down flat to my own side, and taking hold of it by the corner that appear'd; the [pocket]-book came so light into my hand, it was impossible the gentleman should feel the least motion, or any body else see me take it away.[147] (Defoe, *Colonel Jack*)

> About 4 in the afternoon, going from Islington to Newington Green, my chariot was stopt near the turnpike by two men on horseback. One of them came up, on a whitish horse but very dirty, to the chariot door with a pistol and said, 'Damn you, deliver – be quick – your purse, your money, your rings!'[148] (Evidence of Mary Russel against Thomas Taverner, found guilty of highway robbery and taking from her a silk purse, two gold rings and two shillings)

He pretended to have been employ'd in taking care of cattle and driving them to and from Smithfield Market; but the chief way he spent his time was with gangs of wicked and dissolute people, great numbers of which are to be found towards that end of the Town.[149]

> Whereas great numbers of idle persons of loose conversation doe daily go about in the footpaths, public streets etc . . . with wheelbarrow wherein they carry oysters, oranges, decayed cheese, apples, nutts, gingerbread, and other wares to sell . . . and carry with them dice, and encourage unwary passengers and children to play with their dice for some of such their goods and use other unlawful means and practices whereby they defraud several of her Majesties subjects . . . and greatly hinder and obstruct all her Majesties subjects goeing and travelling in and through the said footpaths . . . the driving and useing of such wheelbarrows, etc., is a common nuisance.[150] (Order of Middlesex Sessions, January 1710)

It being Friday and cattle coming in the street, the sash door was shut.

> In my journey was thrown down by a hog, but
> without any hurt.

It made such a noise that we were afraid it would alarm the family, or the watch who stood at the corner of the street.

> She had follow'd, sometimes the business of picking
> up rags and cinders, and at other times that of selling
> fruit and oysters, crying hot-pudding and gray-peas
> in the streets, and the like.

He cry'd faggots five for sixpence, by which he got twenty shillings every week.

> Her employment was to sweep the doors before
> gentlemens houses in Rathbone-place.

I keep a little shed at the corner of Covent Garden, and sell small beer and coffee and a dram for the market people.

> He followed the employment of a porter for fourteen
> years before his death; he constantly plyed or waited
> at a standing as a porter near Great Moor Gate.

He undertook to be a lamp-lighter, which employment he follow'd about Newgate-street and other places without the gate.

> The mob carried the prisoner to St Martins Watch-
> house and put him in the hole below.

He was on foote in the street with her and handed her along the street or over the kennell [an open sewer].

> Near the end of Exeter-street, I slipt into the kennel
> and fell down, for I had been to see a friend and was
> a little in liquor.

The watch was calling past twelve. They ask'd us whither we were going.

> When he had nothing else to do, he begg'd charity in the streets.

About six of the clock of the evening . . . as Gabriel Huge and I were standing together at the doore of the house of one Mr Wright, a stocking maker in Goodmans Fields, a woman being Johanna Randall ran by the doore without any head cloths on and her haire about her eares and holding her pettycoates with her hands as if she were fearfull they would fall off and cryeing out 'Stopp him, stopp him, for God's sake stoppe him, hee will murder me', and I did then see a man pursueing her and just at her heels with a claspe knife unclaspt in his hand.[151] (Evidence of Joseph Tomlinson, stocking-maker)

> As I came along Fleet Street had a mind to attack a whore and did so: went along with her a good way, talked with her tolerably well, and at last left her. Did so with another girl. It makes me a little uneasy for fear somebody that knows me should have seen me.[152] (Dudley Ryder's *Diary*)

William Tilcome [a carter] catched them in naked bed together at his owne house and then whipped him, the said Langley, with only his shirt on with his horse whipp out of his owne house and up the street and Langley left behind his wearing apparell, a watch and money in his pocket.[153] (Evidence of John Jervas, carter)

> She ordered the coachman to drive to the end of Long Acre, where the coach stopped in ye middle of the street and she frequently putting her head out of the coach and singing, with an intent as I believe to pick up some gentleman.[154]

Last Saturday was sevennight between nine and ten at night, I was coming up the Fleet Market and about the middle of it I was surrounded by about half a dozen women, who forced me into a house in Love's Court. They made me go up stairs, and then bade me strip and go to bed.[155] (Evidence of John Cox against Lydia Collett, indicted for stealing his waistcoat, handkerchief and sixpence in money)

> Mary Williams now convicted upon an indictment against her for a trespass and misdemeanour is fined for the said offence one shilling . . . and she is ordered to be stripped naked from the middle upwards and publicly whipped att a carts tayle three severall times round Covent Garden Markett place in the parish of St Paul Covent Garden in this county in a full markett between the hours of twelve att noon and two in the afternoon of such day as the Sheriffe of this county shall forthwith appoint.[156] (New Prison Kalender, February 1730)

Mrs Long . . . was taken up on a generall search night for picking up men in the street and the next day by the Justices of the Peace at St Martin's Vestry sent to Bridewell on that account.[157]

> After 7 o'clock brother called me to go to park with sister . . . Never was walking there before with a lady. A little perplexed how to behave with respect to the giving her the right or left hand when we turned back. At first changed sides with her to keep her on my right hand but at last observing that ceremony not much regarded by others, I kept my own side in going backwards or forwards.[158] (Dudley Ryder's *Diary*)

8   Meeting People

Witnesses in court cases were often asked when and how they first met someone. Their answers provide an insight into the range of networks in the supposed anonymity of the big city.

Relationships, common origins or neighbourhood provide one obvious set of networks.

> I first met/became acquainted with [whoever] . . . by his being my own naturall son . . . by marrying her sister . . . by being her grandson . . . by being his brother's porter's wife . . . by being brother and sisters children . . . by marrying a kinswoman of his . . . by being neighbours' children . . . by being playfellows together in our youth . . . by being schoolfellows together . . . by lodging in the same house with him . . . by being neighbours . . . by being an opposite neighbour . . . by goeing often by her doore.

Work provided another.

> By being of the same trade . . . by living with them as their servant or footman . . . by our being fellow servants together . . . by being shopmates . . . by being shipmates . . . by saileing with him in one ship together . . . by coming to be his apprentice . . . by makeing a furbelow scarfe for her . . . by her often employing me as a mantua maker . . . by doeing plainworke for her . . . by being hired to be her

washerwoman . . . by workeing taylouring worke
together . . . by having lett him blood . . . by
attending her as her nurse during her lyeing in . . .
by being employed to carry letters for her . . . by
meanes of useing him as a pawnebroker . . . by being
hired to drive a hackney coach for him . . . by being
tutor to her brother . . . by means of his being curate
of the parish.

*Buying and selling, eating and drinking opened out the range of
acquaintances still further.*

By means of her being a customer to me . . . by
means of her selling baked potatoes in Covent
Garden Market . . . by buying fruit of her at the door
of the Fleece Tavern in Cornhill . . . by carrying
them bread . . . by buying corn for my mistress's
coach horses from her . . . by means of her frequent
comeing to my cookes shopp to suppe or dine there
. . . by fetching drink from her house . . . by
accidentally drincking with him . . . by his often
breakfasting, dining, supping and drinking tea with
me at my lodging.

*But such categories by no means exhaust the possibilities of meeting people
in the big city.*

By meeting him at a dancing bout in Thistleworth in
Middlesex . . . by her coming to beg something . . .
upon going to him for some money that was owing to
me . . . by means of arresting him . . . by being
fellow prisoners in the Fleet Prison . . . by being
fellow collegiates in Queen's College Oxford . . . by
means of a young gentlewoman, an acquaintance of
her, who came to my house to learn to sing . . . by
his learning mee to write . . . by being a passenger

with her in a stage coach goeing down to Salisbury
. . . by her bringing from Ireland a letter to me . . .
by marching with him in the Blew regiment of the
Trained Bands.

9 Courtship, Sex and Marriage

Magdalena Le Tondu did confess to me that shee
and James Paumier were promised to one another,
and therefore I told her that I was glad to hear it and
wished that it were true and at ye same time told her
that shee ought to have a care of herself for that the
world said and reported that James would make fair
promises to women, but would never perform them.
Shee replyed that shee was not afraid and I will show
you why and then carried me to a press where her
cloathes hung and showed me a scarlett cloth
petticoat with a broad silver galloon lace to it and a
black scarfe lined with blew velvett, and told me that
James had presented them to her which shee said she
accepted upon the account of his promising her
marriage, and she did then treat me with champaign
wine which she said he sent unto her.[159] (Evidence of
Ester Sandham, whose doubts were justified)

I first met Abigail Harris when her father asked me and a
friend to dine with him in June 1699, whither I used to goe
often afterwards to see her, her mother and sister . . . I have
had free access to Abigail at her father's house where I have
been free and familiar with her, and often in the presence of
her sister or some other person in the family kiss and imbrace
her, squeeze her by the hand, sit in her lap, feel her naked
breasts and take up her coats and see her legs. She has
permitted me to feel her belly and thighs, and I have
attempted to feel her privy parts but she has resisted and not
sufferred me.[160] (Evidence of William Barlow, gentleman of
the Inner Temple, aged twenty-four)

One Mr Maw a youngman and reputed a lawyer
would once or twice come to the house and visitte
Jane [Lupton] and stay with her there . . . sometimes halfe an houre or an houre together, in publick
company, and I believe they were never alone
together at any time in private and hee allwayes
carried himselfe very civilly and respectfully towards
her and I doe verily beleive that he had a great love
and affection for her and did designe to have courted
her in the way of marriage, but that Jane always kept
him at too great a distance from giveing him any
opportunity soe to doe.[161] (Evidence of Martha Le
Pong)

Bartholomew Richardson and Margaret Goater were very free
and familiar with each other and carried and behaved
themselves to each other as if they were lovers . . .
Bartholomew was very free in kissing and toying with her and
shee seemed very well pleased therewith. I did verily beleive
that Bartholomew then courted her in the way of marriage
and from her carriage and behaviour towards him I did alsoe
beleive that shee accepted and admitted of such his
courtship.[162] (Evidence of John Mason)

Elizabeth Wildey is generally accounted and reputed
amoung her friends and acquaintances to bee a
matchmaker or a person who getts her livelyhood by
match makeing and pretending to help persons of
both sexes to fortunes for money and reward . . .
During the time of her lodging at my house she told
me that shee was promised a thousand pounds by
Mr Spencer for makeing a marriage up between him
and Sir John St Alban's widdow.[163]

In a very serious and solemn manner William Blair took
Margaret Crawford by the hand and said 'I take you
Margaret to and for my wedded wife' and Margaret holding
William Blair by the hand at the same time said 'I take you
William to and for my wedded husband' and then William
Blair did put a gold ring on her finger and said to her 'With

this ring I thee wed my dear Peggy.' After the said marriage contract was solemnized they looking on themselves to be man and wife did lye together in one and the same bed naked and alone in Mrs Grimeley's house in the Haymarket and had the carnal knowledge each of the other's body.[164]

> After the solemnization of the said marriage [in St George's Southwark], they went to a publick house near St George's Feilds where they dined and sent for severall of her relations thither, and in the evening of ye same day they went to her the said Margaret's father's house in Southwark where they . . . lay that night, where this deponent saw them in bed together.[165] (Description of the wedding of George Bilby to Margaret Harvey by Nicholas Birkhead)

About eighteen months ago I came to live at the Bull and Garter near the Fleet Prison as a servant and as a plyer at Elizabeth Lilly's door to pick up marriages or to perswade people goeing by inclinable or intending to bee married within the Liberty of the Fleet to bee married at her house.[166] (Evidence of Zachary Taylor, who later acquired his own 'house')

> On the first day of September 1721 Mr John Mottram marryed me to my husband William Nicholls at a publick house known by the sign of the Elephant and Castle in Fleet Lane London without banns or licence . . . And in the middle of the form and ceremony of the marriage Mr Mottram demanded his fees for marrying us and, my husband asking him what his fees were, he demanded thirteen shillings and fourpence or thereabouts. And my husband asking him if other people paid as much he expressed these or the like words, 'Damn it, I won't stand disputing to lose my time', and took up his hat and offered to go out of the room. And thereupon my husband gave him a guinea [21 shillings] and bad him take what he was to have and he then took thirteen shillings and some odd pence and when the

marryage was finished he demanded five shillings for
dating the certificate on a day different from the day
whereon we were marryed.[167] (Deposition of
Elizabeth Nicholls, wife of William, watchmaker of
St Brides. The Rev. John Mottram was a well-known
Fleet parson.)

About three or four dayes after the marriage, Elizabeth Russell
came to me and my wife and told us that shee had done a
foolish thing in marrying John King because she was married
to Solomon Russell several years before and had severall
children by him, four whereof were then living, and the
occasion of leaving Solomon Russell was because he was
unkind to her and that she married John King for a
maintenance.[168]

> I have been married to Joseph Price about ten years
> to my best remembrance of ye time, with whom I
> live and cohabite as his wife. I was married to John
> Prestage at ye age of about fourteen or fifteen years,
> with whom I lived as his wife about two years, after
> which he left me and went into Flanders, whereupon
> I married Joseph Price. John Prestage is now living
> and hath another wife and a child by her now living
> . . . I was married to John Prestage at Whitney in
> Oxfordshire by Mr Trumball minister there. I
> cannot recollect where nor by whom I was married
> to Joseph Price.[169] (Evidence of Anne Price, aged
> thirty-three, washerwoman of Cross Lane, St Giles.
> Joseph Price, aged forty-three, described himself as a
> Chelsea Pensioner who made his living by going on
> errands, but he was described by another witness as
> 'a common beggar and beggs at ye corners of streets
> and sweeps ye ways'.)

James Strutt the younger said he had a wife but she had been
a Jezebel and a very unkind woman to him, and that shee
went away from him and lived with one Mr Hales . . . His
wife loved Hales his little finger better than she loved James'
whole body.[170]

I have heard and beleive that the elopements, going abroad, stayings out late and her going to playhouses have been without ye consent and well likeing and contrary to the orders of her husband William Colcott.[171] (Evidence of Mary Templer regarding the behaviour of Frances Colcott)

I have often seen her goe into his chamber when hee hath been in bed and locked the doore after her . . . and at such times I have heard her squeake and cry out . . . but notwithstanding her squeakings I observed that shee alwayes came merry out of his chamber.[172]

> I peeped through a crack or hole in the doore and did there see my mistress on a bed and Maurice Rablin my master's journeyman upon her body on the bed with his breeches downe and shirt upp soe that I see his bare breech.[173]

Hearing his bed crack, I had the curiosity to look through the closet door leading into the chamber and there saw Mr Calvert and Mrs Grove lying upon Mr Calvert's bed with his arms clasped about her neck.[174]

> Between eleaven and twelve of the clock at night, I looked through a hole or large crevice in the parlor where two candles were then burning and there plainely did see Mary Butler lyeing upon her back on the bedd with her pettycoates up.[175]

By and in a peer glasse standing in the dineing roome I did see Diana Dormer there sitting upon a blew and white velvet couch or squabb and Thomas Jones [a footman] standing by and close to her and stooping with his face towards hers as if it were to kisse her.[176]

On or about the twelveth of August last was twelvemonth I was hired to become a servant to Mr Lodowick Lord, a broker, at his house in Monmouth Street. After I had soe lived with him about three or foure dayes, hee both by words and actions severall times attempted my chastity and I opposed his unlawfull desires. After I had there lived with him about a weeke, Lodowick in his lodging roome behind his shopp prevailed on me to drincke some strong waters and thereby intoxicated my braines and then taking the advantage of such my intoxication and by force threw me on a bed and, takeing up my coates, had there the carnal knowledge of my body. From and after that time he severall times had the carnal knowledge of my body, sometimes on my bed in the kitchen and sometimes on a bed up two paire of staires . . . and I particularly remember that on the very day whereon his Majestie King George made his publick entry through the Citty, Lodowick obtained the carnal knowledge of my body on his bed in his lodging roome behind the shop, which was the last time he had the carnal knowledge of my body . . . At the several times of his soe haveing the knowledge of my body hee obtained the same by force and superiority of strength. By meanes of his soe enjoying the use of my body, I was begotten with child by him, of which child being a boy I was delivered on the sixth of June last.[177] (Evidence given 17 August 1716 by Martha Vorse, aged thirty, the widow of a tailor. She later 'performed a penance' for her 'incontinence' in the parish church of St Giles in the Fields.)

Your maid had been hard at work all day a washing and had laine herselfe down upon the bed in the corner of the kitchen and, shee being heavy asleep, you tooke up her coates and putt them over her eyes and knocked her, and thereby her poor thing catched cold. Shee cann never goe downe into the cellar but you must runn after her and joggle her against the butts.[178] (Rebuke by Isaac Wells of Thomas Langley, landlord of a public house)

Diana Dormer would on severall mornings bring a parcell or quantity of the herbe sabine to me and

order me to pound and straine it into a porringer, as
I accordingly did . . . and I did see her very often
drincke the same soe soone as I had soe strained it
and I remember that at one of the said times, she
said to me, 'Betty, don't you think that I am with
child', to which I replied, 'Indeed, Madam, I thincke
nothing of the matter.'[179] (Evidence of Elizabeth
Cotton, laundry-maid. Sabine or savin was a
common means of procuring abortions.)

Although a wife is very lewd, if she lives with her husband he
is chargeable for all necessaries for her, because he took her for
better for worse; and so he is if he runs away from her, or
turns away his wife, in which case he gives her credit where-
ever she goes. But if she runs away from her husband, then as
soon as such separation is notorious, whoever trusts her doth
it at her peril, and the husband is not liable, unless he takes
her in again.[180] (*The Lady's Law*, 1732)

I believe that a day scarce passed over my head . . .
whereof Thomas Byfield did not abuse [Elizabeth,
his wife] in words or threats such as frequently
calling of her whore, damn'd whore, hellcatt bitch
and brimstone bitch and such like ill and
opprobrious names and by curseing her, wishing her
neck broke, that the divle would fetch her, that the
victualls shee eate might choke her to death . . . that
he thought it noe more sin to kill her then to kill a
cat or a dogg . . . that he would make her as
miserable as any bitch in England.[181]

About the latter end of January last [1696] Susan Wilkey, by
reason of the ill usage of Thomas her husband, left him and
absconded herself. And Thomas used afterwards to come to
my house and enquire for her and threaten and swear that if
he could find Susan and, if she was above ground, he would
send her to Newgate and feed her with bread and water and if
it was possible he would send her to Algier.[182] (Evidence of
Elizabeth Beebey, Susan's sister. Algiers was one of the main

bases of Muslim corsairs who enslaved their Christian captives.)

> There came a man and a woman to the inn and
> asked me whether they could not have a lodging in
> the inn for that night . . . and I imagineing by their
> calling each other My Dear and My Love and such
> like kind expressions, that they were man and wife,
> did prepare a bed for them.[183] (Evidence of George
> Green, chamberlain of the Four Swanns in
> Bishopsgate Street)

I have been severall times with Dorothy Purslow at fortune tellers to know when her husband should dye and she hath given them money and hath said to me that, when he dyed, she would send for me and be merry and drink burnt clarrett and play cards for joy. I beleive she hath at times spent at least ten shillings on fortune tellers.[184] (Evidence of Mary Faroh)

> Lady Magrath is a violent tempered and passionate
> person . . . Sitting at dinner and being in a passion
> with Sir John [her husband] she tooke up a knife and
> threw it at him which stuck in his side about half an
> inch . . . She did strike him with a stick with which
> she broke a looking glass and she flung severall
> bottles and tobacco pipes at his head and
> endeavoured to strike him with a box iron which had
> a hot heater in it.[185]

I have often seen Thomas Byfield beat Elizabeth his wife upon the back head face and armes with the full force of his hands, knock her head against the wall with great violence, kick her on the back and belly at such times as shee hath been bigg with child . . . I have alsoe seen him dragg her downe staires by the haire of her head and sometimes by her leggs that her head hath with violence knocked against the staires and from staire to staire all the way he soe dragged her.[186]

Margaret Bates depos'd that she saw the deceased sitting on the bed with her hands on her head, who said she freely forgave her husband and did not believe he threw the poker with a design to strike her; advising all women to forbear provoking language.[187] (Evidence in the trial of Isaac Ingram, indicted for the murder of his wife Mary and found guilty of manslaughter.)

Matthew Duffy a desperate dangerous inhumane person against whom his wife Sara hath duely required sureties for the peace. Hee is committed to the Gatehouse, there to remaine untill he find good sureties personally to appear at the next Quarter Sessions of the peace to bee held for this Liberty to answere and in the meane time to keep the peace towards their majesties and all their liege people and especially towards the said Sara Duffy his wife.[188] (Westminster Gatehouse Calendar, July 1694. Having their husband bound over was one resort of battered wives.)

About the month of November in the year 1700, Henry Leonard did agree with [his wife] Jane to allow her . . . four shillings per week and to pay for a roome and to furnish the said room with a bed and other furniture fit for a bedchamber upon condition that she should live apart from him and no way trouble or molest him.[189] (Henry Leonard was a fairly wealthy man who kept a warehouse and traded in silks and stuffs, so this settlement was hardly generous.)

I have had six husbands. Their names were Richard Williams, John Freeman, John Turner, John Hussey, Thomas Richards and Thomas Smith. Williams was a merchant and lived at Jamaica and was afterwards executed upon the account of the Duke of Monmouths Rebellion. John Freeman was a clergyman and lived and died and was buryed at New York in America. John Turner was a barrister at law and lived in America and coming over to England was taken by the French and carryed to Brest where he dyed and was buryed. John

Hussey was Leiftenant of the Devonshire Man of War and dyed at sea in the year 1693. Thomas Richards was a mariner and dyed at sea and my present husband is also a mariner and is now at sea.[190] (Evidence of Jane Smith of Bermondsey, aged fifty, 12 October 1708)

10   Eating and Drinking

*Londoners normally ate three meals a day, breakfast, supper and dinner, the
main meal, which was eaten at noon. Those who lived in lodgings rarely
cooked food at home, either eating out or sending out to a cook shop or other
catering establishment for their meals. Larger households had their food sent
'upstairs' from the kitchen and would then send what was left back
downstairs for their servants to eat.*

I often observed Elizabeth Vickars do the meanest
and most servile offices for Edward Atwood, such as
dress his victuals and wash the dishes, wait on him
at table, and weed the garden, and to behave herself
in all respects as a common servant . . . I and Mrs
Downes [Edward's niece] and her husband have
several times given money to Elizabeth when we
have dined at Edward's house and Elizabeth used at
such times to attend our going out as a servant and
receive such money, I always giving her half a crown
on these occasions . . . I have gone after such dinners
through the kitchen and seen Elizabeth and a
charwoman that assisted at the house sit together at
a little table therein and she did dine and sup with
the charwoman and with my maid and such servants
as had attended their masters or mistresses at
Edward Atwood's table.[91] (Evidence of Elianor
Coote, spinster, to show that Elizabeth Vickars was
Atwood's servant and not his wife, as she claimed
after his death)

I have severall times observed that when Mr Pereira [a Jewish
merchant] and his wife and daughter have been at dinner in

the parlour, he [Isaac Coronell] hath come down staires into
the kitchen and there waited till they had dined, and then
dined with the servants . . . I wondered why he came in just at
dinner time and did not goe to the table with my master and
mistress, since other gentlemen where I have been alwayes
went to the upper table and did not stay to dine with the
servants, [but] he came sneaking there for a dinner.[192]
(Evidence of Anne Wisher, servant, to show that a) Coronell
was not on intimate terms with the family, b) was not a
gentleman and c) was so mean that he would 'sneak' a dinner
in the kitchen with the servants)

> Thomas Jevon [a woollen-draper] hath bought flesh
> meate of me by the space of a yeare and a halfe and
> uppwards and the same that hee soe bought was
> allwayes of the best for roast and boyled of beefe
> mutton veale lambe and porke as it was in season
> very plentifull and sufficient for such a family as his.
> And I believe that such flesh meates . . . was as
> much as any man (having noe greater a family than
> he) did buy or spend. He allwayes paid the best
> prises for his meate and had therefore the best and
> such as was allwayes sweete and good sent him in to
> be spent in his family.[193] (Evidence of John Whitlock,
> butcher, to counter an apprentice's claim that he was
> poorly fed by his master)

I board and table with William Coles [a merchant dealing in
salt, wine and fish] and have done soe for these four years last
past. He buyes very good food for his family and is reputed to
keep as good a house and table as any man in the parish
where he lives [St Botolph, Billingsgate] of his degree and
quallity. I never knew any want or scarcity of food in his
house.

> William Coles and his wife for ye time I lived there
> which was 17 weekes did usually feed very high and
> of ye best sorts of food, but as to his servants he kept
> an extraordinary bad house. Ye servants did very
> rarely eat of any of ye meat which William Coles and

his wife feed on but what was left at their table above
stares was generally lock'd up and very seldom (unles
some few scrapps or riff raff thereof) brought downe
to ye servants. Ye food wherwith ye servants were
generally fed was very coarse stale mouldy bread and
ranck salt butter, together with some porrage made
of the meat that William Coles and his wife eat
above stares and scraps of fish. Oftentimes they had
dumplings very dry and with very little if any suet or
other ingredients in them. And if it chanced the
servants had any of the meat it was often stale and
corrupt and soe stinking that they could scarcely eat
of it, but yet were inforc'd to eate it for mere
necessity having not to suffice nature of other
victualls. And ye bread and butter and also if there
were at any time chees (which was very seldom and
but ordinary), it was immediately so soon as they
had dyned constantly lock'd up so that the servants
could not come at it. And during all ye time of my
stay there this was the dyet and manner of William
Coles' housekeeping for his servants. And during that
time ye servants very seldome had any breakfasts or
suppers allowed them or if they had it was of such ill
food as they were not able to eate to any content.[194]
(Evidence of Mary Bates, spinster, aged sixteen, and
of Jeremiah Hamond, a schoolmaster and former
servant of Coles. The case was brought by an
apprentice who complained that he did not receive
sufficient or wholesome victuals.)

About two yeares since, I with Joanna New and Mrs Baker
and Henrietta dined at the chambers of Edmund Bromwich in
the Temple, where we were well entertained with a dishe of
fishe, ham and chickens, tarts and wine and other liquors,
which dinner was then said to be dressed at the Swan in
Butcher Row and . . . was brought to his chambers by one
Rhoades a porter.[195] (Evidence of Rose Jones, widow)

Several gentlemen or others came to spend their
money in my mother's house [a coffee-house] and to

smoake and drincke or transact buisnesse . . . One
drancke tea, another drancke two glasses of mumm
. . . another two dishes of tea and a pennyworth of
tobacco and the little gentleman had a dishe of
coffee.[196]

She did not care to sit down at meals with him and seldom
provided a hot dinner for him except on a Sunday.

She sat at the upper end of the table and carved as
mistress of the family.

She was turned out of ye family for not being a housewife nor
understanding her buisnesse as a cooke and I and my then
fellow servants rejoyced and were very glad at her removal.

He came into the Shippe in Green Street in order to
dine there and seated himselfe in an open box in the
publicke roome.

I went with them to Whitcher's house and we had some
salmon and punch and a quartern of brandy.

After the marriage was solemnized they did dine
together on pidgeons pyes which they had from a
cookes shopp.

They had then for [a wedding] dinner some bacon and colly
flower, two fowles roasted and a dish of peas.

Hannah Sutton came at noon or soon after dinner
time to Catherine Lund (who keeps henns in her
yard) for some new laid eggs.

I brought up to the roome four poached eggs for their supper.

We went to a distiller's and had half a pint of gin; we
paid three-halfpence, and scor'd the other three-
halfpence.

He brought me a nosegay and a penny custard.

I have carryed them coffee and chocolett when they
have been in naked bed together.

She and the gentleman dranke ten or twelve shillings worth of
sack or ten or twelve pints (which of them I cannot
remember).

They went into an upper room and called for cakes
and ale that they might bee merry together.

They were a juncating with two strange men and had two
fowls and a salad.

She prevailed on mee and almost forced mee to
drincke a large glass of aniseed water whereby my
braines soone afterwards became intoxicated.

They drank geneva [gin] till they could hardly see one
another.

He was very sickly when he first came to live there
and drancke red cows and asses milk.

I went to market to buy meat for my family . . . and bought
sixteen pounds of beef for half a crown, and a cabbage.

She came to my stall, cheapned [bargained for] some
meat and, after some time, agreed with me for a
piece of beef at two pence a pound.

He set his wife up in Bartholomew-Fair to sell gin and
blackpuddings.

Some sleepy potions [laudanum] which shee
generally took almost every night.

On nights after his master was gon to bed he [an apprentice]
would send for wine and oysters.

My mistress sent me out with a sieve of oysters to sell
in Petticoat Lane.

Her mother made me go with a pitcher and beg milk porridge.

> About nine a clock of ye night of ye same day there
> came a lustly fat black gentleman and a
> gentlewoman to the said lodging [in the Coach and
> Horses near Charing Cross] and I lighted them up
> stairs and made them a fire and carried them a hot
> pot of ale brandy and eggs and warmed the bed.[197]
> (Evidence of Frances Caddy, servant)

James Wasse was very aged [seventy-four]. He used to come
and drink a pint of drink and smoke his pipe at our house. He
seldom clubb'd with any others but generally came alone and
paid for what he called for which seldom exceeded three
pence. My husband and I did generally lead him home though
he was perfectly sober.[198] (Evidence of Elizabeth Ryder,
alehouse-keeper of Kingsland. 'Clubbing' was similar to
buying drinks in rounds.)

> The prisoner in her defence said that about one a
> clock in the morning she was going to buy black
> cherries, and took 3s.6d. with her which she put in
> her mouth, for fear of meeting with rude fellows who
> might pick her pocket; and that she took nothing in
> her pocket but a half penny worth of tobacco, a short
> pipe, and a penny for her morning draught.[199] (Trial
> of Katherine Ward, found guilty and transported for
> picking the pocket of a hackney coachman and
> concealing the money in her mouth)

Hannah Brinsden depos'd, that about nine at night, her
mother (the deceased) sitting on the bed and suckling her
child ask'd her father what she should have for supper. He
answer'd 'Bread and cheese, can't you eat that as well as the
children?' 'No', says she, 'I want a bit of meat.' 'I have no
money to buy you any', says he. 'You know', says the
deceased, 'I have had but little to day.' 'D . . . n ye, ye bitch',

says the prisoner, 'I'll stick ye the next word that ye speak.'
The deceased again askt for meat, and then the prisoner pusht
her back with his left hand, and stabb'd her under the breast
with the knife which he had in his right hand.[200] (Trial of
Matthias Brinsden of St Anne, Blackfriars, found guilty of the
murder of his wife)

> 'Come my dear let's have a dram', says she, and so
> she sends Ann Bowers for a quartern, and it was
> hardly out before she call'd for another, and after
> that for two or three more. And then she was having
> some steaks for supper, which Bowers got ready.[201]
> (Scene in a cook-shop from the trial of Katherine
> Dunster and Ann Bowers, found guilty of theft)

Clay and his wife (being shoemakers) sold gin to their
brethren of the craft . . . day after day, drinking this liquor; of
which the child partook, till it often tumbled about the
floor.[202] (The accused was acquitted of raping the child, aged
two.)

> I am sure I know nothing of the matter. I was very
> much in liquor, and was very sick with drinking
> some out-of-the-way nasty stuff. O pray burn me,
> burn my hand off, but don't send me away; I'll never
> go into a Ginshop any more, if you won't send me
> over sea.[203] (This plea of Hannah Donolly to be
> branded was ignored and she was transported to
> Virginia for theft from a pawnshop.)

11 Entertainment

> Rebecca with a seeming joy came running into the
> chamber to me and told me that now the sunn
> shined (as it then really did) and begg'd that I would
> call upon her at the Dancing Schoole and bring a
> coach along with me, that they might goe out and
> bee merry together.[204] (Evidence of Dorothy Moor,
> servant, relating to a clandestine meeting between
> Rebecca Pereira and Isaac Coronell)

John Todd [apprentice to a merchant] frequently came home
drunk very late at night and put the house into disorder and
trouble to gett him to bed and sometimes lay out all night . . .
He was given much to cursing and sweareing and great
extravagancy in apparrell and as I have heard did use gaming
and the keeping of lewd women company . . . One time he
pawned one of his Misses at hazard for 22 shillings and she
was enforced to leave her petticoate as a pledge for ye same
before she had her liberty to goe away.[205] (Evidence of Ralph
Wyld, brother of John's master)

> On the 25th day of October 1721, he and Dorothy
> Walter had been making merry with his fellow
> witness Henry Howard, a shoemaker, upon the
> account of its being St Crispin's Day at his lodgings
> in the Paved Alley by St James's Market.[206]
> (Evidence of John Murry, shoemaker)

That night being St Patrick's Day, the prisoner [Dennis
Sullivan] got so drunk in honour of St Patrick that he could
hardly stand.[207]

I saw Mary Price go over a stile into a turnip field
[in Kensington], soon after which I saw Mr Gotobed
follow Mary Price over the said stile. About a quarter
of an hour after which I saw Mary Price come back
again. Upon which I said to her 'What, has this old
fellow (meaning ye said Mr Gotobed) been a
knocking of you?' To which she answered, 'Yes,
damn him for an old short prickt dog, as well as he
was able.' I asked her what he had given her and she
told me two sixpences which she then pulled out of
her bosom.[208] (Evidence of William Freeman,
coachman)

Being a gentleman and out of business, I do keepe a house [in
Duke Street] where severall persons of quality and others in
the winter time usually come and dyne privately, and after
dinner they sometimes call for musick, and sometimes for
cards or dyce to divert themselves and pay me what they
please or think fitt.[209] (Evidence of J. J. Heidegger, 9 July
1706. He was later famous as an impresario and promoter of
the opera.)

One time James Sherrard [an apprentice] being at
football chanc'd to have a blow in his eye that did
some hurt to the same and I took a great deal of care
of him and let him keep in bed a day and sent for lice
to one of the Compters [prisons] in order to take
away the blood shott out of his eye.[210] (Evidence of
Ellen Watts, daughter of James's master)

This man took us to the tavern, and offered us a crown apiece
to strip overselves naked, and shew him postures. He gave
Mary Gardner money to fetch a penny-worth of rods, for him
to whip us a-cross the room, and make us good girls; and then
for us to whip him to make him a good boy: But we told him
it was neither a proper time nor place for any such thing, for it
was Sunday night, and others might over-look us in the room
we were in.[211] (Evidence of Susan Brockway, acquitted of
stealing from R.J.)

I do verily beleive that William Palmer [a linen-
draper's apprentice] did frequent cockpits and such
other places because I have seene him to pull out of
his pockets cocks spurrs and implements belonging to
such buisness and I have heard that he did also
frequent playhouses.[212] (Evidence of Anne Swinstead,
former servant in William's master's household)

Last Christmas was twelve month, about 4 a clock in the
afternoon, I went to see a shop-mate of mine, who liv'd in
Bishopsgate-street . . . She and I used to wind silk together.
And there I staid till one a clock in the morning; not that I
use to keep ill hours; for it is very well known that I take an
honest care for a livelihood, but it was holiday time, and we
were willing to be a little merry together.[213] (Evidence of Mary
Batten against John Simmons, acquitted of assaulting and
robbing her on her way home)

About seven or eight times . . . I did in the day time
sett him out of his chariott at a house in Drury Lane
where there was a little milliner or headdressers
shopp and where I sometimes called for him againe
and tooke him up in his chariott about two or three
houres afterwards, generally setting him downe about
two in the afternoone and takeing him up againe
about five.[214] (Evidence of Edward Higgins,
coachman, relating to the Hon. Benedict Calvert)

Lady Martha [Holmes] . . . did in the months of January and
February last (she being then sole and unmarried as I verily
beleive) frequent the withdrawing roome in his Majesties
pallace of St James to which place divers persons of the first
and best quality did resort at times set apart for the
purpose.[215] (Evidence of Walter Blount Esq.)

I did call at Robert Rickard's house and ask for
Thomas Shilling [Rickard's apprentice]. They of the
shop told me that Thomas was at a victualling house
nearby where there was a Billyard table. I going and
finding him there did reprove him for following those

idle courses and neglecting his master's buisnes and
told him that it would be his ruine and he gave me
noe answear but only laughed at me.[216] (Evidence of
John Kendrick)

The first beginning of his misfortunes was frequently going to
the Billiard-Tables; he had learned to play so well that he was
what they call a Tip top player.[217] (Re Robert Ramsey, the
son of 'reputable' parents who was educated at Westminster
and hanged at the age of twenty-seven for theft, on the
evidence of his brother)

> On Monday morning two Running Footmen run
> fourteen times round St James's Park for a wager of
> one hundred guineas; which was performed by the
> winner in an hour and half's time.[218]

Mrs Clap's house was next to the Bunch of Grapes in Feild-
lane, Holbourn. It bore the publick character of a place of
entertainment for sodomites, and for the better conveniency of
her customers, she had provided beds in every room in her
house. She usually had 30 or 40 of such persons there every
night, but more especially on a Sunday.[219] (Trial of Gabriel
Laurence, who was found guilty of sodomy and hanged. Mrs
Clap's house was a notorious 'molly-house'.)

> He is in great expectation of a tumbler you must
> send him for his puppet show; a Punch he has and
> his wife, and a straw king and queen, and ladies of
> honour, and all things but a tumbler, which this
> town [Norwich] cannot afford; it is a wooden fellow
> that turns his heels over his head.[220] (Letter from Sir
> Thomas Browne, 1682, relating to his grandson's
> home puppet theatre)

He carried her to a Jelly house at Richmond and there
attempted to debauch her.

> They played at cards or back gammon or draughts or
> some other innocent diversion.

He had an itching after Game, and came often home naked, having gamed away all his clothes.

> He was a very honest lad and only delighted in Cudgel Playing and Bear Gardens.

I was going with Captain Brown to the Kentish Town Races.

> I made a Holiday to see the Execution.

To get him into a good humour, I invited him to come to a house-warming to my house.

> Ye said apprentice did use to go to the Bear garden and he had a nursery of beargarden dogs abroad.

He would be very often out of dores amongst frenchmen and fidlers and other idle company with whom he spent much of his time.

> Being young and silly, she would gad abroad with idle wenches who indeed were the ruin of her, by carrying her to hops and musick-houses where loose company resort.

A discourse arose about playing at a game called crickett.

> He doth live with his mother who keeps a bowling green and imployes himself in the looking after the bowles.

I was then in Chick-Lane, hearing some girls singing of ballads.

> He said young Bailey and he had been in the fields a birds nesting.

He was making a kite for the children.

Elinor Harper came to me and told me that Mr
Joseph Reynolds had a friend that had lent him a
barge and did design to shew her Hampton Court on
the morrow and desired me to go with her for
company or any other friend that I would take with
me, and I told her I could not go because it was
Dancing Day.[221] (Evidence of Hannah Snapes,
schoolmistress of Islington)

Benjamin Grover [a cooper's apprentice] was a very remiss
idle person and if he were sent to me in Southwark for hoopes
he would many times loyter and idle away his time and not
returne home in three or four houres. Having sometimes
occasion to goe into London a good while after Benjamin had
his errand, I have found him gazeing upon the Thames and I
beleive it was his constant practice soe to doe.[222]

I saw Frances Colcott come out of the Play House in
Lincolns Inn Fields between eight and nine of the clock
in the evening in company with a gentleman . . . and
took coach and went together to the chocolatt house in
Bridges Street, where the coach stopped for about a
quarter of an hour and Frances and the gentleman
drank chocolatt together and from thence [she] went
with the gentleman in ye coach to another chocolatt
house in the Hay Markett, where they stayed a little
while and then returned back in the coach together to
the Rose Tavern in Bridges Street.[223]

The usual time of Anna Nowes' going to bed was about
eleaven or twelve a clock at night and sometimes when she
had been abroad she would sitt up till one or two of the clock
in ye morning. I beleive she did two or three times during the
time I lived there stay out till two of the clock in the morning,
at which times she hath said she had been at the princess's
ball, and she would sometimes after she had come home late
eat some supper, and sitt up till she had taken one or two
pipes of tobacco.[224] (Evidence of Sarah Backwell, housemaid.
Anna Nowes was the wife of a wealthy attorney whose
servants had to stay up until their mistress returned home.)

Edward Day [an apprentice] was very much addicted to play at shoffell board and such like plays and particularly one day last Christmas was twelve months Edward called of me at my master's and told me it was his Holyday and desired me to go abroad with him. Accordingly I did and we went to a publick house in the Strand where we continued all day playing at shoffell board at a game called Rolley Polley where Edward as I beleive lost some money. Edward [also] used frequently to throw with dice at wheel barrows in the street.[225] (Evidence of Daniel Houghton. Shovel-board or shuffle-board was a game similar to shove-halfpenny. Edward also liked to gamble 'at nine pinns'.)

I went at 7 o'clock to the dancing at Mr Fernley's dancing school. It cost me two shillings for wine and three shillings for Mr Fernley and one shilling for a hautboy [oboe]. I think this is too dear for the pleasure I had, the women not being very good company.

Went to church. Was very negligent about the service that was performed. Could not but blame myself for it, expecially since my thoughts were chiefly employed about the ladies, how to get opportunities of looking at them through my glass.

Walked in the Park and then to the Drawing Room . . . Saw the King very plain a great while. I could not help looking smiling and pleased when I looked at him.

Rose at 8. Mr Birch came with some greyhounds to hunt with us. We were very unwilling to leave the ladies for such dull sport. However, we went out and stayed two hours beating the ground to find a hare, without any success. I think this is the dullest sport that can be.

Rose at 6. Drank two bottles of purging waters. A very fine morning. Walked in the long walk. Thought of the being of God.[226] (These last five extracts are from Dudley Ryder's *Diary*.)

12 Clothing

I can positively sweare that all the dresse and
apparrell I now weare is my owne proper dresse and
apparrell except my pinner which my mother lent me
this morning to come out in because my owne was
not cleane. I myself bought and paid for my
apparrell out of money which I have earned by
workeing, except my hood which my mother gave
mee sometime since . . . I have been informed by my
mother that I am neare fourteen yeares of age . . .
and I am worth nothing but my clothes. I am
maintained by my father who receives what I earn by
twineing of silke, haveing a small allowance he makes
me thereout to find me in clothes.[227] (Evidence of
Marie Batteaux of Cock Lane, Stepney, daughter of
Jean Batteaux, weaver)

The cloathes I now weare are my owne and paid for. I bought
my perewigg of Mr Gardian, perewigg maker in Cabinett
Street in Spittlefields. My wife bought my neckcloth and shirt
somewhere in Spittlefields. I bought the cloth for my coate
and wastecoate of a draper near Whitechappell. I bought my
breeches of Mr Morley, a plush weaver in Spittlefields, and
my stockings of a stocking maker in Quaker Street in
Spittlefields and my shoes of Mr Fouchett in Phoenix Street in
Spittlefields. My hatt was given me by the widdow of my
master to whome I was an apprentice.[228] (Evidence of Louis
Mange, silkweaver of Stepney)

My cloathes are my owne, they are all paid for, none
being borrowed. I bought them of the proper persons
who sells such wares, my gowne in Zealand, my

pettycoates of one Mr Ebber in Smock Alley in
Spittlefields, my smock in Zealand, my boddice or
stayes of a woman who sold such things about
streets, my shoes of a stranger in Spittlefields, my
stockings of Mr Deveux behind the markett in
Spittlefields, my rideing hood of a stranger whose
name I know not near the same place, my black
hood of Mary Ginnett now in Ireland, and my
headclothes some where in Spittlefields.[229] (Evidence
of Susanne Bettembeaux, a nurse, aged forty-two,
born in Picardy. Witnesses were occasionally asked
about the provenance of their clothes to determine
whether they had been given or lent by the parties.)

David Church [an apprentice] was constantly allowed a clean
shirt and other linen every weeke to shift himself withall which
were delivered to him after every washing to put into his own
trunck that so he might take them at his pleasure. He had also
cleane bands enough for twice a weeke which were in like
manner delivered for him to put on. And John Gandy [his
master] did likewise furnish David with a very good feather
bedd clean and wholsome and clean sheets constantly once a
month as often as the [household] did wash. David Church
had every thing that an apprentice of his trade and quality
ought to have of meat drink washing lodging and other
necessaries.[230] (Evidence of Mary Bradley, a former servant in
the household. Church's counter-claim is lost, but Bradley's
evidence can be taken as an ideal to be compared with the
following extract.)

William Sherman, when he first came to Thomas
Spratley [his master, a poulterer], had a good suit of
clothes and necessaries provided him by his mother.
But after the same were worne out, Thomas Spratley
took noe care to provide him either with clothes or
other necessaries, but let him goe till he was ragged
and had hardly any shoes to his feet and persons
crying out shame of him and wondring that his
master would let him goe in such manner. Thomas
Spratley did thereupon give him an old coat of his

own that hung almost to ye ground and was in
wraggs and now and then when William was allmost
bare foot he would give him a very old pair of his
shoes that would hang on his feet. In noe sort did he
take care of William as he ought to doe insoemuch
that William became very lowsie and nasty in his
clothes that the lice might be seen crawling on him
and seldom had clean linnen under three weekes
times and that very sorry.[231] (Evidence of Thomas
Taverner. Lice and bugs in clothing and bedding
were a common problem which was normally cured
by boiling or baking the offending garments.)

I told Elizabeth Ellis that I came from Mr Lang who desired
that shee would dress her self and be ready to go with him
that afternoon to the play. I then delivered her the letter [from
Lang] and Elizabeth went towards the window in her chamber
and, as she was reading the letter, I looked into the chamber
and saw a hatt, sword and periwig lying on ye table, a coat,
wastcoat and breaches lying on a chair by the bedside and a
man lying in ye bed, with a napkin about his head . . .
Elizabeth then ordered me to return an answear to Mr Lang
that she would dress herself and be ready at the time
appointed to go to the play.[232] (Evidence of Robert Haynes,
porter)

I with others after they soe were in bed threw a
stocking at them as is customary upon such occasions
of a bride and bridegroomes first bedding
together.[233]

I did severall times see them in naked bed together between
the sheetes, hee being naked to his shirt, and shee naked to her
shift.[234] (This seems to have been the standard nightware,
virtually identical evidence being given in hundreds of
adultery and marriage cases.)

He gave me a white French necklace which I beleive
was worth about halfe a crowne upon my giveing

him a beef stake for his dinner out of two which I
had for my owne dinner.

I saw him pick up a woman in Red Lyon Fields and offer her
a handkerchief if shee would go with him, which shee refused.

He was a little man and usually wore a yellowish
sandy coloured perriwigg.

She was a very genteele neate woman and went lite in her
clothes for a woman of her age.

A man who by his habit, apron and rule that stuck
by his side seemed to be a carpenter.

He appeared by his band to be some parish clerke.

A lusty man in a drayman's apron.

He then turned up her petticoats to feel for her pocket, and
did what he would with her.

Mary White of St Luke Middlesex was indicted for
assaulting Susannah Cuttle, an infant, about the age
of four years and an half and taking from her a
flannel petticoat, a shift, a quilted petticoat, a skirt, a
cap, a knot, a frock, and a stay.[235] (The child was
brought home stark naked.)

A Holland sprig'd gown, value 7s., a pair of stays, value 3s., a
cambrick handkerchief, value 18d., a muslin ditto, value 1s., a
linnen apron, value 2s., a callimanco-quilted coat, value 15s.,
a dimity petticoat, value 3s., a pair of damask shoes, value
2s.6d., a pair of silver buckles, value 8s., a Bermudas hat,
value 7s., a suit of cambrick headcloths laced, value 2s.6d., a
gold ring, value 8s. and ninepence in money.[236] (Clothes stolen
from Elizabeth Pate after she was stripped and raped on her
way home from Tottenham Court Fair in 1737. Her three
attackers left her one petticoat, her shift and her stockings.)

I have seen Margaret [Goater] about seven or eight
times and beleive her to bee about twenty two yeares
of age. She is a middle siz'd woman, pretty thick sett,
of a fairish complection with red colour and brownish
haired and shee often wore black and white cloathes,
but generally red cloathes, and sometimes a blew
sattin.[237] (Evidence of Dulcibella Mason, whose
husband said that 'to his best remembrance'
Margaret wore 'cherry coloured cloathes'. Witnesses
were quite often asked to describe the normal clothes
of the parties, but their descriptions are rarely any
more informative than in this example.)

I had not gone far before I was overtaken by two men in light
colour'd stockings. They past by me without speaking. I was
afraid they were thieves, because of their white stockings, for it
seems white stockings is a mighty fashion amongst thieves.[238]
(Evidence of Elizabeth Bedford against Robert Colson, 1734)

'Mary, if you don't stand by me I am ruined, and if
you will stand by me and swear that Mr Volaw
called me bitch and whore I will give you a new
gowne and pettycoate and it shall bee the best dayes
worke that ever you did in your life.'
   'I will not damne my soule or foresweare myselfe
for a gowne and pettycoate though I am a poor
girle.'[239]
(Evidence of Margaret Rogers re Mary Shackbolt)

Upon Mrs Groves first comeing to lodge, shee appeared to bee
very slender and flatt before and wore stayes and usually then
went straite laced, but after shee had been there some time I
observed that she had left off her stayes and for all the time
afterwards usually went in a loose or undresse and appeared
to me to be with child. I did alsoe observe that dureing her
stay there shee grew bigger and bigger and . . . often heard
her complaine that her leggs aked and that she was soe sick in
the night shee could not sleep and was forced to call her maid
upp.[240]

Frances [Colcott] hath been very extravagant and
expensive in buying and wearing things of great
value and beyond the condition she ought to appear
and live in. I saw her with very good cloathes on and
a gold watch by her side and other ornaments much
too good for her quality as wife [to a hosier].[241]

Isaac Coronell was but very indifferent in his habitt and
linnen but afterwards he appeared more genteel in a new coate
and better linnen but by his readiness in goeing of errands for
my mistress he alwayes appeared to me more like a footman
than a gentleman.[242] (Evidence of Anne Wisher, servant)

Griffith Jones said to Elianour Owens that hee would
be marryed to her in his red coate because he gott his
bread in it, to which Elianour replyed that it was all
one to her if hee wore a blankett, meaning thereby as
I then apprehended and beleive that shee did not
care how hee were dressed soe shee had him.[243]
(Evidence of Jane Williams of Lambeth, 2 January
1712. Griffith Jones was a sergeant in Colonel
Ingoldsby's Regiment of Foot.)

13 Time and Seasons

Most people were quite capable of giving the approximate time of the events they were describing, though expressions like the following were quite commonly used as an aid to remember a year or a date.

In the great hard frost . . . in the late dreadfull storme . . . ever since the sicknesse yeare . . . two or three dayes after the great high wind . . . on the day of the last great eclipse of the sun . . . when White Hall was on fire . . . when ye Pretender was born . . . at the time the races were at Hounslow . . . the evening before Mr Paul and Mr Hall were executed at Tyburn . . . about the time of the last Sessions at the Old Bayley.

There were also aids to remember the time of day . . .

In sermon time . . . immediately after morning prayer . . . about candlelighting in the evening . . . at dinner time of a Sunday . . . at Exchange time when the merchants meet at the Royal Exchange . . . when it was duskish.

the season . . .

At nut time . . . in pea and bean time . . . in damson time.

or the date, though the decline in the number of recognized Saints' Days since the Reformation made this less easy than it had been in medieval times.

About Shrovetide last . . . a little before the Whitsun holy days last . . . about Bartholomew Tide next will be five years . . . on the feast of the Epiphany commonly called Twelfth Day . . . St Valentine's Day . . . last St George's Day . . . Ascension Day . . . St Barnabas's Day last was eight yeares . . . on the fast day for the Fire of London . . . last Lord Mayors Day . . . I don't remember the day of the month, but it was some remarkable day for there was a bonfire.

The passage of the seasons is also sometimes reflected in diaries such as in the following extracts from the 1738/9 diary of Stephen Monteage, accountant to the South Sea Company.

This day finished having a fire in my office for this season [30 April] . . . in the afternoone Grace our milkwoman came with her garland and danced as usuall [4 May] . . . left off bed warming [7 May] . . . left off woollen and put on thread socks for the summer [7 May] . . . heard a cucko first this year [13 May] . . . left off wearing my Great Coat [22 May] . . . a dish of peas for dinner the first this season [24 May] . . . gooseberry pye for supper first this season [3 June] . . . mackarel for dinner, first this season [22 June] . . . put on my woollen socks for the winter season [18 September] . . . this morning began to light fire in my office for the winter season [1 October] . . . put on my plush waistcoat and breaches for the winter season [29 October] . . . a turkey and mince pies for dinner being Christmas Day [25 December].[244]

Appendix on Sources

Much of this book depends on analysis of information provided by London deponents in the Prerogative Court of Canterbury, the Commissary Court, the Consistory Court of the Bishop of London and the Court of Arches.[1] Cases in these Church courts were conducted on the basis of written material. Plaintiffs appointed a proctor, who presented their cases in a written libel, and the defendant did the same, his or her answer being known as an allegation. For the evidence from witnesses, numbered interrogatories were drawn up and the witnesses were examined on these by the registrar 'in some private room, from which all other persons . . . are removed'.[2]

The interrogatories contained questions relating not only to the matter in dispute but also to the persons of the witnesses, with the object of providing the court with some idea of their quality and reliability. These questions varied considerably over time and between individual cases.[3] Nearly everyone was asked to state their age and parish of residence, while all women gave their marital status and nearly all men gave themselves a status or occupational label. In some periods, most witnesses were asked to give their place of birth, while at other times this question was rarely asked. Between 1695 and 1725, witnesses were often asked to say how they got their living or were maintained and the answers provide the data for the analysis of work in this book. Witnesses were also sometimes asked about their wealth, tax commitments, rent and the length of time they had lived in the same parish, while women were often asked how long they had been married and the occupations of their husbands.

The Church courts were closed during the 1640s and 1650s and their records start again in the early or mid-1660s. Four samples of deponents resident in London have been drawn from this material. The first two, the male and female 'origins' samples, consist of 1,994 men and 2,121 women who gave evidence between 1660 and 1725 and whose place of birth is stated in the introductory section of their deposition; the information collected comprises the year of the deposition, age and place of birth of deponent and whether the deposition was signed or marked, this material being used for the analysis of migration and literacy.[4] The other two samples, the male and female 'employment' samples, have been studied in more detail and data from all the types of questions mentioned above have been collected for them. They consist of 1,794 men and 1,436 women who gave evidence between 1695 and 1725, which included information as to how they were maintained or employed.[5]

These depositions provide the researcher with a mass of data which could not be found in any other source. The problem is to determine just how reliable this is and whether the witnesses provide a reasonably unbiased cross-section of the population being studied. The first point is the easiest to evaluate. While there is considerable evidence of coaching by lawyers in the main body of depositions, this is not true of the answers to the personal questions which are at issue here, the answers being clearly individual to the particular witness. The questions asked are also of such a nature that there seems little motive for witnesses to lie. The information gathered for the 'origins' samples, for instance, includes the witnesses' place of birth, age and literacy – the last defined as the ability to sign the deposition. Most people must have known where they were born, though a few seem to have been a little hazy on the subject, as is suggested by the registrar's occasional insertion of the phrase 'ut credit' (as he/she believes) after the name of the place. Using signatures as a proxy for literacy certainly creates problems of interpretation, as discussed in the text, but it seems reasonable to assume that if witnesses could sign, they did.[6] Ages do cause problems, since a fairly high proportion of the middle-aged and elderly rounded their ages to forty, fifty, sixty etc., and, if reported ages are tested for inaccuracy by the Smith Index, only those under thirty give the researcher confidence that they are correct.[7] This problem has been avoided or at least minimized in tables presenting age structure by defining age-groups as 35–44, 45–54, etc., rather

than 40–49, 50–59, etc., on the assumption that most people who
said they were fifty were nearer fifty than forty or sixty.
Nevertheless, if witnesses were so cavalier in reporting their ages,
one suspects that they were also fairly haphazard or forgetful in
reporting the length of time that something had happened in the
past. This will affect the accuracy of calculations based on
counting back from recorded ages, such as the age at marriage,
the age at which immigrants arrived in London and so on, the
inaccuracy being greater the older the witness.

The additional information given by witnesses in the 'employment' sample also seems likely to be fairly accurate. Most people
must have known what they or their husbands did for a living,
where they lived, what rent and taxes they paid and so on. It is
possible that some people claimed to be of rather more distinction than they actually were, giving a socially upward bias to
the data, but it should be remembered that the witnesses were on
oath and their answers could in most cases be easily checked.
Indeed, some interrogatories specifically provided for a check on
witnesses, asking them, for instance, not only what they did for a
living themselves but also what other named witnesses in the
same case did. Naturally, discretion meant that some people
would not disclose the whole truth to the registrar of a Church
court. No one, for instance, said that they gained their livelihood
from prostitution or theft, though other witnesses claimed that
more than one of the sample was a common whore or the mistress
of a bawdy-house. Leaving this aside, it seems probable that
most of the personal information in the depositions was accurate,
certainly accurate enough for our purposes. The representativeness of the samples is, however, much harder to determine. On
the whole, it seems probable that female witnesses are better in
this respect than male witnesses, which is why there has been
much more quantitative analysis of the female sample. The
reasons for this assumption are discussed below.

Female Witnesses
An attempt was made by the present writer in 1989 to determine
the representativeness of female witnesses in the London Church
courts.[8] This concluded that there was a considerable area bias
in the sample, with the West End over-represented and the
northern and southern suburbs under-represented. This would

exaggerate somewhat those things most characteristic of the West End, such as employment in the needle trades. The other main conclusion was that the sample provided a fair reflection of the social structure of London, the most likely bias being that there were rather too few members of the wealthier groups in society, who were probably less likely to be asked personal questions than humbler people. It is also possible that there were too few people from the very lowest unrespectable group in society, though the sample does go a long way down the social scale, including women in very humble occupations and some supported partly or entirely by their parishes.

These conclusions on the social structure of the sample were entirely impressionistic, being based on a general picture of metropolitan society derived from wide reading in manuscript and secondary sources. Such a subjective assessment is not of course entirely satisfactory. However, alternative checks are hard to make since similar quantifiable material on early modern Londoners, and especially London women, is difficult to find anywhere else than in these same Church court depositions.[9] One solution is to do an internal check on the consistency of the samples by splitting them up into two groups and seeing whether both groups present the same general picture.[10]

This will be done by splitting the samples according to the sort of case in which deponents gave their evidence. Two of the courts used – the Prerogative and Commissary Courts – dealt entirely with probate cases in which the disputes related mainly to wills, probate inventories and the relationship of people to the deceased. Witnesses from these courts will be described as 'probate' witnesses in what follows. The third court which has been used – the Consistory Court – dealt in a totally different type of business. The great majority of the cases related to defamation (sexual slander), the legality of marriages and divorce. Finally, the Court of Arches, which acted as both an appeal court and a court of first instance, heard cases of both the above types. However, the great majority of the cases were on similar subjects to those in the Consistory Court and the deponents from these two courts will be grouped together as 'other' witnesses.

It seems a reasonable *a priori* assumption that 'probate' witnesses would not be identical in all characteristics to 'other' witnesses. They were often asked to give evidence on matters which had occurred a long time in the past and so were likely to be older; they were often witnesses of wills and so were more likely to be literate; they were often related to testators and so were more likely to be people of substance or property. Witnesses in defamation suits, on the other hand, were normally those who had heard slanderous words spoken, usually in the street or some other public place. They were therefore likely to be neighbours of the person defamed, who was usually not of very high status, or were very often passers-by or people who earned their living in the street itself. Disputed marriages were normally those of a clandestine nature such as the 'Fleet' marriages, which were rarely resorted to by members of the upper ranks of society, and the witnesses familiar with the circumstances were likely to be people of fairly lowly status. Divorces happened in all ranks of society and some of the witnesses called were of high status, but most were middling or humble people, servants being particularly common as witnesses in such cases. In short, 'probate' witnesses might be expected to be older, more literate and of higher status than 'other' witnesses. If, in spite of this, an analysis of the two groups shows common characteristics and patterns, then one can feel some confidence in using the evidence from the Church courts as a realistic basis for making generalizations about London women as a whole.

A start can be made by comparing the age structure of the two groups, as is done in Table A.1. This confirms the hypothesis above in that 'probate' witnesses are found to be considerably older than 'other' witnesses. Otherwise, despite some anomalies, the figures for the two groups seem to have the same internal logic and draw the same general picture of age structure, suggesting in both cases that relatively few immigrants came to London in their teens and showing that few women could expect to live very long in high-mortality London.

Table A.2 looks at literacy patterns and shows that 'probate' witnesses were much more likely to sign their names than 'other' witnesses. However, both groups demonstrate the same pattern. Migrants have high rates of literacy by national standards and both migrants and the London-born show considerable improvement across the period.[11] Moving on to the data derived from the 'employment' sample, it can be seen in Table A.3 that there was a

TABLE A.1 Age Structure of Female Sample

Age-group	London-born		Immigrants	
	Probate n=990 %	Others n=597 %	Probate n=2208 %	Others n=1408 %
19 & under	6.1	13.7	3.2	4.8
20–24	12.5	19.1	12.6	12.6
25–29	14.1	15.6	12.1	14.7
30–34	16.4	14.9	12.9	16.7
35–44	22.4	19.9	25.4	24.9
45–54	15.7	9.2	18.4	15.1
55–64	9.8	5.2	11.0	7.8
65 & over	3.0	2.4	4.4	3.4
	100.0	100.0	100.0	100.0

Source: All members of female origins sample.[12]

higher proportion of widows and a lower proportion of spinsters in the probate sample, a reflection of the differing age structure of the two groups as shown in Table A.1.

Finally, the distribution of occupations is shown in Table A.4. Rather fewer probate witnesses were gainfully employed, as one might expect of a slightly more prosperous and 'respectable' group. Otherwise, the table shows very much the same general pattern of occupations between the two groups, with a few anomalies. The most obvious one is that there were more than twice the proportion of witnesses engaged in nursing and medicine in the 'probate' group, a finding which is easily explained since nurses were often called to give evidence on the mental and physical state of the deceased at the time that he or

TABLE A.2 Proportion of Female Witnesses Signing Deposition

	Born before 1660		Born 1660 & after	
	Probate %	Others %	Probate %	Others %
Migrants	49	40	63	57
London-born	61	45	78	63

Source: Female origins sample.

TABLE A.3 Marital Status of Female Witnesses

Marital status	Probate (653) %	Others (783) %
Spinsters	23.3	29.0
Wives	45.2	49.8
Widows	31.5	21.2
	100.0	100.0

Source: Female employment sample.

she made the will. This and other anomalies between the two groups hardly make much difference to the analysis of women's work in Chapter 4. This showed that a high proportion of London women were gainfully employed and that the jobs they did mostly fell within a very narrow range of occupations which could be defined as 'women's work'. Whatever the particular numbers culled from the particular sample being analysed, such findings would continue to be valid.

In conclusion, the overall impression gained from this division of the female samples into two groups in that both reflect the same society but that the 'probate' group is rather further along a curve of age, literacy and respectability. It also seems unlikely that these samples do not reflect the society of London women as a whole. The actual percentages may be wrong; a whole sector of down-and-outs may have been missed at the bottom of the society; there may well have been rather more prosperous and 'unemployed' women at the top of society than appear in the tables. However, the general picture of London women presented in this book would seem to be accurate enough and it is, of course, the general picture, the patterns and the trends which interest the social historian and not exact numbers.

Male Witnesses

It is difficult to have the same confidence that the male sample represents a reasonable cross-section of the male population of London. A glance through the deposition books suggest that the profile of male witnesses is distorted by large numbers of men being called to give professional evidence, people such as

TABLE A.4 Distribution of Female Occupations		
Occupation	Probate %	Others %
Domestic service	23.9	26.3
Charring/laundry	7.5	11.5
Nursing/medicine	17.5	8.3
Textile manufacture	5.2	4.4
Needlework	15.8	20.9
Hawking/carrying	5.2	6.9
Shopkeeping	8.6	7.8
Catering/victualling	10.2	7.8
Miscellaneous services	3.4	3.0
Miscellaneous manufacture	1.6	2.0
Hard labour/daywork	1.1	1.1
	100.0	100.0
Total gainfully employed	67.4	72.0
Total unemployed	32.6	28.0
	100.0	100.0

Source: Female employment sample.

clergymen, lawyers, scriveners, apothecaries, surgeons and parish clerks. Such a suspicion is confirmed by counting.

In Table A.5, the occupations of the witnesses in the male employment sample are set out in broad occupational groups and it can be seen at once that the 333 'professionals', who include 201 lawyers, distort the whole picture. A modern American city might have one in nine of its adult male population employed in the law, but hardly early eighteenth-century London.

In any case, it would not be realistic to produce a detailed breakdown of male occupations from such a small sample. This can be done for the women since they engaged in so few occupations. But it is well known from other studies that there were hundreds of different male occupations in early modern London[13] and there is no guarantee that such occupations will be represented in a random fashion in a sample of under 2,000 people. At least ten times as many would seem to be necessary.

TABLE A.5 Occupational Distribution of Male Employment Sample

Occupation	Nos
Army	38
Distribution, transport etc.	218
Building	69
Domestic servants	86
Food, drink & tobacco	137
Victualling houses	125
Leather trades	72
Metalwork	101
Textiles, clothing	204
Wood, furniture	48
Miscellaneous manufacture	34
Merchants, finance etc.	61
Professionals	333
Officials	79
Miscellaneous services	64
Unemployed, living on estate	125
	1794

Numbers could be inflated by using the occupation or status labels recorded by male witnesses in the Latin introductions to their depositions, in addition to the occupations referred to in answer to a specific question about maintenance or employment. But this could be misleading, as can be seen if the labels are compared with the actual occupations as stated in answer to a maintenance question.

No less than 379 people, twenty-one per cent of the whole male employment sample, described themselves as gentlemen, esquires or knights in the status label at the head of their deposition. The breakdown of their actual occupations is shown in Table A.6, but, if they had not answered the maintenance question, the researcher would have no idea what such people did for a living.

Just over a hundred other men in the sample were described in the introduction to their deposition by the formula 'citizen' and the name of a livery company. It is well known that company membership is not a very good guide to occupation by the late seventeenth century and the men in the sample bear this out.

TABLE A.6 Occupations of Gentlemen, Esquires and Knights

Occupation	No.	%
No occupation – 'lives on his estate'	79	20.8
Lawyers	154	40.6
Government office	23	6.1
Army and navy (inc. 11 'other ranks')	40	10.6
Other professionals	14	3.7
Commerce & manufacture	21	5.5
Stewards, book-keepers & clerks	29	7.7
Servants	10	2.6
Others	9	2.4
	379	100.0

Source: Male employment sample.

Only about a third had an occupation which truly reflected the name of their company and in many cases, such as the cloth-workers and merchant-tailors, this was little help in determining the actual nature of their work. Well over half had an occupation which had absolutely nothing to do with the company.

There are problems too with the descriptions in which historians of employment have most confidence, such simple occupational labels as tailor, weaver or carpenter. Just over ten per cent of those so described in the sample were in fact engaged in a totally different occupation; the labels described the trades to which they had been apprenticed or 'bred', but had subsequently abandoned. Many others had a second occupation not mentioned in the introduction to their deposition. And, even when the deponent was exclusively engaged in the occupation by which he styled himself, these occupational labels can be misleading. They very rarely distinguish between master and journeyman or between rich man and poor. They hardly ever give any details about the occupation, which is unfortunate since there is a lot of difference between a Master Cook to the King and a journeyman cook in an East End eating-house, though both may well style themselves 'cook', or between the commander of an East Indiaman and a boy serving on a coaster, though both may describe themselves as 'nauta' or sailor in their depositions.

Such problems suggest that an occupational distribution for

London as a whole based on this data would be a rather dubious proposition. On the other hand, it does seem possible to produce a crude but fairly accurate occupational geography of London, on the assumption that distortions in distribution would be reflected only in the total numbers of individual occupations, while clustering of occupations in particular localities should not be affected. The problem in doing such an exercise lies once again in sample size – less than 2,000 people in the male employment sample, hundreds of different occupations and over 100 parishes in London. The last problem was reduced by dividing London into just seven areas: the West End; the Strand and Fleet Street; Holborn and St Giles; the City; the northern suburbs; the East End; and the area south of the river. The sample size was inflated by adding in the occupations of those men in the larger 'origins' sample who were described by an occupational label, the main female occupations from the women's employment sample and also the occupations of their husbands. The result is a rather artificial sample of both men's and women's occupations with just under 5,000 cases in all.

This exercise suggests that, overall, London was not characterized by a very high degree of occupational concentration. There were thirty-three occupations or occupational groups with forty or more cases in the sample. Only eight of these had over half their numbers in just one of the seven areas. The most concentrated was silk-throwing, an industry dominated by female employment, with over ninety per cent of its work force in the East End. Next in degree of concentration, with sixty-six per cent each, were sailors in the East End and merchants in the City. The other five occupations were male servants and soldiers in the West End, weavers in the northern suburbs, shipwrights in the East End and watermen south of the river. At the other end of the scale, there were twelve occupations which were so widespread that no area had as many as thirty per cent of the total – victuallers, building workers, porters, shoemakers, tailors, joiners, metal-workers, laundrywomen, seamstresses, nurses, clergy and physicians and surgeons.

Despite this wide spread of most occupations, each of the seven areas had its own separate occupational character. This can most easily be illustrated by calculating location quotients, a technique which gets round most of the problems caused by the

TABLE A.7 Location Quotients of Selected Occupations

Occupation	\	\	\	Area	\	\	\	\
	1	2	3	4	5	6	7	No.
ARMY								
Officers	3.6	–	–	–	–	–	–	31
Soldiers	2.4	–	–	–	–	–	–	40
DISTRIBUTION								
Sailors	–	–	–	–	–	3.6	1.7	229
Watermen	–	–	–	–	–	1.5	6.4	64
Shipwrights etc.	–	–	–	–	–	2.8	5.2	50
Coachmen	1.6	–	2.7	–	–	–	–	61
Coachmaking etc.	2.7	–	2.6	–	–	–	1.9	14
Porters	–	–	–	2.1	–	–	–	75
Hawkers*	–	–	1.8	–	–	2.2	–	33
BUILDING								
All workers	–	–	–	–	–	–	–	211
DOMESTIC SERVANTS								
Male servants	2.5	–	–	–	–	–	–	190
Female servants*	1.6	–	–	–	–	–	–	242
Charwomen*	2.0	–	–	–	–	–	–	40
Laundrywomen*	–	–	1.5	–	–	–	–	71
VICTUALLING								
All workers‡	–	1.8	–	–	–	–	–	213
FOOD AND DRINK								
Bakers‡	–	–	–	–	–	1.7	–	63
Butchers	–	–	–	2.5	–	–	–	52
Brewers	–	–	1.6	–	–	1.6	1.5	49
Distillers	–	1.9	–	–	–	2.7	–	30
LEATHER								
Shoemakers	–	–	1.5	–	–	–	–	172
Glovers‡	–	1.8	1.6	–	–	–	1.6	18
Making leather	–	–	–	1.5	–	–	6.4	26
METALWORKING								
Iron & steel	–	–	–	1.9	–	–	–	90
Braziers	–	–	–	2.8	–	–	2.4	12
Wire-drawers	–	–	–	6.4	–	–	–	12
Gold & silversmiths	–	2.4	–	–	2.8	–	–	36
Clock- & watchmakers	–	1.5	–	2.3	–	–	–	33
Locksmiths	1.9	1.9	1.9	–	–	–	–	13
Gun-makers	–	–	–	–	–	3.3	–	26
Sword-cutlers	–	3.1	–	–	1.6	–	–	15

TABLE A.7 *cont.*

Occupation	Area							
	1	2	3	4	5	6	7	*No.*
METALWORKING cont.								
Pewterers	—	1.9	—	1.9	1.9	—	—	20
Needle-makers	—	—	—	5.9	—	—	—	8
TEXTILES								
Dealers‡	—	1.7	—	—	1.9	—	—	133
Salesmen/old clothes‡	—	—	2.8	—	—	1.9	—	37
Weavers	—	—	—	3.4	—	2.1	—	137
Silk-throwers*	—	—	—	—	—	4.8	—	44
Tailors‡	—	1.5	—	—	—	—	—	163
Dressmakers*	2.0	2.1	—	—	—	—	—	55
Seamstresses*	1.5	—	—	—	—	—	—	84
Stocking-makers‡	—	2.1	—	3.8	—	—	—	16
Peruke-makers	2.1	1.5	—	—	—	—	—	56
Hat-makers	—	2.1	—	—	—	—	8.4	18
Clothworkers	—	—	—	—	3.2	—	—	37
Dyers	—	—	—	—	2.3	—	2.0	21
Bodice-makers‡	1.5	—	—	1.9	—	—	—	25
Other clothes etc.	—	1.5	—	1.6	—	—	—	53
WOOD, FURNITURE								
Joiners	—	—	—	—	—	—	—	71
Coopers	—	—	—	1.5	2.2	1.7	—	34
Upholsterers‡	—	2.0	2.2	—	—	—	—	35
Turners	—	—	—	—	1.7	—	—	22
MISC. MANUFACTURE								
Glass-makers	—	—	1.7	—	—	—	4.7	17
Tobacco pipes	—	—	1.7	—	—	3.5	—	8
Comb-makers	—	—	—	—	—	3.3	—	7
Horners	—	1.6	—	—	—	4.2	—	9
Printing	—	—	2.9	2.9	—	—	—	10
MERCHANTS etc.								
Merchants	—	—	—	—	4.1	—	—	106
Finance, broking etc.	—	—	—	—	2.8	—	—	36
PROFESSIONALS								
Lawyers	—	2.5	2.1	—	—	—	—	169
Scriveners & notaries	—	—	—	—	2.2	—	—	136
Physicians & surgeons	—	—	1.6	—	—	—	—	107
Apothecaries	—	—	—	—	1.9	—	—	102
Nurses*	—	—	—	—	—	—	—	107
Clergy	—	1.5	—	—	1.5	—	—	94

Occupation	Area							
	1	2	3	4	5	6	7	No.
OFFICIALS								
Central government	2.6	–	–	–	–	–	–	34
UNEMPLOYED								
On his/her estate‡	2.0	–	–	–	–	–	–	123

Source: Male origins and employment samples, female employment sample (including occupations of husbands). Total sample size was 4,730 cases; not all occupations are included in the above listing.

Method: The percentage distribution of occupations and occupational groupings was calculated for each of the seven areas and these percentages were divided by the percentage distribution of that occupation in the whole sample. The results are known as location quotients and any quotient of 1.5 or more was considered to demonstrate significant occupational clustering. In those lines with no figure, there was no quotient of 1.5, indicating not much clustering by area.

* An occupation in which women predominate or have a monopoly.

‡ An occupation with fair numbers of women.

Key to areas:
1 WEST END (875 cases): St Anne, St James and St Margaret Westminster, St Martin in the Fields.
2 STRAND & FLEET STREET (595): St Paul Covent Garden, St Clement Danes, St Mary le Strand, St Dunstan in the West, St Bride, Temple, Bridewell, Whitefriars, Savoy Precincts.
3 HOLBORN & ST GILES (642): St Andrew Holborn, St Giles in the Fields.
4 NORTH (620): St Sepulcre, Christ Church, St Anne and St Botolph Aldersgate, St James Clerkenwell, St Giles Cripplegate, St Leonard Shoreditch, St Botolph Bishopsgate.
5 CITY (763): All parishes within the walls except Christ Church and St Anne Aldersgate.
6 EAST END (890): St Botolph Aldgate, St Catherine by the Tower, Holy Trinity Minories, Tower Liberty, Spitalfields, Stepney, Whitechapel, Wapping, Shadwell, Limehouse.
7 SOUTH OF RIVER (345): Deptford, Rotherhithe, Bermondsey, Southwark, Newington Butts, Lambeth.

non-random appearance of many occupations and the uneven numbers of cases in the seven areas. The percentage distribution of sixty-five occupations or occupational groups was calculated for each area and these percentages were divided by the percentage distribution of that occupation in the whole sample. Any result of 1.5 or more was considered to demonstrate significant occupational clustering. This figure was chosen because any lower quotient produced too many significant clusters and spoiled the general pattern that emerged, a pattern which in most cases makes intuitive sense.

The location quotients are set out in Table A.7 with the definitions of the seven areas at the end of the table. By running one's eye down the columns 1 to 7, it is possible to discern the occupations in each area which show the greatest degree of clustering. Thus Area 1, the West End, had more than its fair share of soldiers, coachmen, coachmakers, male and female servants, charwomen, locksmiths, dressmakers, seamstresses, peruke-makers, bodice-makers, government officials and gentlemen and ladies of leisure living on their own estates. Such results will surprise no one familiar with early eighteenth-century London and indeed the location quotients for all seven areas reflect very well the expectations provided by general reading. Most historians of the early modern period prefer their quantitative analysis not to be counter-intuitive, so it is encouraging that the analysis here should confirm preconceptions and these location quotients have in fact proved very useful as an input to the description of the city in Chapter 1.

Notes

The notes normally refer to the surname of the author, or the first word or words of the titles of anonymous works, and the date of publication. For full details of references, see the Bibliography, p. 303.

1 The Metropolis

1. *Foreigners* (1729), p. 2; Chamberlayne (1707), p. 347; Hatton (1708), p. i.
2. Peking, Edo (Tokyo) and Constantinople were larger. For the population of European cities, see De Vries (1981).
3. See, amongst others, the books cited in note 1 above, Maitland (1739), Parish Clerks (1732) and Strype (1720).
4. References to Pepys's diary are to the edition by Latham & Matthews (1970–83).
5. For studies of Hogarth with indications of the location of his paintings and engravings, see Paulson (1971) and Bindman (1981).
6. See, in particular, Ward (1699) & Ward (1927).
7. Brown (1700).
8. Gay (1716); Swift (1958) i, 84.
9. Gay (1716), pp. 31, 57, 70.
10. Mitchell & Deane (1962), pp. 251, 254–5. On the Gin Age in general, see George (1965), pp. 27–42; Davison (1992).
11. The Swedish visitor Pehr Kalm, who was in London in 1748 (Kalm [1892]), was particularly impressed by the lushness and height of the grass in the meadows and fields around London and has much to say about the carriage of manure from the city; Hatton (1708), p. i.
12. *Foreigners* (1729), pp. 8–10; the description of the growth of London which follows rests mainly on Summerson (1962); Defoe (1962) i, 314–21; Brett-James (1935) and a comparison of the maps in this work with those in Hatton (1708) and John Roque's map of 1747 as reproduced in Guildhall (1981).
13. Although Defoe, amongst others, was prepared to cross the Isle of Dogs and include Blackwall within the metropolis. Defoe (1962) i, 314.
14. For two different experiences of the view or lack of it, see Uffenbach (1934), p. 32 and Kalm (1892), p. 26.
15. Quoted by Summerson (1962), p. 41.
16. *Foreigners* (1729), pp. 26, 122.
17. Uffenbach (1934), p. 56; Defoe (1962) i, 315.
18. This description of housing depends mainly on Summerson (1962). See also Power (1986).
19. Strype (1720) ii, 63.
20. On the rebuilding, see Reddaway (1940) and Bell (1923).
21. Strype (1720) ii, 28, 29 (New Rents & Ewers Street).
22. On East London housing, see Power (1972) and for more on the housing of the poor, see below pp. 165–71.
23. Macky (1722), p. 167.
24. This general survey of the geography of occupations in London rests on a very wide range of incidental information and on the analysis of location quotients (see Appendix, pp. 274–6). The metropolitan economy is described at much greater length with many references in Earle (1989a), pp. 17–81.
25. For useful discussions of the population of London, see Sutherland (1972); Wrigley (1967); Finlay & Shearer (1986). For a very valuable

recent survey of the field, see Harding (1990). Wrigley's estimates are normally accepted as good enough for most general purposes – 400,000 in 1650; 575,000 in 1700; 675,000 in 1750 – though it is possible that the 1650 figure is rather too low.

26. See de Vries (1981) and also Wrigley (1985), who has an interesting analysis of the different experience of English and continental towns during this period. English provincial towns taken together were growing faster than London.

27. On the decline of vagrancy, see Beier (1985), pp. 171–5.

28. For a good study of the administration of poor relief within the City of London, see S. Macfarlane (1986). Not much work has been done on the big parishes outside the City where the problem of poverty was greater and the administrative difficulties of dealing with it very considerable.

29. For some examples, see *Account* (1725).

30. Price indices are not very satisfactory for this period and historians have to rely mainly on Phelps-Brown & Hopkins (1956).

31. I know of no study of London rents during this period and this passage is pure speculation.

32. On wages, see Phelps-Brown & Hopkins (1956); Gilboy (1934); Tucker (1936).

33. On infant and child mortality in London, see Finlay (1981a), ch. 5; Landers (1987). Infant mortality rates were to fall quite spectacularly in the second half of the eighteenth century. See Schwarz (1992), ch. 5. For some indications of adult mortality, see Earle (1989a), pp. 306–10.

2 Upbringing and Origins

1. Gough (1981), p. 196; translation on p. 327.

2. King in Thirsk & Cooper (1972), p. 773; *ON*, 13 Jan 1752 (Beacham).

3. On infant and child mortality rates, see, for the first half of the seventeenth century, Finlay (1981a), pp. 16, 102. Rates did not improve in our period, as is shown by Landers (1987), pp. 65–6. Estimates of the proportion of London-born in the adult population are derived from the 'origins' sample analysed for this book; see Tables 2.4 and 2.5, pp. 47, 48.

4. *ON*, 13 Jan 1742 (Joseph Laycock); 11 Aug 1736 (John Kelsey).

5. Quoted by Faller (1987), p. 59; Defoe (1715), p. 78.

6. Campbell (1747), pp. 4, 15; Wadsworth (1712), p. 58.

7. On reading and teaching generally, see Neuburg (1971); Spufford (1981), ch. 2; for a good general survey of education, see O'Day (1982).

8. Kennett (1706), p. 15; the standard book on charity schools is Jones (1938) but this has recently been severely criticized by Rose (1991). The most famous contemporary critic of the charity schools was Mandeville (1723).

9. Quoted by Jones (1938), p. 86; cf. Firmin (1678), p. 5 and Watts (1728), p. 15.

10. For details of these establishments, see *Account* (1713); *Account* (1725); *Account* (1732).

11. Brokesby (1701), p. 3; Collyer (1761), pp. 20–1; on the new schools, see Hans (1951).

12. On girls' education, see Gardiner (1929) and O'Day (1982), ch. 10. Numbers of schools were probably rising in the later seventeenth century and certainly after 1700 when the growth of charity schools considerably increased the provision of a minimum education for poor girls. The low quality of education received by even upper- and middle-class girls was subject to some criticism, usually on the grounds that ignorant women made poor companions for their husbands. Very little was done to improve the situation. See, for example, Astell (1697) and Defoe (1697), pp. 282–304.

13. Gardiner (1929), p. 238; Jones (1938), p. 77; Fielding (1748), p. 1; Simon (1968), p. 35. On needlework training, see Kendrick (1967), pp. 118–19, 159.

14. PROB 24/56 f. 234; Eee 10 f. 151; PROB 24/44 f. 426; DLC 250 f. 498; PROB 24/40 f. 336; 24/54 f. 333v; 24/52 f. 149.

15. The full title of this publication is *The Ordinary of Newgate, his Account of the Behaviour, Confession, and Dying Words, of the Malefactors, who were executed at Tyburn* [and the date]. They exist in many collections; see Linebaugh (1977). The ones used in this study are from the Guildhall Library (SL 43/1) and the British Library (1852. d.4 & PP 1349 a).

16. Thompson (1975), p. 194; cf. Faller (1987), p. 54; Beattie (1986), p. 251.

17. For examples of hanged Etonians, see *ON*, 19 Dec 1716 (Hudson) and 23 Feb 1719 (Edward Bird, who went to Westminster as well). For two more Old Westminsters, see 8 March 1731 (Wych) and 13 Jan 1742 (Ramsay).

18. *ON*, 16 June 1731; cf. 19 July 1738 (Fellows) and 11 Feb 1751 (Edward Smith).

19. *ON*, 31 July 1741; cf. 6 Aug 1740 (John Clark).

20. *ON*, 5 July 1721 (Perkins & Spencer); cf. 4 Feb 1736 (Bulker).

21. *ON*, 5 Oct 1744 (Wright); 18 Nov 1743 (Homan); 29 Jan 1720 (Sheppard).

22. *ON*, 17 June 1751 (Talbot); 13 Jan 1742 (Dean).

23. *ON*, 8 March 1731 (Andrews); 26 July 1731 (Davis).

24. *ON*, 25 March 1751 (Atkins); 17 June 1751 (Peacock); 1 June 1752 (Brown); 27 April 1752 (Basset).

25. *ON*, 23 Oct 1751 (Ireland); 13 April 1743 (Kelley); 7 Nov 1744 (Lee); 12 June 1741 (Johnson); for two examples of Charity School boys, see 6 Aug 1740 (Foster) and 22 Nov 1742 (Hinton).

26. *ON*, 13 Jan 1752 (Dickenson).

27. *ON*, 18 March 1741 (Cassody).

28. *ON*, 16 Sep 1741 (Cook).

29. Collyer (1761), p. 22 and see pp. 22–5 for his rather feeble proposals to

fill up the time. One reason for teaching Latin was to give children something difficult to do during the last years of their schooling.

30. *ON*, 14 March 1739 (Marsland); 18 March 1741 (Brabant).

31. *ON*, 8 March 1731 (Maynee); 11 Aug 1736 (Kelsey); 26 May 1738 (Toon); 3 Aug 1739 (Bridge).

32. *ON*, 31 July 1741 (Lineham); 31 Dec 1750 (Connor).

33. *ON*, 25 Aug 1743 (Hazzard); 18 May 1743 (Wilmhurst).

34. Cressy (1980), pp. 54–5; Schofield (1972–3), pp. 440–1; Spufford (1981), pp. 19–44. See also my suspicions that many women learned to sign their names, and that only, when they were adults: Earle (1989b), p. 336.

35. Spufford (1981), p. 22; PROB 24/50 f. 486 (Dybel) and see PRO PROB 24/53 fos 315–19 for witnesses who answered a question about their ability to read.

36. Cressy (1980), p. 177; Schofield (1972–3), p. 445.

37. For some foreign comparisons, see Houston (1988), ch. 7.

38. For more details, see below p. 120.

39. Defoe (1724), p. 86.

40. Chamberlayne (1707), p. 352.

41. Graunt (1676), pp. 57, 63; Wrigley (1987), p. 135; for a similar analysis of Dutch cities, see de Vries (1974), pp. 109–118.

42. Finlay (1981a), pp. 140–2; see also Elliott (1978), pp. 216–20. Such a change is indicated by an analysis of burial registers, the reasonable assumption being that the sex ratio of those who died in the city will reflect the sex ratio of the living.

43. It should also be noted that households in the earlier period would have contained a larger number of, mainly male, apprentices whose numbers were to decline both relative to the city population and absolutely in the course of the seventeenth and eighteenth centuries. See below pp. 60–3.

44. Earle (1989a), p. 219.

45. Monter (1980), pp. 189, 200; Fairchilds (1984), pp. 15–16; Ringrose (1983), pp. 56–7.

46. Hélin (1963), pp. 113–14.

47. Roche (1987), p. 31.

48. Sharlin (1978), pp. 126–38; cf. Mols (1955) ii, 391. For criticism of Sharlin's article, see Finlay (1981b).

49. Ringrose (1983), pp. 34–63; Roche (1987), pp. 18–31, quotation from p. 18.

50. Ringrose (1983), p. 53 (and see fn. 22 for references to similar patterns in other cities); Roche (1987), p. 27; Fairchilds (1984), pp. 61–6.

51. These generalizations are based mainly on the cases collected for the 'origins' samples (see p. 264) which provide information on both place of birth and occupation. It is difficult to see any real bias towards the London-born in this material.

52. Garrioch (1986), p. 7 and Roche (1987), pp. 29–30 both note the colonization of areas or particular streets of Paris by immigrant groups from different *pays* and also show that there was a traditional geography of work in Paris, e.g. water-carriers from the Auvergne, chimney-sweeps from

Savoy, masons from Normandy and Limousin etc. There seems to have been little or none of this sort of differentiation in London.

53. On the chapbooks, see Spufford (1981), pp. 56, 182–3. Scots, Irish and German/Dutch accents were often ridiculed in the reports of Old Bailey trials in *OBSP*. On clubs, see Clark (1987).

54. Eee 9 f. 7; DLC 248 f. 13.

55. *ON*, 24 Nov 1740, William Duell (Griffin).

56. Blum & Houdaille (1986), p. 264 (Graphique 2); Ringrose (1983), p. 35.

57. One other possibility is that the flow of migrants remained constant in all age-groups, which is unlikely and contrary to what evidence we have, though it is easy to find individual examples of elderly immigrants.

58. For a summary of a number of studies on this subject, see Wareing (1980). Some studies use different but similar sources, e.g. Glass (1969), p. 387, which is based on the records of freemen, and Kitch (1986), which uses the records of the tax on apprenticeship premiums which was introduced in 1711. For other useful studies of rural-urban migration in England, see Patten (1973), Clark (1979) and Souden (1984).

59. Although many hypotheses have been put forward, the one most in favour relates high or low migration from an area (normally a county) to high or low 'birth surplus' in that area, a birth surplus being an excess of baptisms over burials in parish registers. See, for example, Wrigley (1987), pp. 136–7; Elliott (1978), pp. 173–85; Kitch (1986), pp. 228, 244.

60. See above p. 42. The only study of female migration to London that I know is Elliott (1978), pp. 166–7, where she analyses the migration experience of 604 migrant single women whose place of birth is stated in their marriage allegations, 1597–1619.

61. On this, see below pp. 60–3.

62. Clark (1972), esp. pp. 134–50.

63. On the vagrants, see Beier (1985) and see pp. 171–5 for the improvements in our period.

64. *ON*, 23 Oct 1751; cf. *ON*, 23 Dec 1715 (Ann Body); 5 Oct 1737 (Totterdale) and many others.

65. *ON*, 13 Jan 1752 (Dickenson); 31 Dec 1750 (Beckenfield); 18 March 1741 (Young, alias Jenny Diver). Cf. Little (1973), pp. 15–28; Denich (1970), p. 140 for modern studies of rural-urban migration showing that rural restraint and boredom and the attractions of urban life and amusements were a major motivation. Beattie (1975), pp. 96–101, has some interesting comments on the comparative freedom of city life for women.

66. Gough (1981), pp. 101, 182–3, 122, 221–2.

67. DLC 249 f. 238; PROB 24/52 f. 1.

68. *ON*, 4 May 1741 (MacManus); Chartres (1977a), pp. 31–2; Crofts (1967), pp. 22–3; Defoe (1725), p. 86; PROB 24/49 f. 410. This journey was particularly slow, most carriers doing about 15 to 20 miles a day.

69. Defoe (1722a), p. 17; DLC 258 fos 88, 162; Gough (1981), pp. 170–1; *ON*, 4 May 1741 (Carr).

70. Gough (1981); Hey (1974), pp. 192–4. There were representatives in

London of 15 out of the 91 families resident in Myddle at the time of the Hearth Tax of 1672. *ON*, 14 March 1738 (Adamson).

71. PRO PROB 18/29. Interrogatory in the case of Palmer v. Frobisher, question 2. The answers to such questions in Church court depositions provide the information analysed in the 'employment' samples: see Appendix, pp. 263–5.

3 Men's Work

1. Mandeville (1723), p. 326.
2. Rappaport (1989), p. 53.
3. For a discussion of the samples, see Appendix, pp. 263–5.
4. *ON*, 20 May 1717.
5. *ON*, 6 Aug 1740 (Clark); 16 June 1731 (Burroughs); 19 July 1738 (Fellows).
6. *ON*, 1 Feb 1717 (Whitehead); 19 Dec 1716 (Dean); WCL F.2020 f. 190 (Poplett).
7. E.g. WCL F.5020 f. 190. On the climbing boys, see Hanway (1785).
8. Eee 11 f. 247; *ON*, 13 Jan 1742 (Newman).
9. *ON*, 28 May 1714 (Roderick Awdry, aged 16); 22 Dec 1714 (John Awdry, aged 26); 11 May 1715 (Samuel Awdry, aged 20).
10. *ON*, 7 April 1742 (Jordan); s.d. (Walden); Defoe (1725), p. 20.
11. *ON*, 5 Oct 1744.
12. GHMS 9065 A/11 f. 332 (Irwin); PROB 24/60 f. 164 (Moor); *ON*, 19 Sep 1712 (Johnson); 11 Feb 1751 (Clements); 18 May 1709 (Dove).
13. Finlay (1981a), p. 67, drawing on work by Elliott; Kitch (1986), p. 226. The 1600 percentage seems impossibly high. In general on the decline of apprenticeship, see Kellett (1957–8), pp. 388–9, Kahl (1956), Glass (1969), p. 385.
14. There were 92 who had been apprenticed and 99 who had not in the sample studied. On the drop-out problem, see Kitch (1986), p. 226, S. R. Smith (1973), pp. 197–8, Ben-Amos (1991).
15. *ON*, 11 Oct 1752 (Lee); GHMS 9065 A/11 f. 332.
16. A more detailed discussion of apprenticeship, especially in 'middle-class' occupations, can be found in Earle (1989a), ch. 3.
17. *ON*, 21 April 1714 (Gearish).
18. Examples of premiums can be found in Campbell (1747), Collyer (1761) and in PRO IR 1 (the records of the tax on apprenticeship premiums). For some seventeenth-century examples, see Earle (1989a), p. 94.
19. *ON*, 26 July 1731 (Davis).
20. Excerpts from a typical indenture. See Earle (1989a), p. 93; *ON*, 3 March 1737 (Sutton).
21. *ON*, 8 Feb 1721 (Bond).
22. Rappaport (1989), pp. 334–8.
23. For a more detailed discussion of these changes, see Earle (1989a),

pp. 18–34 and in general on the eighteenth-century labour force, see George (1965), especially ch. 4, and Schwarz (1992), ch. 1.

24. *ON*, 19 Sep 1716.
25. Quoted by Federer (1980), p. 10.
26. PROB 24/58 f. 219.
27. See in general on this subject, Dobson (1980).
28. GHMS 9065 A/9, 25 May 1700; PROB 24/53 f. 113.
29. DLC 252 f. 413; DLC 247 f. 171.
30. PROB 24/47 f. 332; Eee 10 f. 232; PROB 24/45 f. 72.
31. On investment by London businessmen, see Earle (1989a), ch. 5.
32. PROB 24/40 f. 70; PROB 24/41 f. 424v; PROB 24/52 f. 231.
33. *ON*, 13 April 1743; DLC 258 f. 343.
34. *ON*, 13 July 1752 (Gibbons); *ON*, 13 Jan 1742 (Buquois); DLC 252 f. 215v (Duncan).
35. *ON*, 14 March 1738 (Johnson).
36. For details, see Campbell (1747); Collyer (1761).
37. On these and many other perquisites and their decline in the course of the eighteenth century, see Linebaugh (1991).
38. *Review*, 14 April 1705, quoted by George (1965), p. 160.
39. Quoted by George (1965), p. 181; Campbell (1747), p. 193.
40. *ON*, 10 March 1714 (Gibson).
41. Gregory King thought that the total seafaring population in the 1690s was 50,000 men; Maitland estimated that London's merchant fleet of 1732 employed just under 22,000 sailors. Ehrman (1953), pp. 110–11; Maitland (1739), pp. 618–21.
42. PROB 24/49 f. 172 (Aubin); HCA 13/82 f. 182 (Gibson).
43. *ON*, 11 Feb 1751 (Sullivan).
44. Based on 372 cases with this information in HCA 13/80–85.
45. HCA 13/80 nf, 12 May 1690.
46. PROB 24/37 f. 411; PROB 24/46 f. 328.
47. There are many examples of this in *ON*, e.g. 21 April 1714 (Gearish); 19 Dec 1716 (Rogers); 4 Feb 1736 (Bulker) and many others.
48. On the manning of the Royal Navy, see, amongst many other works, Baugh (1965), ch. 4; Rodger (1986), ch. 5; Ehrman (1953), ch. 4. Landsmen were exempt from the press, but they were attracted by naval pay even though this did not rise much, if at all, in wartime.
49. For seamen's pay and conditions, see Davis (1962), ch. 7 and Rediker (1987), ch. 3 & Appendix C.
50. HCA 13/83 f. 151. Parents seem to have been a party to the signing on of boys. See HCA 13/82 f. 403 where William Vineard, aged 14, was hired for a voyage to Ireland in the presence of his mother.
51. HCA 30/654, account book of *Content*; HCA 13/80 nf, 9 July 1692, evidence of Henry King of Yarmouth re the Newcastle trade; HCA 30/664, account book of *Cadiz Merchant*.
52. HCA 13/83 f. 385 (Seagerts); *ON*, 19 July 1738 (George).
53. Some writers suggest that discipline even on merchant ships was very strict. See for example Rediker (1987), ch. 5. But the evidence used is

normally of violence by individual officers rather than of consistently harsh discipline and such violence could easily be found ashore, in the relations between masters and apprentices for instance. Writers on the Royal Navy do not find a particularly oppressive discipline. See Rodger (1986), ch. 6; Baugh (1965), pp. 225–6.

54. As examples, see HCA 13/83 f. 315, Stephen Crosskeys, pot-maker of Lambeth, wrecked in Mounts Bay; f. 403, William Redford of Wapping who gave evidence on the conditions faced by English hostages of privateers in Calais; HCA 13/80, 10 Sep 1691, James MacDonell, who was trepanned by a corsair of Leghorn who forced him to serve five years as gunner without pay; HCA 13/80, 23 Oct 1690, William Hunt, who had received the King's pardon for buccaneering; PROB 24/60 f. 156, John Morgan of Rotherhithe who was a slave in Tangiers for six years and had also served on Capt. Woodes Rogers' famous privateering voyage round the world.

55. DLC 250 f. 243.

56. HCA 13/80 nf, 13 Oct 1691, evidence of Nicolas Wilkins.

57. E.g. PROB 24/38, evidence of Margaret Gordon.

58. HCA 13/82 f. 193 (Worley); on the ages of seamen, see Rediker (1987), Appendix A.

59. HCA 13/82 f. 487 (Parr).

60. Smollett, *Humphrey Clinker*, quoted in Hecht (1956), p. 14.

61. Hanway (1767) ii, 158.

62. The best guide to the scale of male staffs comes after the end of our period in the returns to the 1777 tax on male servants. See PRO T47/8.

63. DLC 252 f. 457 (Francis). There are many examples of farm labourers who became servants in *ON*, e.g. 22 Dec 1714 (Hoskins), 4 May 1741 (Carr), 22 June 1748 (Thomas).

64. Maitland (1739), pp. 354ff. There was one person keeping a coach for every 42 houses in the City and one for every 15 houses in Westminster.

65. PROB 24/35 f. 292 (Hamilton); DLC 251 f. 223 (Hyatt); PROB 24/55 f. 9 (White).

66. On wages, see Hecht (1956), pp. 143–60. The value of board and lodging would presumably be roughly equivalent to board wages, which were about 7s. a week in 1730 (£18 p.a.). Several of the male servants in the sample were worth over £100.

67. Beresford (1927); DLC 255 f. 162 (Morrice); f. 133 (White); f. 145 (Morris).

68. PROB 24/54 f. 11 (Dale); 24/56 f. 253 (Griffith).

69. *Collection for the Improvement of Husbandry and Trade*, 19 July 1695.

70. For two good introductions to the subject, see Holmes (1982), pp. 115–65; Prest (1987).

71. PROB 24/38 f. 15 (Taylor); PROB 24/59 f. 343 (Spooner); House of Commons, *Sessions Papers* xiii, 442–3.

72. PROB 24/49 f. 39 (Pewsey); Eee 11 f. 45 (Deblois).

73. PROB 24/34 f. 352 (Granger); on the civil service, see Holmes (1982), ch. 8 and Brewer (1989), ch. 3.

74. DLC 251 f. 116 (Shirley).
75. PROB 24/36 f. 204 (Purcell).
76. DLC 250 f. 281 (Oldecop); ibid. f. 486 (Selby).
77. DLC 253 f. 260 (Barrett); PROB 24/53 f. 329 – William Young, brewer's clerk, worth £1,000. Collecting rents and debts on commission could be profitable work, as can be seen from the worth of those dealing in sailors' tickets and of estate stewards. PROB 24/58 f. 239 (Webb).
78. PROB 24/57 f. 150 (Leche); DLC 252 f. 474 (Hayne).
79. DLC 252 f. 474 (Hayne); PROB 24/46 f. 482 (Gostlin); PROB 24/60 f. 47 (Clarke); PROB 24/52 f. 239 (Swaine).
80. *ON*, 4 Feb 1736 (Brace).
81. *Gentleman's Magazine* iii (Feb 1733), p. 88, quoted by Webbs (1903), p. 26.
82. King in PRO T64/302; Maitland (1739), p. 531; in general on the victualling trades in this period, see Clark (1983), chs 8–10 and on the Gin Age, see George (1965), pp. 41–55 and Davison (1992). For a description of London's drinking establishments, see Earle (1989a), pp. 51–6.
83. This is suggested by a register of male inn-servants in the Guildhall Library. GHMS 6658.
84. Vintners are much the commonest masters of apprentices entering the drink trades in PRO IR1/2. DLC 243 f. 4v (Hall); PROB 24/38 f. 447 (Willis).
85. Eee 12 f. 167 (Luddington); *Case* (1729), pp. 8–9.
86. PROB 24/59 f. 235 (Taylor); PROB 24/54 f. 149 (Dobson); *ON*, 9 Oct 1732 (Bumpus); PROB 24/60 f. 352 (Stoakes).
87. PROB 24/42 f. 259 (Higgins).
88. On licensing of the gin trade, see Davison (1992); the quotation is from Clark (1983), p. 239.
89. GHMS 9065 A/11 f. 7 (Dennis); PROB 24/39 f. 404 (Blake); PROB 24/40 f. 95 (Pratt).
90. DLC 258 f. 49 (Denby).
91. Stedman-Jones (1971), esp. chs 3–5.
92. On the porters, see Stern (1960) and for the 1708 articles of agreement of a gang of porters, see CLRO Deeds 30/11.
93. On the coal-heavers, see George (1927).
94. *ON*, 9 Oct 1732 (Griffith).
95. Collyer (1761), p. 221; Eee 12 f. 23 (Bull); *ON*, 7 Nov 1744 (Ellard); PROB 24/53 f. 206 (Gascoyne); PROB 24/43 f. 372 (Havers).
96. About 3,000 ticket-porters, 1,000 fellowship-porters and 1,000 coal-heavers. Stern (1960), pp. 50–1, 85; R. Smith (1961), p. 49.
97. PROB 24/57 f. 285 (Laman); 24/37 f. 443 (Tasker); *ON*, 16 April 1753 (Higgins).
98. CLRO MC6/413A.
99. *ON*, 13 April 1743 (Kelley); PROB 24/54 f. 53 (Peacock).
100. *ON*, 18 March 1741 (Quail, Lipscomb).
101. Hay (1982).
102. Defoe (1719), p. 229.

103. DLC 262 f. 258 (Le Grand); PROB 24/57 f. 147 (Fenwick); PROB 24/52 f. 189 (Peers).
104. PROB 24/48 f. 539 (Jones); PROB 24/55 f. 75 (Jennings).
105. PROB 24/52 f. 148 (Harris); 24/44 f. 65 (Chaplin); DLC 258 f. 385 (Gransdon); DLC 632 f. 197 (Smith). For an analysis of businessmen's inventories showing the tendency to invest more in 'rentier' assets with age, see Earle (1989), pp. 144–5; PROB 24/53 f. 90 (Buckland, who also owned a brewery).
106. DLC 632 f. 181 (Coleman); DLC 252 f. 278 (Ison). Most old women as well as most old men worked until they dropped. See Earle (1989b), pp. 345–6.
107. PROB 24/56 f. 253 (Griffith).
108. PROB 24/36 f. 114 (Brooks); DLC 251 f. 278 (Adson); PROB 24/43 f. 343 (Jaques).
109. GLRO DLC 152 f. 95.
110. PROB 24/34 f. 31 (Podewill); PROB 24/52 f. 183 (Barrington).
111. For an analysis showing similar results from inventories, see Earle (1986).
112. DLC 255 f. 235 (Atkinson); PROB 24/40 f. 325 (London); ibid. f. 395 (Knapp); PROB 24/59 f. 225 (Walcot).
113. For this, see Earle (1989a), especially pp. 32, 36. Too few overseas merchants answered this question for separate analysis, but those who did are included under the heading 'dealers' and most of these were worth over £1,000.
114. PROB 24/48 f. 1 (Jansen); DLC 248 f. 5 (Sill); PROB 24/61 f. 225 (Brent).

4 Women's Work

1. Clark (1919), p. 5. For the 'descent from paradise', see Cahn (1987), who uses the proverbial saying that England was a paradise for women as a starting point, though the proverb was in fact still in use in the early eighteenth century. The 'bon vieux temps' is discussed in Hufton (1983), who notes (p. 126) that it 'has proved remarkably elusive', as new research pushes the good times further back into the past. Similar doubts are expressed in Bennett (1988) and Bennett (1992). The locus classicus of the deterioration of women's lives in the early modern period is Clark (1919). Much of the generalization in this section rests on Clark (1919) and Cahn (1987). Other valuable insights have been obtained from Brown & Goodman (1980), Clawson (1980), Honeyman & Goodman (1991), Hamilton (1978), Howell (1986), Lacey (1985), Prior (1985) and Wiesner (1987).
2. Hamilton (1978), p. 11. This book sets out the feminist (i.e. patriarchal) and marxist (i.e. capitalist) interpretations of women's increasing subordination in the early modern period.
3. Hartmann (1981), p. 372.

4. Quoted in Pinchbeck (1930), p. 233. This section is a development with a larger sample of the argument in Earle (1989b).

5. Alexander (1983), p. 12.

6. The difference is less strong for married women, as might be expected, since their family commitments were likely to be an important factor.

7. *Census, 1851* (P.P. 1852–3, lxxxviii, pt I), Table xxviii; 85 per cent were in these three groups in 1851 compared to 66 per cent in our sample. The biggest change is in domestic service, which had risen from 25 to 40 per cent of the total, but this may simply reflect the fact that this was an occupation which was normally recorded in 1851, while many other women's jobs were not. On the shortcomings of the Census, see Alexander (1983) and Higgs (1987). For a recent comparison between female employment as revealed by the 1851 Census and various estimates for earlier periods, see Schwarz (1992), pp. 14–22.

8. On this industry, see Wadsworth & Mann (1931), pp. 106–7, Rothstein (1961), pp. 131–2 and Stern (1956). Contemporaries claimed huge numbers working in the industry, which was organized in small workshops, each employing some 10 or 12 women and girls whose work was subdivided into different skills, such as reelers who controlled the speed of the operation, winders and doublers. The East End industry began to decline from the late seventeenth century as masters sought out even cheaper labour in the countryside, a process accelerated from the 1720s by the development of water-driven throwing-mills in Cheshire and Derbyshire.

9. In both industries the important technical change was the development of a labour-saving machine – the Dutch loom or ribbon-mill and knitting-frame. Few women were employed on the ribbon mills or on the broadlooms producing fabrics in Spitalfields, while most women in the machine-knitting industry were engaged in trimming and sewing up rather than working on the frames.

10. See above, pp. 80–1. DLC 252 f. 130.

11. The occupations in this section come from a variety of cases in *OBSP* and *ON*. The quotations are from *OBSP*, Dec 1742/79; *ON*, 21 Dec 1739; *OBSP*, Sep 1739/434.

12. This information on apprenticeship comes from PRO IR 1/4–5 covering the years 1715–17. No tax was payable if no premium was charged, nor if the premium was paid by a parish or charity, so most of the really poor apprentices were probably left out. The registers have numerous other problems for the analyst. Many entries do not state the whereabouts of the master or mistress, so one cannot be certain if an entry relates to London. Many masters and mistresses are simply listed as widow, gentleman, etc. without any occupation and many more as members of a City livery company which by this date is little help in identifying occupations (see Earle [1989a], p. 252). A further difficulty arises from the fact that when a girl is listed as apprentice to a man in a particular trade, one can never be certain that she did not in fact receive her training from the man's wife in another trade. Such ambiguities arise from the legal situation in which most married women were technically unable to own property or make

contracts and can be found in other sources, e.g. criminal indictments, where property stolen from shops is listed as belonging to a man though the actual prosecution is conducted by his wife who ran the shop quite independently of him. For more information on the needle trades, see below pp. 139–43 and for premiums paid by male apprentices, see above pp. 63–4.

13. See above, pp. 24–5.
14. Firmin (1678), p. 18.
15. Wages are difficult to get much information on, but see Earle (1989b), pp. 342–3 for some data.
16. Clark (1919), p. 235.
17. Ecc 9 fos 295, 523.
18. DLC 251 fo. 262; Ecc 8 fo. 697; DLC 250 fo. 217.
19. *ON*, 29 June 1737 (Mudd).
20. Defoe (1725), p. 4; Defoe (1724), p. 139; Hanway (1767) ii, 158. The best general though biased information on servants is in Defoe (1724 and 1725); see also Hecht (1956), Earle (1989a), pp. 219–29 and, for a good discussion of housework, Davidson (1983).For male servants in London, see above pp. 82–6.
21. *London Chronicle* (1758) iii, 327c; Davidson (1983), pp. 179–81; McBride (1976), p. 45.
22. Angeloni (1756) ii, 38; cf. Miège (1691), p. 267 and for many other such comments, see Hecht (1956).
23. On food, see Earle (1989a), pp. 279–80; for examples of inventories showing maids' bedrooms, see CLRO Orphans 510, 993, 1378, 1712, 1837, 1849, 2297. Maids tended to have much better furnishings and softer beds than menservants.
24. Defoe (1725), pp. 18–19; DLC 250 fo. 453; for specialization and definition of tasks in Pepys's household, see Earle (1989a), pp. 220–9.
25. DLC 250 fo. 197.
26. E.g. Anne More who left her home on Sunday night to be ready for the Monday wash-day at her employers. In Pepys's household, wash-day began at two in the morning. GLRO MJ/SP/April 1705/48; Earle (1989a), p. 222.
27. E.g. *OBSP*, Dec 1744/22; April 1740/230 (£30 or £40 worth of linen in a washerwoman's room); DLC 247 fo. 357, where Hannah Elliott reports a client saying, 'God damn you, you may stop my linnen then, for I have not money to give you.' In addition to non-specific washer-women, there were a number of specialist skilled trades in the clothes cleaning business, such as clear-starching and the cleaning of silks and gloves, which bore similar financial responsibilities. On Victorian laundresses, see Malcomsen (1981).
28. De Saussure (1902), p. 157; for a good description of the arduous nature of household tasks, see Davidson (1983).
29. *Servants* (1725), pp. 14–15.
30. Elliott (1978), p. 225.
31. DLC 244 fo. 426; DLC 248 fo. 214; for 'laundresses to the Temple', see PROB 24/38 fo. 928; /53 fo. 165; /55 fos 15, 27. Here, too, there was an

opportunity for female enterprise; Rachel Crossley had 'the care of seven chambers' in the Temple and subcontracted the work to other women. *OBSP*, Oct 1744/450.

32. Based on settlement examinations in WCL F.5013–5020. Although some servants were 'hired covenant servants by the year', this was unusual and the normal arrangement was for a month's notice by either side. Searching for jobs was made relatively easy by agencies, which began in the late seventeenth century, and by a well-organized information network amongst women such as chandlers, street hawkers and other servants who would know where a place was available.

33. PROB 24/42 f. 378; DLC 255 f. 122. Most books on the history of medicine tend to concentrate on the official and mainly male world of professional medicine, though this bias has been mitigated in recent years. For two valuable books which portray the world of suffering and healing in a more realistic way, see L. Beier (1987) and Porter & Porter (1988).

34. For quack medicine, see Porter (1989). See also Holmes (1982), p. 185 for comments on the decline of stoicism.

35. For lists of surgeons and apothecaries, see BL 777 l. 1. For physicians, see Bloom & James (1935). For women applying for licences, see Wyman (1984), pp. 36–41.

36. For a number of examples, see Porter (1989) and see also Crawford (1984).

37. DLC 247 fo. 332. Cf. Mrs Jane Pernell of Southwark whose first husband was a doctor of physick and whose second was a surgeon and who successfully applied for a licence to practise both 'physicke and chyrurgery' in 1685. Wyman (1984), p. 36.

38. PROB 24/48 fo. 239 (the apothecary Elizabeth Smithson); for the fortunes of male apothecaries, see Earle (1989a), p. 72; DLC 252 n.f. (Hester Reed); PROB 24/42 fo. 378; DLC 251 fo. 144; for Radcliffe's earnings, see Pittis (1715), p. 13.

39. Quoted in Poynter (1961), p. 9.

40. Schofield (1986), pp. 230–3; Eccles (1982), p. 125 gives a figure for England as a whole of 25 per 1,000, even higher than the London figures. See also Cellier (1745), p. 136. In general on midwifery, see Aveling (1872) and Eccles (1982).

41. Roberts (1975), p. xxviii; Eccles (1982), p. 121.

42. Willughby (1863), p. 73; GHMS 9065A/11 fo. 304 (Mary Browne; for her mother, Sarah Goble, see fo. 302); Bloom & James (1935), p. 11; also on the licensing process, see Forbes (1964).

43. E.g. Seymer (1954), ch. 4.

44. E.g. *OBSP*, Jan 1743/97; April 1743/230.

45. Fildes (1988a); Fildes (1988b), ch. 6; see also Gillian Clark (1987). See also Pollock (1983), pp. 212–18 for some interesting comments on wet-nursing drawn from her study of diaries.

46. DLC 253 fo. 383; DLC 252 fo. 410. There are many other examples. Country women might also come into London to be a live-in wet-nurse, such as Sara Wilkinson, the wife of a Hammersmith fisherman, who 'hath

followed the employment of nursing children either at home or abroad' and had nursed her last two foster-children for periods of 12 and 16 months.

47. On St Katherine Coleman, see S. Macfarlane (1986), p. 160. This was a fairly standard rate around 1700. For an example of private payment, see the petition of Martha Workman who was trying to recover just over £5 due for 27 weeks' wet-nursing in 1696, an annual rate of £9 15s. GLRO MJ/SP/OCT 1696/22. The 1674 inventory of the widow of a cook includes payment owing to a wet-nurse at 3s. a week, or £7 16s. a year. CLRO, Orphans 940.

48. DLC 255 fo. 102.

49. E.g. Seymer (1954), ch. 4; Clark (1919), pp. 243–53. On hospitals, see, amongst many other works, Poynter (1964).

50. E.g. Kunitz (1983), pp. 354–5.

51. Clark (1919), pp. 244–5; Fuller quoted by Seymer (1954), p. 63. For some examples of the pay of private nurses, see PROB 24/55 fo. 27 (10s. a week); 24/60 fo. 81 (8s.).

52. See L. Beier (1987), pp. 202–3 for a description of the nurses who assisted Jane Josselin during her pregnancies.

53. GHMS 9065A/10 fo. 327.

54. Eee 9 f. 569.

55. PROB 24/37 fos 463, 474; 24/44 fo. 351. Recognition and collection of herbs was also part of the training of apothecaries. See Earle (1989a), p. 255.

56. Opening quotation from Campbell (1747), p. 208; Earle (1989a), pp. 21–2 & 343, note 18; Ginsburg (1972), p. 67.

57. Ginsburg (1972), p. 64; details on some needle trades can be found in Campbell (1747) – see under 'mantuamaker', 'milliner', 'staymaker' etc.

58. DLC 255 fo. 242.

59. *OBSP*, May 1745/258; PROB 24/59 fo. 304.

60. *ON*, 13 March 1713.

61. On this, see George (1965), pp. 174–5 and see, in general, 'women, occupations of', in her index. On the early nineteenth century, see Alexander (1983), pp. 30–3. See also Schwarz (1992), ch. 7.

62. Campbell (1747) – see under particular occupations.

63. *OBSP*, Dec 1744/33; Gay (1716), p. 128.

64. Mayhew (1967) i, 457–68.

65. GLRO MJ/SP/Feb 1695/21; DLC 251 fo. 358.

66. *OBSP*, May 1744/262.

67. *Proposals* (1706), p. 9; Orchard & May (1933), pp. 32–3; cf. *CJ* xxv, pp. 45–8, evidence of pawnbrokers to a Commons committee of 1745; *OBSP*, July 1740/322; Sep 1740/423.

68. DLC 247 fo. 261; *OBSP*, Sep 1743/402.

69. Sun 40965 and 43253; the policy registers of the Sun Fire Office are in GHMS 11936. This material was also used in Earle (1989a), ch. 6.

70. My thanks to Dr Keith Fairclough for this information about gunpowder supply. Another example of a woman running what one might expect to be a male business is Mary Scarth, who for 18 years ran the

scavenging business of the parish of St Giles in the Fields. PROB 24/60
fo. 391. (See below, pp. 206–7.)

71. In the minority of policies which give the marital status of the women,
80 per cent were widows, 18 per cent spinsters and only 2 per cent wives.
For valuable studies on the common law status of married women, see
Kenny (1879) and Holdsworth (1903–72) iii, 520–33 and for a brief
summary of the position see Earle (1989a), pp. 158–60. There was a legal
loophole provided by the Custom of London which could convert the wife
of a freeman from the servile status of *feme covert* into a *feme sole merchant*
with the same legal rights as a male trader. However, there are few
references to women using the Custom in this respect in the sources used
for this book.

72. Sun 40545 and 41595. Businesses run by men were often insured for
much more than this.

73. DLC 633 n.f. (18 June 1716); Eee 9 fo. 696.

74. DLC 249 f. 132; Eee 9 f. 395.

75. For some indications of the proportions of pensioners in the population
of City parishes, see S. Macfarlane (1986), pp. 254–7.

76. GHMS 9065A/9 n.f. (20 June 1701); DLC 245 fo. 414.

77. Alimony payments to women were of the same order – see Earle
(1989a), p. 373, note 48.

78. PROB 24/40 fo. 343.

79. DLC 249 fo. 141 (Holt); DLC 258 fo. 175 (Jackson); DLC 252 fo. 330
(Batteaux).

80. DLC 255 fo. 57.

81. DLC fo. 238 (Birkhead); DLC 262 fo. 85 (Bolland); cf. DLC 248
fo. 268; DLC 260 fo. 193; PROB 24/36 fo. 359; 24/37 fo. 350; 24/42 fo. 80;
24/59 fo. 347. Separate estate was normally established by pre-contract
with a husband before marriage. See Kenny (1879), pp. 98–115;
Holdsworth (1903–72) v, 310–14; vi, 644–6; xii, 275–6; Okin (1983).

82. PROB 24/60 fo. 188; DLC 252 fo. 443.

83. DLC 252 n.f. (Overton, 6 June 1711); DLC 257 f. 1 (Jones); PROB 24/
36 fo. 359 (Herbert); PROB 24/42 fo. 597 (Overy).

84. The best sources for such information are post-mortem inventories
which normally list the assets, if any, from which the deceased woman
drew her income. For some examples, see Earle (1989a), pp. 171–4.

85. On the Financial Revolution, see Dickson (1967) and see pp. 249–303
for women as investors. For a general discussion of investment in the late
seventeenth and early eighteenth centuries, see Earle (1989a), ch. 5.

5 Londoners at Home

1. Brown (1760) iii, 55; Baxter (1673), p. 481. There is a huge bibliography
on marriage and the family, but see Stone (1977), A. Macfarlane (1986),
Gillis (1985), Houlbrooke (1984) and Pollock (1983) for some big and
informative books.

2. For an excellent discussion of the legal side of marriage in this period,

see Stone (1990), part I on 'The Making of Marriage', and for case studies of marriage drawn from the records of the Church courts, see Stone (1992). For recent work on licence weddings, see Boulton (1991) and on the Fleet marriages, see Brown (1981).

3. Wrigley and Schofield (paperback ed., 1989), pp. 255–65 & Table 7.28 (p. 260).

4. Thirsk & Cooper (1972), p. 773.

5. Defoe (1722), p. 18; Habakkuk (1950), p. 24.

6. Finlay (1981), p. 137. His study of four London parishes does however confirm the early age at first marriage discussed below.

7. Elliott (1981), pp. 84–6.

8. See Earle (1989a), pp. 181–2 for similar results to those of Elliott.

9. Brodsky (1986); see table of lengths of marriages on p. 136.

10. Based on those members of the sample discussed in Earle (1989a), pp. 394–404, for whom it was possible to calculate the bride's age at marriage.

11. Brodsky (1986); Thirsk & Cooper (1972), p. 773.

12. For the high fertility, see Finlay (1979), pp. 28–30; Thirsk & Cooper (1972), p. 773; Brodsky (1986), p. 136.

13. Wrightson (1982), p. 66; Brodsky (1986), p. 124.

14. Quoted in George (1965), pp. 96–7. Chapter 2 of this book has some excellent material on London housing, mostly relating to the second half of the eighteenth century.

15. Defoe (1722a), p. 9; Eee 9 f. 291; *OBSP*, Dec 1742/31.

16. For cheap housing in Shadwell, see Power (1972); for Southwark, see Boulton (1987), ch. 7.

17. One gets the impression from George (1965), ch. 2 that housing deteriorated seriously after 1750 when there was once again a rapid increase in population.

18. For a table showing continuity of residence, see Earle (1989a), p. 241.

19. The exemption of lodgers was often manifested in answers to the Church courts.

20. Maitland (1739), pp. 354ff. provides information on the number of houses and the amount spent on the poor for all the parishes in London. Many witnesses in the Church courts were asked what contribution they made, but not enough for detailed analysis. GHMS 9065 A/9 nf, 22 Feb 1700 (Miller); PROB 24/43 f. 316 (Lee).

21. For some examples of the rents of aristocratic houses in the West End, see Jones (1991), p. 141; for rents in the City, see Alexander (1989). His analysis is based on the records of the 1694 4/- in the £ tax (5 W & M c.1).

22. PROB 24/34 f. 127 (Bradhurst). Not many deponents were asked what rent they paid, but enough to get a general picture.

23. De Saussure (1902), p. 165; PROB 24/61 f. 489 (Harrison); Swift (1948) i, 34.

24. E.g. Eee 9 f. 612; PROB 24/36 f. 359; PROB 24/40 f. 329. Thomas Kite, a woolcomber, had a variety of lodgings north and south of the river 'and generally paid from 18d to 2/6 a week for his lodging'. Eee 10 f. 73.

25. Ecc 12 f. 117 (Bagshaw); PROB 24/39 f. 151 (Askew); for some evidence on the cost of 'diet', see Earle (1989a), p. 383, fn. 6.

26. George (1965), pp. 97–8 for information on common lodging-houses; DLC f. 389 (Chiswell), f. 393 (Morgan); cf. PROB 24/34 f. 127; 24/42 f. 459; *OBSP*, Feb 1739/182 (Sarah Main).

27. PROB 24/40 f. 343 (Booth); DLC 257 f. 337 (Johnson); cf. DLC 251 f. 233 (Sparkes).

28. DLC 252 f. 402 (Roberts).

29. The best study of the influence of neighbourhood on city life in the early modern period is that by Garrioch (1986) of Paris in the second half of the eighteenth century, especially ch. 1. Much of what he says is just as relevant to London as it is to Paris. See also Boulton (1987), especially ch. 9, for neighbourhood relationships in early seventeenth-century Southwark and Earle (1989a), pp. 240–50.

30. For several examples of this, see below pp. 211–13.

31. For servants spying, see Stone (1990), pp. 14, 29, 211–15 and see Earle (1989a), p. 225 for a discussion of the problem in Pepys's household. See also below p. 234.

32. The duality in male and female reputation was exactly the same in Paris. See Garrioch (1986), pp. 38–9. For a discussion of the double standard, see Thomas (1959).

33. Earle (1989a), p. 201. For an example, see below pp. 214.

34. *OBSP*, Feb 1730, p. 15.

35. GLRO DLC Consistory Court depositions, *passim*. For examples of abuse, see below pp. 217–21.

36. Shoemaker (1991), esp. chs 5 and 8.

37. Shoemaker (1987); for examples of skimmingtons and charivaris, see DLC 246 f. 90, Misson (1698), p. 70. In general, see Thompson (1972).

38. For Paris, see Garrioch (1986), pp. 23–4.

39. Shoemaker (1991), ch. 9 and Shoemaker (1992).

40. DLC 251 f. 180v.

41. Cruso (1697), p. 56.

42. PROB 24/35 fos 253–4; on this aspect of middle-class life, see Earle (1989a), pp. 244–8.

43. DLC 249 f. 206.

44. See above p. 158; Boulton (1987), p. 281; the observation about the numbers of communicants is impressionistic, but there are sufficient responses in depositions to the question about communion to provide the basis of a study of this subject.

45. Hitchcock (1992), p. 152. This article has some very interesting insights into the work of the SPCK. See also Rose (1991) on the charity schools.

Part Two: Voices of Londoners

To save space most of the references for the shorter extracts have been omitted. Almost all of them come from DLC or *OBSP*.

1. DLC 633 f. 374.

2. DLC 248 f. 125.
3. DLC 631 f. 304.
4. DLC 249 f. 56v.
5. WCL F. 5017 f. 125.
6. DLC 631 f. 314.
7. DLC 251 f. 225v.
8. DLC 248 f. 237v.
9. DLC 245 f. 204.
10. DLC 251 f. 181.
11. DLC 250 f. 62.
12. DLC 245 f. 382v.
13. *OBSP*, May 1745/275.
14. *ON*, 5 Oct 1744.
15. PROB 24/59 fos 297v–299.
16. DLC 255 f. 146.
17. DLC 255 f. 138v.
18. PROB 24/51 fos 59v–60.
19. PROB 24/51 f. 11v, 21 June 1711.
20. *ON*, 6 Aug 1740.
21. DLC 251 f. 8.
22. HCA 13/80 nf, 23 Oct 1690.
23. PROB 24/59 f. 311.
24. PROB 24/61 f. 617.
25. DLC 259 fos 479v–480, 6 Sep 1709.
26. *ON*, 1 Feb 1717.
27. DLC 244, f. 368.
28. GHMS 9065A/10 f. 127.
29. DLC 248 f. 71.
30. GHMS 9065A/11 f. 57.
31. DLC 249 f. 126.
32. PROB 24/36 f. 206.
33. DLC 249 f. 151.
34. PROB 24/36 f. 334.
35. DLC 249 f. 280.
36. PROB 24/37 f. 87.
37. DLC 249 f. 312.
38. DLC 250 f. 502.
39. DLC 249 f. 383v.
40. PROB 24/41 f. 295.
41. DLC 250 f. 313.
42. PROB 24/42 f. 492.
43. DLC 250 f. 353.
44. Eee 10 f. 73.
45. DLC 250 f. 447.
46. PROB 24/45 f. 250.
47. DLC 252 f. 69.
48. PROB 24/46 f. 418.

49. DLC 632 f. 99.
50. PROB 24/51 f. 350.
51. DLC 632 f. 445v.
52. PROB 24/52 f. 83.
53. DLC 253 f. 26.
54. PROB 24/56 f. 51.
55. DLC 633 f. 376.
56. PROB 24/56 f. 187.
57. DLC 256 f. 222.
58. PROB 24/56 f. 234.
59. DLC 634 f. 165.
60. PROB 24/57 f. 112.
61. DLC 261 f. 73.
62. DLC 253 f. 228.
63. GHMS 9065A/9 nf, Elizabeth Cheyney, 19 April 1700.
64. PROB 24/57 f. 210.
65. GHMS 9065A/11 f. 337.
66. PROB 24/61 f. 469.
67. Eee 8 f. 135.
68. Eee 9 f. 449.
69. Eee 9 f. 72.
70. Eee 9 f. 509.
71. Eee 11 f. 79.
72. Eee 10 f. 182.
73. Eee 9 f. 523.
74. DLC 246 f. 92.
75. Eee 11 f. 173.
76. DLC 249 f. 194.
77. PROB 24/35 f. 188.
78. DLC 249 f. 356.
79. PROB 24/37 f. 354v.
80. DLC 250 f. 343.
81. PROB 24/40 f. 392.
82. DLC 250 f. 488.
83. PROB 24/42 f. 382.
84. DLC 250 f. 498.
85. PROB 24/42 f. 500.
86. DLC 252 f. 304.
87. PROB 24/42 f. 603.
88. DLC 254 f. 49.
89. PROB 24/43 f. 250.
90. DLC 255 f. 423.
91. PROB 24/43 f. 317.
92. DLC 255 f. 215.
93. PROB 24/46 f. 212.
94. DLC 258 f. 100.
95. PROB 24/54 f. 333.

96. DLC 252 f. 200.
97. PROB 24/47 f. 176.
98. DLC 249 f. 479.
99. DLC 253 f. 150.
100. DLC 245 f. 350.
101. DLC 253 f. 9.
102. DLC 245 fos 80–1.
103. DLC 245 f. 309.
104. DLC 245 f. 305.
105. DLC 248 f. 83.
106. DLC 252 fos 294–6.
107. GLRO MJ/SP/APR 1696.
108. DLC 253 f. 118v.
109. DLC 253 f. 152.
110. *OBSP*, Sep 1738/28.
111. PROB 24/60 fos 82, 84v.
112. PROB 24/60 f. 391v.
113. DLC 251 f. 19v.
114. DLC 255 fos 367, 383.
115. Stackhouse (1722), p. 86.
116. DLC 243 f. 436v.
117. PROB 24/60 f. 81.
118. DLC 245 f. 302.
119. PROB 24/36 f. 49.
120. Fielding (1749), p. 412.
121. DLC 252 f. 328.
122. DLC 246, f. 288. Evidence of Mary Brown.
123. DLC 260 f. 34.
124. GLRO MJ/SP/AUG 1705.
125. DLC 255 f. 375.
126. CLRO MC6/457A.
127. PROB 24/34 f. 225v.
128. DLC 261 f. 97.
129. PRO C107/140.
130. *OBSP*, May 1726.
131. DLC 270 f. 78.
132. DLC 632 f. 291v.
133. DLC 248 f. 411.
134. DLC 247 f. 225v.
135. DLC 247 f. 244.
136. CLRO MC6/552B.
137. DLC 246 f. 295.
138. DLC 255 f. 309.
139. DLC 255 f. 242.
140. DLC 249 f. 141.
141. DLC 255 f. 462.
142. *Foreigners* (1729), p. 132.

143. *OBSP*, Dec 1734/13, evidence of William Tims.
144. *OBSP*, Oct 1722.
145. *OBSP*, Oct 1733/9.
146. *OBSP*, Dec 1734/37.
147. Defoe (1722a), p. 46.
148. *OBSP*, May 1734/4.
149. *ON*, 14 March 1738, Peregrine Audley.
150. GLRO MJ/SBB/677.
151. DLC 251, f. 142.
152. Ryder (1939), pp. 71–2.
153. DLC 249 f. 480.
154. DLC 245 f. 302.
155. *OBSP*, Feb 1744.
156. GLRO MJ/CP/P/42.
157. DLC 254 f. 254, evidence of Susan Collins.
158. Ryder (1939), p. 31.
159. DLC 246 f. 300.
160. DLC 247 f. 89. For much more about Abigail Harris, see Stone
     (1992), pp. 48–67.
161. DLC 251 f. 273.
162. DLC 633 f. 62.
163. DLC 252 f. 362, evidence of Margaret Stebbin.
164. DLC 165 f. 233v.
165. DLC 245 f. 312.
166. DLC 258 f. 371.
167. PROB 24/60 f. 132.
168. DLC 246 f. 296.
169. DLC 260 f. 208v.
170. PROB 24/37 f. 441.
171. DLC 245 f. 287v.
172. DLC 252 f. 274.
173. DLC 251 f. 3.
174. DLC 251 f. 166v.
175. DLC 253 f. 167.
176. DLC 255 f. 80.
177. DLC 633 f. 226.
178. DLC 251 f. 298.
179. DLC 255 f. 138.
180. *Treatise* (1732), pp. 91–2.
181. DLC 252 f. 272v.
182. DLC 245 f. 109.
183. DLC 245 f. 185.
184. DLC 247 f. 48v.
185. DLC 247 fos 190, 192.
186. DLC 252 f. 273.
187. *OBSP*, 28 Feb 1721/2.
188. GLRO WJ/CP/P/3.

189. DLC 247 f. 248.
190. PROB 24/47 f. 72v.
191. PROB 24/54 f. 93.
192. DLC 252 f. 111v.
193. CLRO MC6/49A.
194. CLRO MC6/391.
195. DLC 253 f. 123v.
196. DLC 252 f. 74v.
197. DLC 247 f. 131.
198. PROB 24/52 f. 145v.
199. *OBSP*, Sep 1722.
200. *OBSP*, Sep 1722.
201. *OBSP*, Dec 1725.
202. *OBSP*, April 1738/72.
203. *OBSP*, Sep 1737/21.
204. DLC 252 f. 13v.
205. CLRO MC6/358B.
206. DLC 260 f. 109.
207. *OBSP*, Feb 1735/27. Evidence of Mrs Bressan.
208. DLC 249 f. 58.
209. Ecc 9 f. 499. For various aspects of Heidegger's career, see Rogers (1985).
210. CLRO MC6/474B.
211. *OBSP*, Aug 1725.
212. CLRO MC6/382B.
213. *OBSP*, March 1726.
214. DLC 251 f. 230.
215. DLC 255 f. 272.
216. CLRO MC6/451.
217. *ON*, 13 Jan 1742.
218. *London Journal*, 11 Feb 1720.
219. *OBSP*, April 1726.
220. Quoted by Speaight (1955), p. 84.
221. DLC 631 f. 5.
222. CLRO MC6/415B, evidence of Rowland Fry.
223. DLC 245 f. 301.
224. DLC 246 f. 43.
225. CLRO MC6/534B.
226. Ryder (1939), pp. 192, 191, 62, 334, 50.
227. DLC 252 f. 330v.
228. DLC 252 f. 419.
229. DLC 252 f. 417.
230. CLRO MC6/414.
231. CLRO MC6/508A.
232. DLC 631 f. 125.
233. DLC 632 f. 25v.
234. DLC 632 f. 4.

235. *OBSP*, May 1743/262.
236. *OBSP*, April 1737, trial of Charles Donnahough.
237. DLC 633 f. 67.
238. *OBSP*, Sep 1734/41.
239. DLC 252 f. 402.
240. DLC 251 f. 175, evidence of Sarah Gaines.
241. DLC 245 f. 305v.
242. DLC 252 f. 112v.
243. DLC 632 f. 100.
244. GHMS 205/2–3.

Appendix on Sources

1. The records of the Prerogative Court are in the Public Record Office, the Commissary Court in the Guildhall Library, the Consistory Court in the Greater London Record Ofice and the Court of Arches in Lambeth Palace Library. Most studies of the Church courts relate to the period before the Civil War, though many are still valuable for an understanding of the period after 1660. See Marchaunt (1969); Owen (1970), esp. ch. 6; Houlbrooke (1979); Wunderli (1981); Sharpe (1981); Ingram (1987). For the later period, see Stone (1990), especially pp. 33–44, and for case studies of marriages drawn from the records of the Church courts, see Stone (1992).
2. Law (1831), p. 225; see also on the practice of the courts, Consett (1685) and Owen (1970), pp. 36–8.
3. Although the same interrogatory might be used for the examination of all witnesses, not all the questions were put to all the witnesses nor did all the witnesses answer all the questions put to them. The bias seems to be that female and poorer witnesses were asked and answered personal questions more often than male and richer witnesses.
4. Witnesses from the Prerogative Court were omitted from the 'origins' sample, so the sample consists of all deponents who gave their date of birth in GLRO DLC 236–262, 631–634; GHMS 9065A/8–11 and LPL Eee 1–11. Only witnesses who gave their birth in the Latin introduction to their depositions (using adjectives such as 'natus', 'oriundus' or 'ortus') have been included. Other witnesses, when asked how long they had lived in the same parish, said that they had lived there since birth. These have been excluded, since their presence in the sample would have unrealistically swelled the London-born.
5. Questions on maintenance were sometimes asked outside these dates, but most of them fall within this period. Why this should be is not known, but the pattern is the same for all four courts. The deponents are drawn from GLRO DLC 244–262, 631–634; GHMS 9065A/9–11; LPL Eee 8–11 and PRO PROB 24/34–61.
6. See above pp. 35–7. It is sometimes thought that the literate brides of illiterate grooms might be reluctant to shame their husbands by signing marriage registers (a useful source for literacy studies), but this would not

be relevant in the present study since husbands were not present when
their wives gave evidence.

7. The Smith Index enumerates the number of stated ages ending in 1, 3, 7
& 9 and expresses them as a percentage of forty per cent of the total
recorded ages, so the higher the score the more likely that the ages
reported are accurate. The actual scores were:

Declared Ages	Men	Women
20–29	101.9	94.7
30–39	76.0	75.4
40–49	67.0	53.5
50–59	59.3	37.7

8. Earle (1989b), pp. 331–3.

9. Most studies of social structure are based on tax data, which are biased
both by gender and wealth (i.e. they mainly tell us about male
householders) and rarely cover the whole of the metropolis. See, for
example, Glass (1969); Jones & Judges (1935); Power (1986). Studies of
occupations arc based on stated occupations in tax assessments or parish
registers, but these very rarely give the occupations of women other than
domestic servants. See for example, Beier (1986); Alexander (1989).

10. My thanks are due to Professor James Foreman-Peck who suggested
this approach.

11. See above p. 36.

12. The 'origins' sample for this exercise includes witnesses from the
Prerogative Court (cf. note 4 above).

13. See, for example, Beier (1986); Alexander (1989).

Bibliography

The works listed are those which have been referred to in the Notes, where references are given by the author or the first word of anonymous works and the date of publication. Place of publication is London unless otherwise stated. Where there is a second publication date in parentheses, the second one has been consulted. For abbreviations of journals etc., see p. 278.

Account (1725): *An Account of Several Workhouses*
Account (1732): *An Account of Several Workhouses*
Account (1713): *An Account of the Corporation for the Poor of London*
Alexander (1989): James Alexander, 'The economic and social structure of the City of London, c. 1700', London Ph.D.
Alexander (1983): Sally Alexander, *Women's work in nineteenth-century London: a study of the years 1820–50*
Angeloni (1756): Battista Angeloni, *Letters on the English Nation* (2 vols)
Astell (1697): Mary Astell, *A Serious Proposal to the Ladies for the advancement of their true and greatest interest*
Aveling (1872): J. H. Aveling, *English Midwives: their history and prospects.*
Baugh (1965): Daniel A. Baugh, *British Naval Administration in the Age of Walpole* (Princeton)
Baxter (1673): Richard Baxter, *A Christian Directory*
Beattie (1986): J. M. Beattie, *Crime and the Courts in England, 1660–1800* (Oxford)
Beattie (1975): J. M. Beattie, 'The criminality of women in eighteenth-century England', *JSocH* viii
Beier (1986): A. L. Beier, 'Engine of manufacture: the trades of London' in Beier & Finlay (1986)
Beier (1985): A. L. Beier, *Masterless Men: the vagrancy problem in England, 1560–1640*
Beier & Finlay (1986): A. L. Beier & R. A. P. Finlay, *The Making of the Metropolis: London, 1500–1700*
Beier (1987): Lucinda Beier, *Sufferers and Healers: the experience of illness in seventeenth-century England*
Bell (1923): W. G. Bell, *The Great Fire of London in 1666*

Ben-Amos (1991): I. K. Ben-Amos, 'Failure to become freemen: urban apprentices in early modern England', *SocH* xvi

Bennett (1988): J. M. Bennett, 'History that stands still; women's work in the European past', *Feminist Studies* xiv

Bennett (1992): J. M. Bennett, 'Medieval women, modern women: across the great divide' in David Aers (ed.), *Culture and History, 1350–1600*

Beresford (1927): John Beresford (ed.), *Memoirs of an Eighteenth-century Footman*

Bindman (1981): David Bindman, *Hogarth*

Bloom & James (1935): J. H. Bloom & R. R. James, *Medical Practitioners in the Diocese of London . . . 1529–1725* (Cambridge)

Blum & Houdaille (1986): A. Blum & J. Houdaille, '12,000 Parisiens en 1793; sondage dans les cartes de civisme', *Population* xli

Borsay (1990): Peter Borsay (ed.), *The Eighteenth-century Town: a reader in English urban history, 1688–1820*

Boulton (1991): Jeremy Boulton, 'Itching after Private Marryings? marriage customs in seventeenth-century London', *LJ* xvi

Boulton (1987): Jeremy Boulton, *Neighbourhood and Society: a London suburb in the seventeenth century* (Cambridge)

Brett-James (1935): N. G. Brett-James, *The Growth of Stuart London*

Brewer (1989): John Brewer, *The Sinews of Power: war, money and the English state, 1688–1783*

Brodsky (1986): V. Brodsky, 'Widows in late Elizabethan London: remarriage, economic opportunity and family orientations', in L. Bonfield et al, *The World we have Gained* (Oxford)

Brokesby (1701): Francis Brokesby, *Of Education with respect to Grammar Schools*

Brown (1981): R. L. Brown, 'The rise and fall of the Fleet marriages' in R. B. Outhwaite (ed.), *Marriage and Society*

Brown (1700): Thomas Brown, *Amusements serious and comical, calculated for the meridian of London* reprinted in *Works* (1715) iii, 1–96

Brown (1760): Thomas Brown, *Works*

Brown & Goodman (1980): J. C. Brown & J. Goodman, 'Women and industry in Florence', *JEH* xl

Cahn (1987): Susan Cahn, *Industry of Devotion: the transformation of women's work in England, 1500–1660* (New York)

Campbell (1747): R. Campbell, *The London Tradesman*

Case (1729): *The case between the proprietors of news-papers and the coffee-men of London and Westminster*

Cellier (1745): Elizabeth Cellier, 'A scheme for the foundation of a Royal Hospital . . . ' (1687) in *Harleian Miscellany* vi

Chamberlayne (1707): J. Chamberlayne, *Angliae Notitia* (22nd ed.)

Chartres (1977a): J. A. Chartres, 'The capital's provincial eyes: London's inns in the early eighteenth century', *LJ* iii

Chartres (1977b): J. A. Chartres, 'Road carrying in England in the seventeenth century: myth and reality', *EcHR* 2nd ser. xxx

Clark (1919): Alice Clark, *The Working Life of Women in the Seventeenth Century*

Clark (1987): Gillian Clark, 'A study of nurse children, 1550–1750', *Local Population Studies* xxxix

Clark (1983): Peter Clark, *The English Alehouse: a social history, 1200–1830*

Clark (1972): Peter Clark, 'The migrant in Kentish towns, 1580–1640' in Peter Clark & Paul Slack, *Crisis and Order in English Towns, 1500–1700*

Clark (1987): Peter Clark, 'Migrants in the city: the process of social adaptation in English towns, 1500–1800' in Clark & Souden (1987)

Clark (1979): Peter Clark, 'Migration in England during the late seventeenth and early eighteenth centuries', *P&P* lxxxiii

Clark & Souden (1987): Peter Clark & David Souden, *Migration and Society in Early Modern England*

Clarke (1639): John Clarke, *Paraemiologia Anglo-Latina*

Clawson (1980): M. A. Clawson, 'Early modern fraternalism and the patriarchal family', *Feminist Studies* xvi

Collyer (1761): Joseph Collyer, *The Parent's and Guardian's Directory*

Consett (1685): H. Consett, *The Practice of the Spiritual or Ecclesiastical Courts*

Corfield (1982): P. Corfield, *The Impact of Eighteenth-century Towns*

Crawford (1984): Patricia Crawford, 'Printed advertisements for women medical practitioners in London, 1670–1710', *Bulletin of the Society for the Social History of Medicine* xxxv

Cressy (1980): David Cressy, *Literacy and the Social Order: reading and writing in Tudor and Stuart England* (Cambridge)

Crofts (1967): J. Crofts, *Packhorse, Waggon and Post*

Cruso (1697): Timothy Cruso, *Discourses upon the Rich Man and Lazarus*

Davidson (1983): C. A. Davidson, *A Woman's Work is Never Done: A History of Housework in the British Isles, 1650–1950*

Davis (1962): Ralph Davis, *The Rise of the English Shipping Industry in the 17th and 18th centuries*

Davison (1992): Lee Davison, 'Experiments in the social regulation of industry: gin legislation, 1729–51' in Davison et al (1992)

Davison et al (1992): L. Davison, T. Hitchcock, T. Keirn & R. B. Shoemaker (eds), *Stilling the Grumbling Hive: the responses to social and economic problems in England, 1689–1750* (Stroud)

Defoe (1697): Daniel Defoe, *An Essay upon Projects*

Defoe (1725): Daniel Defoe, *Every-Body's Business is No-Body's Business; or, private abuses, publick grievances*

Defoe (1715): Daniel Defoe, *The Family Instructor*

Defoe (1722): Daniel Defoe, *The Fortunes and Misfortunes of the famous Moll Flanders* (Everyman, 1972)

Defoe (1719): Daniel Defoe, *The Farther Adventures of Robinson Crusoe* (Everyman, 1972)

Defoe (1724): Daniel Defoe, *The Great Law of Subordination Consider'd; or, the insolence and unsufferable behaviour of servants*

Defoe (1722a): Daniel Defoe, *The History and Remarkable Life of the Truly Honourable Col. Jacque* (1970)

Defoe (1962): Daniel Defoe, *A Tour through the Whole Island of Great Britain* (Everyman edition, 2 vols)

De Muralt (1726): B. L. de Muralt, *Letters describing the character and customs of the English and French nations*

Denich (1970): B. S. Denich, 'Migration and network manipulation in Yugoslavia' in R. F. Spencer (ed.), *Migration and Anthropology* (Seattle)

De Saussure (1902): C. de Saussure, *A Foreign View of England in the Reigns of George I and II*

De Vries (1974): J. de Vries, *The Dutch Rural Economy in the Golden Age, 1500–1700* (New Haven)

De Vries (1981): J. de Vries, 'Patterns of urbanization in pre-industrial Europe, 1500–1800' in H. Schmal (ed.), *Patterns of European urbanization since 1500*

Dickson (1967): P. G. M. Dickson, *The Financial Revolution in England*

Dobson (1980): C. R. Dobson, *Masters and Journeymen: a prehistory of industrial relations, 1717–1800*

Earle (1986): P. Earle, 'Age and accumulation in the London business community' in Neil McKendrick & R. B. Outhwaite (eds), *Business Life and Public Policy* (Cambridge)

Earle (1989a): P. Earle, *The Making of the English Middle Class: business, society and family life in London, 1660–1730*

Earle (1989b): P. Earle, 'The female labour market in London in the late seventeenth and early eighteenth centuries', *EcHR* 2nd ser. xlii

Eccles (1982): Audrey Eccles, *Obstetrics and Gynaecology in Tudor and Stuart England*

Ehrman (1953): John Ehrman, *The Navy in the War of William III*

Elliott (1978): V. B. Elliott, 'Mobility and marriage in pre-industrial England', Cambridge Ph.D.

Elliott (1981): V. B. Elliott, 'Single women in the London marriage market: age, status and mobility, 1598–1619' in R. B. Outhwaite (ed.), *Marriage and Society*

Fairchilds (1984): Cissie Fairchilds, *Domestic Enemies: servants and their masters in Old Regime France* (Baltimore)

Faller (1987): Lincoln B. Faller, *Turned to Account: the forms and functions of criminal biography in late seventeenth- and early eighteenth-century England* (Cambridge)

Federer (1980): Andrew Federer, 'Payment, credit and the organization of work in eighteenth-century Westminster', Paper given at the SSRC Conference on Manufacture in Town and Country before the Factory, September 1980

Fielding (1749): Henry Fielding, *The History of Tom Jones* (1966 Penguin ed.)

Fielding (1748): Sarah Fielding: *The Governess, or the Little Female Academy*

Fildes (1988a): Valerie Fildes, 'The English wet-nurse and her role in infant care, 1538–1800', *MedH* xxxii

Fildes (1988b): Valerie Fildes, *Wet Nursing: a history from antiquity to the present* (Oxford)

Finlay (1981b): R. A. P. Finlay, 'Natural decrease in early modern cities', *P&P* 92

Finlay (1979): R.A.P. Finlay, 'Population and fertility in London, 1580–1650', *Journal of Family History* iv

Finlay (1981a): R. A. P. Finlay, *Population and Metropolis: the demography of London, 1580–1650* (Cambridge)

Finlay & Shearer (1986): R. Finlay & B. Shearer, 'Population growth and suburban expansion' in Beier & Finlay (1986)

Firmin (1678): Thomas Firmin, *Some Proposals for the imploying of the poor, especially in and about the City of London*

Forbes (1976): T. R. Forbes, 'By what disease or casualty: the changing face of death in London', *JHistMed* xxxi

Forbes (1964): T. R. Forbes, 'The regulation of English midwives in the sixteenth and seventeenth centuries', *MedH* viii

Foreigners (1729): *A Foreigners Guide to London*

Gardiner (1929): D. Gardiner, *English Girlhood at School* (Oxford)

Garrioch (1986): D. Garrioch, *Neighbourhood and Community in Paris, 1740–1790* (Cambridge)

Gay (1716): John Gay, *Trivia*

George (1927): M. D. George, 'London coalheavers', *Economic History* i

George (1965): M. D. George, *London Life in the Eighteenth Century*

Gerhold (1988): Dorian Gerhold, 'The growth of the London carrying trade, 1681–1838', *EcHR* 2nd ser. xli

Gilboy (1934): E. W. Gilboy, *Wages in Eighteenth-century England* (Cambridge, Mass.)

Gillis (1985): J. R. Gillis, *For Better, for Worse: British marriages, 1600 to the present* (Oxford)

Ginsburg (1972): Madeleine Ginsburg, 'The tailoring and dressmaking trades, 1700–1850', *Costume* vi

Glass (1969): D. V. Glass, 'Socio-economic status and occupations in the City of London at the end of the seventeenth century' in A. E. J. Hollaender & W. Kellaway (eds), *Studies in London History*

Gough (1981): Richard Gough, *The History of Myddle* (ed. D. Hey) (Harmondsworth)

Graunt (1676): John Graunt, *Natural and Political Observations upon the Bills of Mortality* (5th ed.)

Guildhall (1981): Guildhall Library, *The A to Z of Georgian London*

Habakkuk (1950): H. J. Habakkuk, 'Marriage settlements in the eighteenth century', *TRHS* 4th ser. xxxii

Hamilton (1978): Roberta Hamilton, *The Liberation of Women: a study of patriarchy and capitalism*

Hans (1951): N. Hans, *New Trends in Education in the Eighteenth Century*

Hanway (1767): Jonas Hanway, *Letters on the Importance of Preserving the Rising Generation*

Hanway (1785): Jonas Hanway, *A sentimental history of chimney-sweepers in London and Westminster*

Harding (1990): V. Harding, 'The population of London, 1550–1700: a review of the published evidence', *LJ* xv

Hartmann (1981): H. I. Hartmann, 'The family as the locus of gender, class and political struggle: the example of housework', *Signs* vi

Hatton (1708): Edward Hatton, *A New View of London* (2 vols)

Hay (1982): D. Hay, 'War, dearth and theft in the eighteenth century', *P&P* xcv

Hecht (1956): J. J. Hecht, *The Domestic Servant Class in Eighteenth-century England*

Hélin (1963): Etienne Hélin, *La démographie de Liège aux XVIIe et XVIIIe siècles* (Brussels)

Hey (1974): D. Hey, *An English Rural Community: Myddle under the Tudors and Stuarts* (Leicester)

Higgs (1987): E. Higgs, 'Women, occupations and work in the nineteenth-century censuses', *History Workshop* xxiii

Hitchcock (1992): Tim Hitchcock, 'Paupers and preachers: the SPCK and the parochial workhouse movement' in Davison et al

Holdsworth (1903–72): Sir W. Holdsworth, *History of English Law*

Holmes (1982): G. Holmes, *Augustan England: professions, state and society, 1680–1730*

Honeyman & Goodman (1991): K. Honeyman & J. Goodman, 'Women's work, gender conflict, and labour markets in Europe, 1500–1900', *EcHR* 2nd ser. xliv

Houghton (1727–8): John Houghton, *A Collection for the Improvement of Husbandry and Trade* 4 vols (ed. R. Bradley)

Houlbrooke (1979): R. A. Houlbrooke, *Church courts and the people during the English Reformation, 1520–1570* (Oxford)

Houlbrooke (1984): R. A. Houlbrooke, *The English Family, 1450–1700*

Houston (1988): R. A. Houston, *Literacy in early modern Europe: culture and education, 1500–1800*

Howell (1986): Martha C. Howell, *Women, Production and Patriarchy in late medieval cities* (Chicago)

Hufton (1983): Olwen Hufton, 'Women in history: early modern Europe', *P&P* 101

Ingram (1987): M. Ingram, *Church Courts, Sex and Marriage in England, 1570–1640* (Cambridge)

Jones (1991): Clyve Jones, 'The London life of a peer in the reign of Anne: a case study from Lord Ossulston's diary', *LJ* xvi

Jones (1938): M. G. Jones, *The Charity School Movement of the Eighteenth Century* (Cambridge)

Jones & Judges (1935): P. E. Jones & A. V. Judges, 'London population in the late seventeenth century', *EcHR* vi

Kahl (1956): W. F. Kahl, 'Apprenticeship and the freedom of the London Livery Companies, 1690–1750', *GM* vii

Kalm (1892): Pehr Kalm, *Visit to England in his way to America in 1748* (trans. J. Lucas)

Kellett (1957–8): J. R. Kellett, 'The breakdown of Guild and Corporation control over the handicraft and retail trades of London', *EcHR* 2nd ser. x

Kendrick (1967): A. F. Kendrick, *English Needlework* (2nd ed.)

Kennett (1706): White Kennett, *The Charity of Schools for Poor Children*

Kenny (1879): C. S. Kenny, *The History of the Law of England as to the effects of marriage on property and on the wife's legal capacity*

Kitch (1986): M. J. Kitch, 'Capital and Kingdom: migration to later Stuart London' in Beier & Finlay (1986)

Kunitz (1983): S. J. Kunitz, 'Speculations on the European mortality decline', *EcHR* 2nd ser. xxxvi

Lacey (1985): Kay Lacey, 'Women and work in fourteenth- and fifteenth-century London' in L. Charles & L. Duffin, *Women and work in pre-industrial England*

Landers (1987): John Landers, 'Mortality and metropolis: the case of London, 1675–1825', *Population Studies* xli

Law (1831): J. T. Law, *Forms of ecclesiastical law: or, the mode of conducting suits in the Consistory Courts, being a translation of the first part of Oughton's Ordo Judiciorum*

Linebaugh (1991): Peter Linebaugh, *The London Hanged: crime and civil society in the eighteenth century*

Linebaugh (1977): Peter Linebaugh, 'The Ordinary of Newgate and his *Account*' in J. S. Cockburn (ed.), *Crime in England, 1550–1800* (Princeton)

Little (1973): K. Little, *African Women in Towns* (Cambridge)

McBride (1976): T. M. McBride, *The Domestic Revolution: the modernization of household service in England and France, 1820–1920*

Macfarlane (1986): Alan Macfarlane, *Marriage and Love in England: modes of reproduction, 1300–1840* (Oxford)

Macfarlane (1986): S. Macfarlane, 'Social policy and the poor in the later seventeenth century' in Beier & Finlay (1986)

Macky (1722): John Macky, *A Journey through England*

Maitland (1739): W. Maitland, *History and Survey of London*

Malcomsen (1981): P. Malcomsen, 'Laundresses and the laundry trade in Victorian England', *Victorian Studies* xxiv

Mandeville (1723): Bernard de Mandeville, *An Essay on Charity and Charity-Schools*

Marchaunt (1969): R. A. Marchaunt, *The Church under the Law: justice, administration and discipline in the diocese of York, 1560–1640* (Cambridge)

Mayhew (1967): Henry Mayhew, *London Labour and the London Poor*

Miège (1691): Guy Miège, *The New State of England*

Misson (1698): Henri Misson, *Mémoires et observations faites par un voyageur en Angleterre*

Mitchell & Deane (1962): B. R. Mitchell & P. Deane, *Abstract of British Historical Statistics* (Cambridge)

Mols (1955): Roger Mols, *Introduction à la démographie historique des villes d'Europe du XIVe au XVIIIe siècle* (Louvain)

Monter (1980): E. W. Monter, 'Women in Calvinist Geneva (1550–1800)', *Signs* vi

Neuburg (1971): Victor E. Neuburg, *Popular Education in Eighteenth-century England*

O'Day (1982): Rosemary O'Day, *Education and Society, 1500–1800: the social foundations of education in early modern Britain*

Okin (1983): S. M. Okin, 'Patriarchy and married women's property in England: questions on some current views', *Eighteenth-century Studies* xvii

Orchard & May (1933): D. J. Orchard & G. May, *Moneylending in Great Britain*

Owen (1970): D. M. Owen, *The records of the established church in England, excluding parochial records*

Parish Clerks (1732): *New Remarks of London . . . collected by the Company of Parish Clerks*

Parkes (1925): Joan Parkes, *Travel in England in the Seventeenth Century* (Oxford)

Patten (1973): John Patten, *Rural-urban Migration in Pre-industrial England* (Oxford)

Paulson (1971): Ronald Paulson, *Hogarth: his life, art and times*

Pepys: *The Diary of Samuel Pepys* 11 vols (1970–83) (ed. Latham & Matthews)

Phelps-Brown & Hopkins (1956): E. H. Phelps-Brown & S. V. Hopkins, 'Seven centuries of the prices of consumables, compared with builders' wage-rates', *Economica* n.s. xxiii

Pinchbeck (1930): Ivy Pinchbeck, *Women Workers and the Industrial Revolution, 1750–1850*

Pittis (1715): W. Pittis, *Some Memoirs of the late J. Radcliffe*

Pollock (1983): Linda A. Pollock, *Forgotten Children: parent-child relations from 1500 to 1900* (Cambridge)

Porter (1989): Roy Porter, *Health for Sale: Quackery in England, 1650–1850* (Manchester)

Porter & Porter (1988): R. & D. Porter, *In Sickness and in Health: the British experience, 1650–1850*

Power (1972): M. J. Power, 'East London housing in the seventeenth century' in P. Clark & P. Slack, *Crisis and Order in English Towns, 1500–1700*

Power (1986): M. J. Power, 'The social topography of Restoration London' in Beier & Finlay (1986)

Poynter (1964): F. N. L. Poynter, *The Evolution of Hospitals in Britain*

Poynter (1961): F. N. L. Poynter, 'The influence of government legislation on medical practice in Britain' in ibid. (ed.), *The Evolution of Medical Practice in Britain*

Prest (1987): Wilfrid Prest, 'Lawyers' in ibid. (ed.), *The Professions in Early Modern England*

Prior (1985): Mary Prior, 'Women and the urban economy: Oxford, 1500–1800' in ibid. (ed.), *Women in English Society, 1500–1800*

Proposals (1706): *Proposals for Establishing a Charitable Fund in the City of London*

Rappaport (1989): Steve Rappaport, *World within worlds: structures of life in sixteenth-century London* (Cambridge)

Reddaway (1940): T. F. Reddaway, *The Rebuilding of London after the Great Fire*

Rediker (1987): Marcus Rediker, *Between the Devil and the Deep Blue Sea: merchant seamen, pirates, and the Anglo-American maritime world, 1700–1750* (Cambridge)

Ringrose (1983): D. R. Ringrose, *Madrid and the Spanish Economy, 1560–1850* (Berkeley)

Roberts (1975): P. Roberts (ed.), *The Diary of Sir David Hamilton, 1709–1714* (Oxford)

Roche (1987): Daniel Roche, *The People of Paris* (Leamington Spa)

Rodger (1986): N. A. M. Rodger, *The Wooden World: an anatomy of the Georgian Navy*

Rogers (1985): Pat Rogers, *Literature and Print Culture in eighteenth-century England* (Brighton)

Rose (1991): Craig Rose, 'Evangelical philanthropy and Anglican revival: the charity schools of Augustan London, 1698–1740', *LJ* xvi

Rothstein (1961): N. K. A. Rothstein, 'The silk industry in London, 1702–66', London M.A.

Ryder (1939): Dudley Ryder, *Diary* (ed. W. Matthews)

Schofield (1986): R. S. Schofield, 'Did the mothers really die?' in L. Bonfield et al (eds), *The World we have Gained* (Oxford)

Schofield (1972–3): R. S. Schofield, 'Dimensions of illiteracy, 1750–1850', *Explorations in Economic History* x

Schwarz (1992): L. D. Schwarz, *London in the age of industrialisation: entrepreneurs, labour force and living conditions, 1700–1850* (Cambridge)

Servants (1725): *The Servants Calling*

Seymer (1954): L. R. Seymer, *A General History of Nursing*

Sharlin (1978): A. Sharlin, 'Natural decrease in early modern cities: a reconsideration', *P&P* 79

Sharpe (1981): J. A. Sharpe, *Defamation and sexual slander in early modern England: the church courts at York* (York)

Sharpe (1987): J. A. Sharpe, *Early Modern England: a social history, 1550–1760*

Shoemaker (1987): R. B. Shoemaker, 'The London "mob" in the early eighteenth century', *J of British Studies* xxvi, reprinted in Borsay (1990)

Shoemaker (1991): R. B. Shoemaker, *Prosecution and punishment: petty crime and the law in London and rural Middlesex, c. 1660–1725* (Cambridge)

Shoemaker (1992): R. B. Shoemaker, 'Reforming the City: the Reformation of Manners campaign in London, 1690–1738' in Davison et al (1992)

Simon (1968): Brian Simon (ed.), *Education in Leicestershire, 1540–1940* (Leicester)

Smith (1961): R. Smith, *Sea Coal for London: history of the coal factors in the London market*

Smith (1973): S. R. Smith, 'The social and geographical origins of the London apprentices, 1630–1660', *GM* iv

Souden (1984): David Souden, 'Migrants and the population structure of later seventeenth-century provincial cities and market towns' in P. Clark (ed.), *The Transformation of English Provincial Towns, 1600–1800*

Speaight (1955): G. Speaight, *The History of the English Puppet Theatre*

Spufford (1981): M. Spufford, *Small Books and Pleasant Histories: popular fiction and its readership in seventeenth-century England*

Stackhouse (1722): Thomas Stackhouse, *The Miseries and Great Hardships of the Inferiour Clergy, in and about London*

Stedman Jones (1971): G. Stedman Jones, *Outcast London* (Oxford)

Stern (1960): W. M. Stern, *The Porters of London*

Stern (1956): W. M. Stern, 'The trade, art or mistery of silk throwers of the city of London in the seventeenth century', *GM* vi

Stone (1977): L. Stone, *The Family, Sex and Marriage in England, 1500–1800*

Stone (1990): L. Stone, *Road to Divorce: England, 1530–1987* (Oxford)

Stone (1992): L. Stone, *Uncertain Unions: marriage in England, 1660–1753* (Oxford)

Strype (1720): John Strype, *A Survey of the Cities of London and Westminster*

Summerson (1962): Sir John Summerson, *Georgian London* (2nd ed.)

Sutherland (1972): I. Sutherland, 'When was the Great Plague? Mortality in London, 1563 to 1665' in D. V. Glass & R. Revelle (eds), *Population and Social Change*

Swift (1958): Jonathan Swift, *Collected Poems* (ed. Horrell)

Swift (1948): Jonathan Swift, *A Journal to Stella* (ed. Williams)

Thirsk & Cooper (1972): J. Thirsk & J. P. Cooper, *Seventeenth-century Economic Documents* (Oxford)

Thomas (1959): Keith Thomas, 'The Double Standard', *Journal of the History of Ideas* xx

Thompson (1972): E. P. Thompson, 'Rough Music: le charivari anglais', *Annales* xxvii

Thompson (1975): E. P. Thompson, *Whigs and Hunters: the origins of the Black Act*

Treatise (1732): *A Treatise of Feme Coverts: or the Lady's Law*

Tucker (1936): R. F. Tucker, 'Real wages of artisans in London, 1729–1935', *Journal of the American Statistical Association* xxxi

Uffenbach (1934): Z. C. von Uffenbach, *London in 1710*

Wadsworth (1712): Benjamin Wadsworth, *The Well-ordered Family* (Boston)

Wadsworth & Mann (1931): A. P. Wadsworth & J. de L. Mann, *The Cotton Trade and Industrial Lancashire, 1600–1780* (Manchester)

Ward (1927): E. Ward, *The London Spy* (ed. Hayward)

Ward (1699): E. Ward, *A Walk to Islington*

Wareing (1980): J. Wareing, 'Changes in the geographical distribution of the recruitment of apprentices to the London Companies, 1486–1750', *JHGeog* vi

Watts (1728): Isaac Watts, *An Essay towards the Encouragement of Charity Schools*

Webbs (1903): S. & B. Webb, *History of Liquor Licensing, 1700–1830*

Wiesner (1987): M. E. Wiesner, 'Women's work in the changing city economy, 1500–1600' in M. J. Boxer & J. H. Quateart, *Connecting Spheres: Women in the Western World, 1500 to the Present*

Willughby (1863): Percivall Willughby, *Observations in Midwifery* (ed. Henry Blenkinsop, Warwick)

Wrightson (1982): Keith Wrightson, *English Society, 1580–1680*

Wrigley (1987): E. A. Wrigley, *People, Cities and Wealth: the transformation of traditional society* (Oxford)

Wrigley (1967): E. A. Wrigley, 'A simple model of London's importance in changing English society and economy, 1650–1750', *P&P* xxxvii, reprinted in Wrigley (1987)

Wrigley (1985): E. A. Wrigley, 'Urban growth and agricultural change: England and the continent in the early modern period', *Journal of Interdisciplinary History* xv, reprinted in Wrigley (1987)

Wrigley & Schofield (1983): E. A. Wrigley & R.S. Schofield, 'English population history from family reconstitution: summary results, 1600–1799', *Population Studies* xxxvii

Wrigley & Schofield (1989): E. A. Wrigley & R. S. Schofield, *The Population History of England, 1541–1871: a reconstruction* (Cambridge)

Wunderli (1981): R. M. Wunderli, *London church courts and society on the eve of the Reformation* (Cambridge, Mass.)

Wyman (1984): A. L. Wyman, 'The surgeoness: the female practitioner of surgery, 1400–1800', *MedH* xxviii

Index

In order to keep the index to a reasonable length, most names of people used as examples or quoted in the text have been omitted. Many topographical references have also not been indexed.